WAYNE
Rooney

WAYNE
Rooney

The Story
of Football's
Wonder Kid

HARRY HARRIS
& DANNY FULLBROOK

ROBSON BOOKS

This new edition first published in Great Britian in 2004 by Robson Books, The Chrysalis Building, Bramley Road, London W10 6SP

An imprint of Chrysalis Books Group

British Library Cataloguing in Publication Data
A catalogue record for this title is available from the British Library.

ISBN 1 86105 820 9

Picture Credits
Pages 1 to 3, top page 4, top page 5 and top page 6 – Mercury Press
Bottom page 4 and top page 7 (Dale Cherry) – Rex Features
Bottom page 5, bottom page 6 and bottom page 7 (Matthew Ashton) – Empics
Page 8 (top: Dylan Martinez; bottom: Mike Finn-Kelcey) – Reuters

Typeset by SX Composing DTP, Rayleigh, Essex
Printed by Creative Print & Design (Wales), Ebbw Vale

Contents

Introduction

'The phenomenal talent displayed by Wayne over the last year, and in this tournament in particular, have made him one of the most sought-after commodities in the media and marketing world. My task is to ensure a co-ordinated and coherent approach to the media, which embraces his football club, the Football Association and all his sponsors.'

– Ian Monk, head of the PR agency managing Rooney's image, after Rooney's performance in the Euro 2004 Championships

Wayne Rooney's goals, his fierce competitiveness and sheer genius electrified Euro 2004, turning a teenager who was unknown outside England into the game's newest global superstar. From Pelé to Eusebio, from TV pundits to the front-page leader writers, just about everyone expressed their opinions about the boy wonder the England players called 'Wazza', as the tournament catapulted him into the general public awareness the way Italia 90 illuminated the career of Paul Gascoigne. For Gazza's tears, there were Wazza's goals, and arguably only his cruel foot injury deprived England of glory in the tournament.

As Rooney's valuation soared to the Fantasy Football realms of £50m, the chances of a more realistic £30m transfer from Everton intensified. After England were eliminated by Euro hosts Portugal, and Rooney was in hospital having his right foot immobilised in plaster, the England coach, Sven Goran Eriksson, told the youngster that his life was about to change in a way he had never imagined.

Rooney might not be anywhere near as good-looking as England captain and fashion icon David Beckham, but he brought back the sport's feel-good factor – until his fractured metatarsal ended his formidable presence in the tournament. Now everyone craves a piece of Rooney. There will be an unprecedented demand on his time, and endless offers of endorsements because of his newly found iconic status.

Rooney and his fiancée, Colleen McLoughlin, have already been described as the new Posh 'n' Becks, but the firm hired to manage the wonder kid's PR is planning to cultivate a different image. The rugged Rooney will never be as pretty as Becks, but he is the new generation, superseding the 29-year-old England skipper as the nation's talisman.

The Rooney PR machine will, instead, cultivate his grass-roots football appeal and wholesome boy-next-door image. Ian Monk Associates, the agency appointed to manage Rooney's media image, is under virtual siege from journalists and media organisations from around the world seeking to tap into the 'Roo-mania' generated by his goalscoring exploits in Euro 2004. Rather than the glitz and glamour that surrounds the Beckhams' celebrity lifestyle, Rooney's PR team will be playing on his humble origins and street credibility. Headed by Ian Monk, the agency says it is handling a deluge of media requests from around the globe. Monk is a former newspaper executive who moved into the PR business six years ago and set up Ian Monk Associates in 2003.

As well as the intense press interest, a range of global consumer brands are chasing endorsement or sponsorship deals. Proactive Sports Group, the firm that manages Rooney's commercial interests, has already signed a range of contracts on behalf of the player. Sports analysts have suggested Rooney could earn up to £100m during his career. Compared to the Brazilian soccer legend Pelé by the England coach, Rooney already has personal endorsement contracts with Ford, Coca-Cola, snack brand Pringles and football-boot supplier Nike, which are estimated to be worth around £10m.

While Colleen isn't exactly one of the Spice Girls, she has already become something of a media star, and has had to get used to the limelight with incredible speed. Last year she missed Wayne's full competitive debut as he starred in England's 2–0 win over Turkey at the Euro 2004 qualifying stage, since she was still a schoolgirl performing in a production of *Bugsy Malone* at St John Bosco school. Colleen, who has two younger brothers and a younger sister, since dropped out of her A-level studies to pursue a career as an actress, and she has now made an appearance in *Hollyoaks*.

Alongside her old pals from Croxteth, Liverpool, Colleen can now count among her social circle the ultimate footballer's wife, Victoria Beckham. Colleen flew out to the posh Spanish sporting paradise La Manga to join Wayne at the England training camp prior to Euro 2004. It was her first time alone on a plane and her first taste of being a 'footballer's wife'. She recalls: 'I was dead scared. I was on the phone to Wayne, who was already out there. I didn't know what clothes to wear or what to do. I was really nervous.' But with cool sunglasses and a shopping trip to Burberry, where she picked up a dazzling red bikini, Colleen was ready to take her place by the pool. She reverted to a more casual look, strolling around in a blue vest top and shorts.

Six years ago, the Rooney family was so poor Wayne was playing in a pair of filthy trainers with a hole in one toe. 'What's happened is really mad,' said Colleen just before Rooney walked on to the pitch for England's opening game against France at Lisbon's magnificent Stadium of Light. 'I remember Wayne playing football with my brothers in the street. We used to spend hours hanging around on the street corner talking to each other.'

Although the couple had been friends for six years, their first date was a trip to the cinema. Colleen says of the crazy turn her and Rooney's life together has taken: 'Sometimes I have to pinch myself.'

Less than two years ago, the Liverpool teenager was still an £80-a-week apprentice at Everton. The first to benefit from his new-found wealth was his family. He splashed out £20,000 on a cruise on the new *Queen Mary II* for Mother's Day and paid £30,000 for a family holiday in Mexico. Colleen received a £2,000 diamond-encrusted designer watch. Following their engagement in October 2003, he bought a £1m eight-bedroom executive mansion eleven miles away in affluent Formby. But when Rooney celebrated his eighteenth birthday in the same month, his mother offered to make sausage rolls and butties for the party at Aintree racecourse to save on money. In March this year, he took advantage of the council's right-to-buy scheme to snap up his three-bedroom childhood home in Croxteth. It cost him £18,360, less than two weeks' wages.

Controversy was never far away, though, for example when an eighteenth birthday party he organised for Colleen at the three-star Devonshire House Hotel in Liverpool erupted in highly publicised fisticuffs – allegedly after the £10,000 which he had put behind the bar ran out.

He was spending the pounds, but also gaining them in weight. Last summer when he returned to Everton, his club manager David Moyes went public with his concerns and even Eriksson admitted that England fitness coach Ivan Carminati had been forced to put the youngster through extended extra sessions to reduce his weight after he arrived in Sardinia. That was after barely ten days off from the end of the season. The Portuguese press dubbed him 'McRooney'. But Rooney made his mark with his four goals, making him joint top scorer before he was cruelly cut down by injury. Eriksson said:

After the France game I was surprised at how well Wayne performed. Because when we met up in Sardinia, he wasn't 100 per cent fit, he was heavy and we had to do a lot of extra work with him. He did that and came on very well. Yet to see him that strong and quick after what we saw surprised even me. I expected him to play well, but not at that level given the problems he had in Sardinia.

Wayne's mum, Jeanette, proudly watched him collect successive Man of the Match awards, the only trophies the England squad brought back from the tournament.

Rooney's foot injury agony was made even worse when he reached hospital and Portuguese medics began celebrating their victory around him. He was already gutted when an X-ray revealed the break at Lisbon's Hospital de Santa Mariato. Dr Oliviera Marceus said: 'Portuguese people know how to celebrate and we were all celebrating our win, even though we were working. We were all very excited, but Rooney was not because he's English. He was very quiet and sad. But it was very nice to have him here.'

But all the experts agreed on Rooney's invaluable contribution to the England cause. With him, England stood a chance – without him, well, out they went. David Seaman was typical of the expert analysis when he said:

When Rooney went off Portugal knew a massive threat had gone and it had an effect on us as well, but it shouldn't have done. We had to deal with it and we didn't. We have played two big games the same way, letting our opponents dictate the game. Losing Rooney didn't help, of course. We missed a player who is great at holding the ball and takes the pressure off. We needed to keep it for thirty seconds and we could not do it.

There's no doubt we are good enough to win a tournament. The squad is basically young and as long as it keeps together it will get stronger. Wayne Rooney will get better, John Terry will gain from the experience, Sol Campbell has been superb, while Ashley Cole was fantastic and still so young. There are also players like Ledley King coming through and of course Rio Ferdinand to come back. Let's try and cut the hype though, even if, in our hearts, we think it looks good for the future.

Gary Lineker also felt England relied far too much on Rooney. The BBC anchorman and former England striker criticised Eriksson for failing to vary his tactics once Rooney limped off:

The most disturbing thing was how we proved that we have no Plan B. Plan A was to allow Wayne Rooney to play opponents virtually on his own, filling up all the space between the forwards and midfield, as well as scoring most of the goals. When Rooney went off we didn't know what to do, we lost all shape and there was no linkman to the forwards. That is slightly disconcerting when you consider all that happened was we lost an eighteen-year-old boy – albeit a world-class player. The whole back four just stood five yards from goal, where any sort of contact on the ball from the attacker is likely to end in a goal.

After their quarterfinal defeat, Eriksson promised:

I am confident that we can win the World Cup in 2006. I had a short meeting with the players and I can tell you one of the things I told them. I said that in three and a half years we have lost three competitive games and the way we lost all of them shows the difference between winning and losing is nothing. That gives me the confidence that we can beat any team. I talked about 2006 and that I'm committed to taking this team through.

When Eriksson suggested he had not seen a young player make such an impact in a major tournament since Pelé, it was inevitably interpreted as a comparison with the world's greatest. Not quite intended as such by the England coach, it nonetheless provoked worldwide debate. Portugal coach Luis Felipe Scolari said: 'Rooney is an excellent player but Pelé is unique and there will be no one like him in 1,000 years – not even in a computer game.'

The Portuguese legend Eusebio, who played against Pelé in the infamous 1966 World Cup match at Goodison Park where Brazil were humbled and Pelé brutalised, said:

I do not like the comparisons. Rooney is a youngster with immense talent who could turn out to be one of the best players in Europe or the world – but no one can compare him to Pelé. We must have great respect for my great friend Pelé. I can say we are like brothers. Pelé is Pelé and there is only one in the world like him. Rooney has plenty of time to become great and I advise him to keep his feet on the ground and to work hard to become a great player. There should not be comparisons like this. There should be more respect.

But Eriksson was not the first person to make the comparison with the Brazilian legend. Even before Rooney's exhilarating, phenomenal full England debut, Sir Bobby Robson called the teenager 'a jewel in the crown', and talked about him in terms of another seventeen-year-old who made an impact on the global game. But Sir Bobby is not senile quite yet. Writing exclusively in the *Mail on Sunday*, the 71-year-old former England coach put forward a powerful case for Rooney's inclusion against Turkey, even for such a vital European Championship qualifier: 'Sven Goran Eriksson is truly blessed by the emergence of the wonderfully talented Wayne Rooney. His is a phenomenal talent that must not be denied or restricted. I have watched the boy play on several occasions. He takes my breath away – he is sensational. He can do things which are way out of reach of any other player. The great Pelé was a mere seventeen when he was unveiled to the world by Brazil, and that was in a World Cup.

Rooney has the perfect name for a natural-born winner. His surname, found mainly in Ireland, dates back to the thirteenth century. Apparently 'Rooney' is the anglicised version of 'O Ruanaidh', from 'Ruanadh', an Irish personal name meaning 'champion'. Rooney's performances ensured his place in the Euro 2004 all-stars line-up and the debate will linger whether, had he not been injured, England would have gone on and beaten Portugal.

Everton confirmed that Rooney would be out of action for about eight weeks and would miss the start of the Premiership season. Everton's head physiotherapist, Mick Rathbone, said: 'The injury is a cracked fifth metatarsal. He should be able to start his rehabilitation, to include cycling and swimming, within three to four weeks' time.' But when he is fit, the big question is whether he would still be at Goodison Park or, perhaps inevitably, be sold to another club, possibly Chelsea or Manchester United. On signing his first professional forms for Everton in January 2003, with a £13,000-a-week contract, Rooney declared: 'I hope and I feel that I can achieve my ambitions here, and they are playing for Everton, for England one day – and scoring the winner against Liverpool in the derby!' Such loyalty would be put to the test after his phenomenal impact at Euro 2004.

Sir Alex Ferguson wanted him before the tournament and had hoped to tie up a deal, just in case he made such an impact in Portugal that it would inspire Roman Abramovich to enter the bidding.

During the Euro 2004 Championship, Rooney overshadowed the likes of David Beckham, Steven Gerrard, Paul Scholes and Michael Owen to such an extent that it's now impossible to imagine an England side without him. Eriksson said:

Wayne is one of our jewels now and will just get better and better. It's not just about his goals, it's about how he plays football and the thought behind it. He's always a thought-process ahead in the positions he takes, in how he links up our game; it's fantastic. It's easy for us to play out with the ball when he's playing. You can target him and he'll keep it or if he doesn't, it's because he's been fouled and bought us a free kick. Wayne Rooney confirmed how good he is in Euro 2004 and proved he's even better than we thought and he's respected because of it. Now he's a big name in Europe and even around the world, I guess, because these matches have been watched all over. He's a big name for today and for the future. And I think he can handle the pressure which will come from being more heavily marked and more photographed away from football.

He's quiet, but he's smiling and happy and not trying to be the big star. Of course, when he's back in England it will be Rooney fever so it's very important his advisors, his agent and his family and friends support him in the right way. He will be a star of the World Cup in 2006, the European Championship in 2008 and well beyond that because he's only eighteen.

Wayne Rooney's life so far has been nothing short of pure theatre. So it seems just about right that Everton owner and deputy chairman Bill Kenwright is a theatre lover, because he knows more than anybody how to deal with a great drama. And that is exactly what Rooney's rise to the pinnacle of the game and the England team has been, given that he is only eighteen.

But if there is a comment that proves that, while Rooney may be English football's saviour, the teenager is still a kid performing in a grown-ups' world, it is this one. When asked at the end of his first season who he feared most, his Everton manager David Moyes, England boss Sven Goran Eriksson or his mum, Rooney replied: 'I think I would have to say my mum, because if I take a step out of line, she is right there and ready to give me a slap.'

Rooney-mania spread at such a ridiculous rate in his debut season that he was vying with John Lennon, Dixie Dean and Billy Fury in a BBC Radio Merseyside poll to find the Greatest Liverpudlian. Although he came nowhere in the final poll, it illustrated his remarkable climb into the public's perception.

It was just a year since Wayne Rooney was queuing up in the canteen with the other pupils at De La Salle school for his favourite meal of sausage, chips and beans. PE teacher Joe Henningham said: 'The thing you noticed about Wayne was his size. He was the biggest lad in his class. I've always said you've got to be strong to get a muffin in the dinner queue at De La Salle.'

Everton deputy chairman Bill Kenwright said in July 2002: 'I did a radio interview yesterday and I tried to play down Rooney, but you can't play down Rooney. How can you play down the greatest thing around in football? He will make an impact this season and I hope he does. You have to try to protect him from us, our fans and our hopes, but we have a great manager and I hope he will get that point across.'

His Premiership debut came in a 2–2 home draw with Tottenham Hotspur on the opening day of the 2002–03 season – and Rooney created the first goal for Mark Pembridge. His first goal came in October 2002 against one of the best teams in Europe, Arsenal, and, in what has now become the stuff of legend, Rooney's success in his inaugural senior season continued at international level when he was fast-tracked into the England team – becoming the youngest player to wear the Three Lions when he made his debut against Australia in February 2003 at the age of seventeen.

After what, for him, might have been considered a quiet second season on the domestic front, Rooney blazed a trail through the early stages of Euro 2004 to give England a real, if fleeting, hope of lifting the trophy.

With Rooney as the new jewel, who needs a diamond formation?

1

A Star is Born

'The thing you noticed about Wayne was his size. He was the biggest lad in his class. I've always said you've got to be strong to get a muffin in the dinner queue at De La Salle.'

— Wayne's PE teacher Joe Henningham

A star is born from humble beginnings in a close-knit devout Roman Catholic environment, in a council estate in Croxteth, three miles from Goodison Park. Before Rooney-mania exploded their house looked like any other in the area. There were three Everton pennants and an Everton car registration plate on show in the front bedroom window. It could have been one of any number of Blue-blooded families on Merseyside. But this was a very special house. This was the house where Goodison Park wonder kid Wayne Rooney lived until fame and fortune meant a move became inevitable.

'Young Wayne' shared it with his proud-as-punch parents, Wayne senior, a Liverpool-Irish former amateur boxer, and Jeanette, a school dinner lady, together with younger brothers Graham and John. His family has always been Everton barmy – his dad bought him a blue shirt on the day he was born, 24 October 1985. His family has a piece of the Goodison Park turf at home.

The house was much like any other in the area, but if you were trying to guess who lived there, then all you would have to do would be to look at the framed pictures on the wall and the trophies on top of the TV. This is nothing, though, compared to the masses of photographs bulging from the Rooney scrapbook.

One framed picture stands out above all else. An eleven-year-old Wayne is standing in the Anfield centre circle alongside then

Everton captain Dave Watson and former Liverpool skipper John Barnes. The youngster was the Blues' mascot for the derby that took place on 20 November 1996.

The game ended 1–1 (Robbie Fowler scored for Liverpool and Gary Speed for Everton). Another photo from that night, of a smiling Stan Collymore and unsmiling Wayne Rooney is apparently kept on the floor behind a chair. Other pictures that adorned the rooms included one of Duncan Ferguson, a second-half substitute in that derby, standing with his arms around Wayne and his brothers at Everton's Bellefield training ground the following season. There is no way that Big Dunc would ever have predicted that he'd be playing alongside young Wayne just a few years later.

Wayne's brother Graham, a pupil at De La Salle, is now concentrating on his boxing, while John, who has recently started at the secondary school, is still at the Everton Academy, where Graham once was, and is a promising midfielder in its youth team. But it is the eldest Rooney who has gone from a kid kicking the ball about on the streets of Liverpool to a world star.

Wayne kicked a ball as soon as he could walk and wore holes in the pebble dash at his grandmother's house by thumping a football against the wall. Wayne's nineteen-year-old cousin Thomas Rooney recalled: 'He'd be there at 7 a.m. just kicking a ball. Nan didn't think it was funny. She'd hear the stones fall and yell, "Wa-a-ayne!" and he'd get a slap. Sometimes it would be me or Gilly [cousin Stephen Rooney] but we'd tell her it was Wayne. Whatever we did, we did it together. If we went away to the caravan park in Wales, we'd find a gang and arrange a game. It was crazy.'

Like brother Graham, who was once the Northwest schoolboy boxing champion, Wayne used to box, but he gave up in favour of his life-consuming football. You might think that because of his size and talent Wayne would have succeeded at any sport he chose, and Thomas stands that up by saying: 'He could have made it at boxing. We sparred a lot, he hit like a heavyweight.'

With all three Rooney boys once on Everton's books, Wayne senior prayed one would make the grade, saying: 'You don't really think it's going to happen at the time. Wayne began to kick a ball as soon as he could walk. And, like me, he has always been an

Evertonian. His first game at Goodison? I can't remember, but he was probably about six months old!'

His mum Jeanette can remember exactly when his first game as a player was. She said: 'He played his first proper game when he was seven. It was for an under-11s or under-12s team from the Western Approaches pub in Storrington Avenue. Despite only being seven, he came on as a sub and scored!'

Typical Rooney by the sound of it. Jeanette added: 'He also played for the Copplehouse pub team in Fazakerley when he was nine and other teams, including East Villa and Pye FC. He won the Golden Boot for them, after scoring the most goals in the BT Challenge Cup competition.

'He also scored loads of goals in his first year at De La Salle – he won a league and cup double with them but then stopped to concentrate on playing for the Everton Academy. He actually scored 99 goals in one season for the Academy's under-10s. And he broke the goalscoring record for Liverpool Schools' FA under-11s, which he still holds.'

Wayne was always among the most popular lads at school because of his footballing skills, and typically he was a record-breaker wherever he went. That included Our Lady and St Swithin's Primary School where he even banged the goals in wearing a pair of old ripped trainers.

Rooney's former headmaster Tony McCaul said the Goodison idol was by far and away the best player in the school: 'Wayne was always a special boy who absolutely loved his football. It was obvious from a young age he was going to become a player. Wayne was head and shoulders above the other boys in the playground and would have been out there all the time if he could have been – he absolutely loves the game.

'He was a very well-behaved pupil and is a credit to St Swithin's. Everybody at the school is delighted by Wayne's success and we wish him all the best for the future.'

Most of his team-mates from St Swithin's are either out working or still studying at school. One of his friends from his primary-school days is John Ryan, who played alongside Rooney in the school team. As he studied for his A levels, he said the Everton forward was always destined for greatness. 'Wayne was a great lad and a fantastic player. I support Liverpool but still hope Wayne does brilliantly in his career. He deserves everything he gets. We all still see him around but he has to concentrate on playing for Everton and probably doesn't have much spare time.'

The primary school's goalkeeper, Daniel Hinnigan, who shares the same birthday as Rooney but is a year younger, said: 'Everybody is really happy about what Wayne is achieving and he was the best player in school by a long way.'

Margaret Carnell lives in the same Croxteth neighbourhood as the Rooneys and said the community is right behind him. She said: 'He is a lovely lad and he has got a lot of supporters in the area. The Rooneys are just an ordinary local family. They've done really well with their three lads and with Wayne's success. It's great to see a lad from such humble roots become a successful footballer.'

The whole family knew that Wayne would one day make it as a professional, as his brother Graham said: 'I knew Wayne would do it. And I think John could follow in his footsteps as well.'

Wayne Rooney is a dream come true in every sense. He has already packed into a couple of years the kind of success most players have in their entire careers. Wayne was not the brightest at school but he was big for his age, strong and could do more intricate tricks with the ball than he could manage on his BMX bikes at the De La Salle Catholic Boys' School, which was also attended by Francis Jeffers, Mick Lyons and Paul Jewell.

He still rides a BMX and enjoys some stunts and, in true clichéd fashion, until recently jumpers for goalposts were still on the agenda as he liked nothing better than a kickabout with his mates on the local park. He's a fan of the Stereophonics and pop diva J-Lo, plays table tennis at the local club, and enjoys boxing with his mates. His idol is Alan Shearer.

But despite what has happened to him as he has been catapulted from schoolboy to England hero he has not changed, according to his cousin Thomas who said at the end of Wayne's amazing first season: 'The thing people on the outside don't realise about Wayne is that nothing that's happened to him over the last year has changed him. He's still our Wayne.

'He does normal things, he will just ring us and ask where we are, then come and just sit around talking. That's what he did after playing for England against Turkey. The only difference was we all wanted to know about the players. We were like, "What's Beckham like? What about Gerrard?" Wayne was just, yeah, they're OK.

'He was too shy to ask for autographs but we've got Shearer's. We think he's the best. It's amazing Wayne meets these people now. We both still have their posters on our walls.'

Wayne represented Liverpool Schools and broke their goalscoring record, netting 72 times in one season (out of a team total of 158 goals) for the under-11s in the 1996–97 season. He smashed the record that had been held since the late 1970s by Steve Redmond, who later made a name for himself as a defender at Manchester City.

It was also the season Wayne won his first European trophy, after the team competed in an international tournament in Holland. Tim O'Keefe, his then manager, recalls in an interview before his England debut:

Wayne had strength, aggression, pace and a great ability to finish with his right or left foot, or his head. Wayne was a very quiet boy but popular with the other lads and the staff. I would rate him alongside former Liverpool schoolboy players Robbie Fowler and Steve McManaman at that age. They all had that bit of magic which helped them stand out from the others.

A lot of lads are quiet off the pitch but different on it. But with Wayne, it was a case of controlled aggression when he was playing. At times he could be annoying, because he would go against everything in the coaching manuals. You'd think, 'He can't do anything from there,' and then you'd see him put the ball in the net. Yet he was a good listener and did take things on board.

But there was a famous occasion when Wayne ignored everyone and everything except his own goalscoring instinct. His dad was shouting encouraging words from the touchline, as were manager Tim O'Keefe and his assistant Jim Milne. Wayne was in a central position heading deep into the opponents' half: 'Take him on, take him on,' shouted his dad. 'Pass it wide, pass it wide,' shouted the coaches. The youngster did neither. He simply let fly an unstoppable shot from thirty yards or more. Another Wayne Rooney goal.

Coach Jim Milne said of him: 'He took no prisoners on the pitch. It was obvious to us he was destined for greater things. He was a strong, powerful boy, but he was also sensible.'

Tim said: 'It was always satisfying for us to see players go on and do well. Wayne had so much natural ability he was always going to succeed. I think he will eventually play for England [what a prophecy that was]. And the good news for Evertonians is that he has always been a strong Blue and his family are all Blues. I think he will want to stay at Everton for as long as they want him to stay.'

'I don't think he's changed at all,' added Tim. He's still got short hair. He still looks intimidating.'

The only thing that Rooney hated about playing schools football was that sometimes he had to play in the red strip of archrivals Liverpool. Evertonian Tim explains: 'It was the city team's colour, although I should point out that whenever we played at Goodison Park, we always wore blue!'

Typically Rooney is already setting an example for other talented young Merseysiders trying to make a career for themselves. 'Any young player who goes to watch Wayne Rooney play football will be looking at a good role model,' says Tim Johnson, vice-chairman of the Liverpool Schools' FA and school-sports editor of the *Liverpool Echo*. 'He's a player of exceptional ability, who will hopefully continue to develop over the next few years.'

Obviously Rooney's talent was soon spotted by scouts from Everton and rivals Liverpool. He was given a trial at Anfield when he was nine. But Rooney insisted on wearing his Everton kit throughout, declining invitations to change into the strip that had been provided – somehow he was always destined for the Toffees.

Contrary to local folklore, he wasn't sent home and told to come back only when he had a 'better attitude'. Unlike fellow Evertonians Robbie Fowler, Steve McManaman and Michael Owen there was only one place the young Rooney wanted to be, and that was Goodison Park.

The self-confessed Evertonian describes how he could have been snapped up by their Merseyside rivals. In an interview with the *Evertonian* magazine, Rooney said: 'I actually had a trial for them. I was playing for Copplehouse under-9s at the time and after the game I was approached by a Liverpool scout who invited me to Melwood. I went along but after going there just once I got the phone call from Bob Pendleton [Everton's scout]. It was the call I had desperately wanted and that was it for me. I gave Liverpool a "swerve" after that.'

He added: 'As a young lad wanting to be a professional footballer, I had to go to Liverpool when I was asked because there was no other club interested in me then. But as soon as Everton came in there was never a single doubt in my mind.' As if to emphasise this, when he scored in the FA Youth Cup final against Aston Villa he lifted his shirt to show a T-shirt – 'Once a Blue, always a Blue'.

As his mum has said, Wayne's first club side was the under-12s of local pub the Western Approaches, for whom he scored on his debut aged seven. Stories are told of how, when he was just ten, he scored a spectacular overhead kick for Everton's schoolboys at Manchester United, which stunned the crowd first into silence and then thunderous applause.

At twelve, Rooney suddenly shot up in size and became the biggest boy in his class. His body strength added to his natural ability. His former school, De La Salle, is only a stone's throw from Goodison Park, and just around the corner from the old family home on the Croxteth estate in Liverpool. Rooney's former head of year, John Hennigan, who was teaching Wayne until he left school in 2002, aged sixteen, is an Everton season-ticket holder. In the 2002–03 season, instead of watching Rooney sat behind his desk he was watching him on the pitch from his seat in Goodison's Park End.

He said before the season started: 'It'll be a little bit special watching someone I know – an ex-pupil – playing for the team I support. Let's hope it's a good season for Wayne and a good season for Everton. We don't want to go overboard, but he has certainly got a lot of potential.

'Wayne's not an academic lad; he does his talking with his boots. I have never coached him, but he's undoubtedly a great athlete, the sort of lad who, apart from being a great footballer, could win the high jump and the one hundred metres.'

John was worried about what effect Rooney's stardom would have on him and predicted the changes he would have to go through: 'Like any other school leaver, he has been used to mixing with his peers. But now he'll be spending a lot of time with people who are quite a bit older than him. He's going to need a lot of luck along the way and it was comforting to hear Everton manager David Moyes say he is going to look after him. If you've got a special young talent you've got to look after it.'

He was also worried before the start of the season about Rooney being protected on the pitch. He said: 'If you earn yourself a name, there will be people determined to take it off you and a lot of established professionals, some of them internationals, won't want to be embarrassed by a sixteen-year-old striker.'

John's colleague, Graham North, was Wayne's head of year in his second, third and fourth years at De La Salle. Graham says: 'Wayne has been good for the school and the school has been good for Wayne, supporting him whenever it could. He was never any problem. He came in and got on with his work. He was a rather quiet lad who took things in his stride, nothing seemed to bother him too much. I've been teaching here for twenty-five years and I've seen so many talented footballers, but very few make it.'

Until early 2003 Wayne and his family still lived in the council house he grew up in. But after the money-spinning impact of his first season, and the interest in the wonder kid, they moved to a £500,000 detached home in Sandfield Park, near Everton's Bellefield training ground. In October 2003, Rooney bought a £1-million eight-bedroom executive mansion eleven miles away in affluent Formby.

Everton have always been terrified of losing Rooney to a multi-million-pound bid from one of the world's biggest clubs, and even more so after his stunning impact at Euro 2004. But cousin Thomas doesn't think Wayne will ever leave his beloved Everton. In any case, there is something else that everyone at Everton is even more afraid of . . . Wayne's mum.

Jeanette Rooney may have been a £100-a-week dinner lady until recently, but she's afraid of no one when it comes to looking after her boys. So she took a dim view when youngest son John, who was

signed up in February 2003 to Everton's youth team, was dumped
for being overweight.

'Jeanette was fuming,' a family friend said. 'She stormed down to
the training ground and had it out with the coaches, insisting John
had the potential to be every bit as good as Wayne. Jeanette made it
clear that if Wayne heard about this harsh treatment he wouldn't be
happy. It goes without saying that John was put back on the squad.'

The friend added: 'Jeanette's not a pushy mum. She's not in it for
the money and the glory. She just knows what's best for her lads and
she believes in them. She's what you might call a strong character.
Everyone at Everton's terrified of her.'

She has an equally stern reputation at Wayne's former school, De
La Salle, where she was renowned as a strict lunch-time supervisor
and for her pride in her three children. Peter McIntosh, Wayne's
former agent, said Jeanette knew exactly what she wanted. 'She isn't
one of these women who don't know anything about football. She
knew about the offside rule, she knew when a player was playing
well or badly. She never criticised Wayne. She was always upbeat
and she told him he was doing well,' he said. 'She was a very strong
woman, a lot like Wayne in many ways. She was a very silent,
independent type who just got on with life.'

While Jeanette and her brood are now among the most famous
faces in Liverpool, for many years she supported her family with two
jobs, as McIntosh explained: 'In the day she would work as a dinner
lady and at night she would go to another job. I remember she did so
many hours she didn't have time to go and watch her son play for
Everton.

'She was the breadwinner because Wayne's dad was out of work.
She knew that everything relied on her. Wayne never wanted for
anything, whether it was training shoes or money for going out. Both
Wayne's parents went without so they could do the best for their sons.'

Jeanette is determined to keep Wayne's feet on the ground. Apart
from the new house, most of his pay is invested for him. Jeanette also
fully approves of Wayne's 'other woman', an aspiring actress called
Colleen McLoughlin who used to live just around the corner.

Wayne is said to be besotted by the blonde he has been dating for
over two years, so much so that he splashed out on a £2,000

diamond-encrusted designer watch for her. Until recently Colleen, who has two younger brothers and a younger sister, was an A-level student at Liverpool's St John Bosco school, where Wayne would pop in and wait in the common room for her to finish classes. Colleen dropped out of her studies to pursue an acting career, and has now made an appearance in *Hollyoaks*.

Colleen missed Wayne's big night against Turkey because she was appearing in a school version of the musical *Bugsy Malone*, and later ran home to watch a video of the match. The next day Colleen was again unable to see Wayne, as she joined the rest of the show's cast at a pizza restaurant. But he had a surprise for her.

'At about 8.30 p.m., Wayne walked in. He had a salad and a Coca-Cola for himself and then paid for Colleen and all her friends. He dotes on her,' said a manager at Deep Pan Pizza at a nearby cinema multiplex. 'He arrived late and she was surprised and happy. But he didn't have a pizza, so was obviously thinking of his training.'

Wayne's precocious talent is such that Jeanette and others around him are almost afraid of what it will do. Everton FC bosses banned him from giving media interviews until he turned eighteen, and have graphically explained the perils of superstardom. When Wayne signed his first professional contract at the club in January 2003, he was told that if he succumbed to the traditional temptations of drink, drugs and women he would lose it all. The faded figure of Paul Gascoigne was held up to him as an example not to follow.

At home, Wayne is so loyal to his brothers that at one boxing match where a decision went against Graham, Wayne came out fighting. 'He climbed up to the ropes and went nose to nose with the referee. He didn't agree with the decision and you could say he made his feelings clear,' said one witness.

Occasionally Wayne 'enjoys a few beers' but most of the time settles for a Coke in his local pub, the Western Approaches.His idea of an evening out is the four-course set menu at his local Shangri-La Chinese restaurant.

'Wayne eats anything off the menu. He loves it all,' manager Kenny Po said. 'He comes in with a big gang of mates, sometimes lads, other times with their girlfriends. He doesn't flash his cash about. He's a big tipper and is generous and polite.'

Thomas Rooney, just a year older, in 2002 was earning £80 a week at Tranmere as a trainee. He talked about how they spent their leisure time. He said: 'We go to the pictures, normally me, Wayne and our cousin Gilly. The whole family are close, but us three are always together. And we go to the centre where my uncle runs the boxing. It's a big gym with Sky TV.

'We just hang around. At nights we play table tennis and snooker at the local club. We also play football in the street. We have one game where two people cross and the keeper has to catch five headers or volleys to come out of goal. Wayne's good at that, even in goal. He could make it there, you know. If ever they need an emergency keeper, he is Boss.'

Vinny and Billy Morrey, his uncles, enjoyed modest careers in the game. Billy played semi-professionally for England. The background and private life of the Rooneys have been under the glare of public examination to the extent that, when his family booked a holiday to Butlins in Minehead, the story did not stay a secret and attracted plenty of criticism.

Wayne feels most comfortable surrounded by his mates in familiar surroundings, as Thomas added: 'No one bothers him here as everyone knows him. A few might ask for autographs but it's like it's just Wayne – nothing special. He's still got his BMX bike. He's really good and can do lots of tricks and jumps, and we're both into music, we like the Stereophonics, Cast and Oasis. Sometimes we go to gigs with our uncle Eugene. Wayne had tickets to see Kylie. He'll kill me for saying that, but he couldn't go so his girlfriend Colleen took a couple of our cousins. We saw *8 Mile* at the pictures a few weeks ago and we like Eminem. But Wayne's favourite is Chubby Brown. He knows every word of his *Jingle B*@!cks* DVD. He likes the Spanish look and thinks Jennifer Lopez is gorgeous.'

Peter McIntosh predicted that Wayne's impoverished upbringing and a mum dedicated to him will help him show flair on the pitch and humility off it. 'He's a pure one-off. He's not a big-time-Charlie footballer who's going to go off the rails. He goes to the pictures once in a while. He doesn't even say much,' said Peter. 'He's focused on his football. It's his life. He lives and breathes it.' Just as England now live and breathe Wayne Rooney.

2

Spotted

'It doesn't matter what Liverpool would have said to him, he wouldn't have gone there.'

– Blues scout Bob Pendleton

Imagine the scene. All over the country on foggy Saturday and Sunday mornings young boys play football in front of their screaming parents. As the spectators proudly look on and cheer and yelp at every touch from their offspring, it does not really matter how good they are. But just a row back, mingling in with the parents, are the professional scouts who live and breathe football as if it is all that matters in their lives. You have to be dedicated to the cause to drag yourself out of bed at the weekends just in case you come across something very special. But these guys have eyes like hawks and have been involved in the game for ever.

To spot a 'young un' before anybody else is the challenge, and in areas of the country like Merseyside and Tyneside, as well as east London, the scouts at least know that there is a chance they will stumble upon a future star, because these places are rich with talent and have already provided so many professional footballers over the years.

Bob Pendleton has been trying to unearth gems for Everton for years. It was his sideline while he worked as a train driver. Since retiring from his job the 65-year-old has put even more effort into his scouting role, and in 1994 he came up trumps. Many people have suggested that it was not difficult to spot Wayne Rooney considering his record-breaking rampage through junior football on Merseyside. But whatever people like to say, Pendleton is the

12

proud scout who saw a nine-year-old Rooney plying his trade and said to himself, 'this boy is something special'. Bob's place in history is now assured.

The moment of discovery, when the hairs on the back of Bob's neck stood on end, came when Wayne was playing for Copplehouse under-10s in the Walton and Kirkdale Junior Football League, where Francis Jeffers, Robbie Fowler and Steve McManaman had previously played. Pendleton described the first time he spotted Rooney playing for Copplehouse Juniors in the autumn of 1994, just around his ninth birthday: 'It was on a Sunday morning at the Merseyside Youth Association's Jeffreys Humble playing fields in Long Lane, on the border of Aintree and Fazakerley.

'You could tell he was special straight away. When you see someone special, which he was, you just know. I approached their manager, Big Neville, and asked him: "Who's the little fellow?" He looked at me and groaned: "Oh Bobby, we've only just signed him. Leave him alone." I said: "Leave him alone? You must be joking.'''

Pendleton added: 'You could see it then. He was strong and dedicated, and he couldn't help scoring goals. But Liverpool had already seen him playing in a Saturday league in the Bootle area. He had one or two training sessions at Melwood.'

But having grown up a true Blue, there was never any choice for Wayne. He and his family were dyed-in-the-wool Everton fans, so Pendleton knew he was on to a winner and he could not quite contain his excitement. Bob added: 'He only ever wanted to do one thing and that was play for Everton. It doesn't matter what Liverpool would have said to him, he wouldn't have gone there. His dad, Wayne senior, also said he wasn't going anywhere else. And he was also adamant he wasn't going to Liverpool.'

Bob, who also tipped off the Blues about young defender Tony Hibbert, knew he had to get Wayne down to the Everton Academy to meet the Director of Youth, Ray Hall, as quickly as possible, because there was no way he was passing up this chance.

Ray Hall's HQ is a modest, humble Portakabin in the corner of Everton's Bellefield training ground. It has proven to be a conveyor belt of raw young talent over many years. The fact is Hall signed the ten-year-old Rooney after one training session. But he probably did not even need that. Pendleton added before the 2002–03 season started: 'Within days I took young Wayne down with his dad to meet Ray Hall, Everton's academy director. Ray saw him training and backed me a hundred per cent, signing him there and then. And now he's looking forward to playing in the Premiership for the team he's always supported, at the age of sixteen. It's a real *Roy of the Rovers* story.'

Hall spends all his life assessing the youngsters that come knocking on his door with their dads or chaperoned by experienced scouts. But with regard to Pendleton and his first visit to Bellefield to talk about Rooney, Hall said: 'I did not need his scoring record as proof or even one training session. You get an experienced scout sitting there with his tea cup quivering while you're talking to the lad and you know he's special.'

Hall takes great pride in what he does and the youngsters that he produces, so you can imagine how he felt when Rooney was paired with former Everton youngster Franny Jeffers for England in the second half against Australia on 12 February, and then watched Wayne move on to make his first England start against Turkey.

As Rooney was playing in that memorable game at the Stadium of Light, Jeffers equalled Alan Shearer's thirteen-goal scoring record for the England under-21s. The similarities between the two rising stars are uncanny. Academy director Hall, who has worked on Everton youth development for thirteen years, said:

Franny came here aged nine and was in the first team as a teenager. Wayne was the same age when he arrived and everyone knows what's happened to him this season.

They are both local lads, they went to the same junior and secondary schools and they made their full England debuts together against Australia. You can never be sure how far a young boy will progress in football but Franny and Wayne were always at the top of their age groups for ability and potential.

I remember the first time I saw Franny and it was obvious he was an intelligent and gifted lad. He scores most of his goals inside the penalty area but that is a knack in itself. With Wayne, the goals can come from anywhere because he is physically the stronger of the pair.

Hall heads up one of the biggest departments at Everton, because producing their own talent is crucial for the cash-strapped club. He puts the roll call of winners down to sheer hard graft and a willingness to work all hours. He said: 'There is something about this area – because it has always produced outstanding talent, not only for us but also Liverpool and Tranmere. It must be in the genes.

'In recent years, we have produced four England internationals in Jeffers, Rooney, Michael Ball and Gavin McCann, plus Richard Dunne for the Republic of Ireland. And five of the ten youngest goalscorers in the Premiership came from here – Jeffers and Rooney again, plus Ball, Michael Branch and Danny Cadamateri. Since our academy was established in 1995, seventeen players have gone on to play for the first team.'

What is most wonderful for Rooney is that, while he may have exploded on to the Premiership and England stage so young, his support unit around him is still there from his schooldays and, of course, people still care. His then manager O'Keefe says: 'In the photos I've got, even aged ten you can pick Wayne out. His shape hasn't actually changed. He's always been built like a battleship.

'I think he'll be fine. In some ways he plays the same as when he was ten. He gets the ball, turns and goes at defenders. Strength, speed, aggression. Irrepressible, the way Scousers are. What he appears to have acquired at Everton is vision.'

Pendleton takes massive pride in what he does, and with Wayne he has hit the big time. But at the end of the day he has just become a friend of the family and wants Rooney to do well like any doting grandad or uncle would: 'I've kept in regular touch with Wayne and his family and they're smashing, down-to-earth people. If Wayne continues to listen to the right people I'm sure he'll have a great future.'

That is one hell of an understatement.

3

Whiz-Kid Wayne

'I did not even need that as proof. You get an experienced scout sitting there with his cup of tea quivering while you're talking to the lad, and you know he's special.'
— Everton Youth Academy supremo Ray Hall talking about Rooney's first trial session for Everton

Wayne Rooney was just nine years old when he first breezed into Bellefield at the start of a journey that would reach superstardom inside eight years. Even at that tender age it was obvious he wasn't your average impressionable youngster.

The prospect would chill the bones of every Everton fan who has revelled in his meteoric rise but, like so many world-class local stars before him, Rooney could have ended up wearing the red of Liverpool. The autumn of 1994 was a bleak time for the Blues as they made their worst ever start to a league season under Mike Walker to become the butt of countless jokes and relegation certainties until former Goodison legend Joe Royle came to the rescue.

At exactly the same time, and a million miles away from the Premiership, the seeds of their long-term recovery were sown when the kid from Croxteth walked in to rewrite the history books.

Merseyside rivals Liverpool had also spotted the young Rooney playing in a local junior game in Bootle, and invited him to Melwood in the hope that the star would change his allegiance from blue to red. But with Rooney and his entire family adamant that there was only one club for him – and Rooney turning up at his trial with Liverpool wearing his Everton kit! – he held out and was soon spotted by Bob Pendleton playing for Copplehouse Juniors, taken to one of the twice-weekly youth training sessions at Everton's Bellefield training ground and signed on the spot by the club's Academy director Ray Hall.

Before he had reached his tenth birthday Rooney was officially a Blue. And the rest, as they say . . .

Even the earliest signs suggested this was a player destined for greatness. He was into double figures in goals long before he was into double figures in years, with his first full season on the Goodison books a staggering success. In just one season Rooney scored 99 goals for the Academy under-10s team, and soon broke the goalscoring record for Liverpool Schoolboys under-11s, grabbing 72 out of a team total of 158 goals.

The striker continued to devote all his time to playing for local sides and school teams but Everton, like all professional Academies, soon wanted him exclusively under their tutelage. It was a blow for De La Salle School that their finest player could no longer represent them, so soon after making the step up from Our Lady and St Swithin's primary, though both schools were soon to share in plenty of reflected glory. When Francis Jeffers partnered Rooney up front on the night he became the youngest ever England international against Australia, it was surely a national-curriculum first that the entire England attack was produced by the same two schools.

Before then, however, Rooney was on the fast track through the Academy ranks. Typically, Wayne represented Everton's under-15s as a thirteen-year-old, before the only real blip of his career saw his progress slowed by his rapid physical development. The stature that would help him brush aside defenders in the Premiership initially upset his natural balance and skill.

But once adolescence was negotiated, the pattern continued and the goals flowed again. Six years after joining the Academy, at the age of fifteen, he was not only promoted to Everton's FA Premier Academy under-17s side, but the 2000–01 season saw him elevated to the under-19s set-up too.

The word had long gone out on Rooney around Merseyside by that stage, though, and, in a policy that lasted throughout his debut season in the Premiership, the staff at the Everton Academy were left the thankless task of trying to keep public praise to a minimum in an effort to keep expectations in check. It was a virtually impossible task as Rooney's football continued to do the talking week in, week out.

In the week he was called up for England under-15s duty against Holland and Germany in February 2001, the Blues striker scored his second goal in two games for the club's under-19s side in a 3–0 win over Bolton Wanderers that took Everton to the top of the Academy League.

Nick Chadwick, four years his strike partner's senior, grabbed the other two that day to take his tally to seventeen for the season. While Chadwick would go on to make his senior debut within two months, the real Rooney bandwagon had begun.

By the start of the 2001–02 season, Rooney was a regular in Colin Harvey's senior Academy side. But for FA rules barring schoolboys from playing league football, it was a campaign that would have ended with a Premiership start. As it was, his involvement in the top flight was restricted to an unused substitute appearance at Southampton a week after leaving De La Salle, but at Academy level thrilling chapters were being written with almost every outing.

Former youth sensation and later thrice Everton boss Howard Kendall recalls a conversation with his old team-mate Colin Harvey, who was the Goodison youth-team coach from 1997 until his retirement last season, and himself a teenage debutant for Everton.

'I asked if there was anybody special coming through the ranks. Now Colin's not the sort of man to get excited about anything, he's seen a legion of promising players come and go, so he's very pragmatic about it all. I've never heard him so animated as he was when he told me about Wayne. I can't remember there being this air of excitement about the place for a long time.'

After a difficult start to the season Rooney marked his sixteenth birthday in superb style as the under-19s' long wait for a first league win ended emphatically in mid-October. The youngster scored four times as Everton crushed Wrexham 5–0, opening the scoring with a flying header in the first half before completing his hat trick with two goals in a minute, then adding a poacher's fourth.

Coach Harvey, a key influence on Rooney's development and the first to handle the prodigy with fatherly care, simply said afterwards: 'I've actually seen Wayne play a lot better than that, but he took his goals very well.' Despite playing with and against more senior, more developed players that season, Rooney continued to shine.

Peter Beardsley knows a thing or two about playing for England and star strikers, so praise from him is something to be cherished. But he could not believe what he saw when he watched Wayne play for the first time. He said: 'I had first-hand experience with Wayne when he played for Everton against our under-19 team at Newcastle. He was only a schoolboy at the time but he made the difference between the two teams. He gave our boys a torrid time and scored two goals.'

By 5 November he'd notched his seventh of the season when he curled in a wonderful free kick with his right foot from 25 yards in a 1–1 draw at Bolton, while the following month delivered two memorable moments for the boyhood Evertonian.

Liverpool have long had reason to curse Rooney's rise across the other side of Stanley Park and December 2001 delivered two major headaches for the Anfield club.

The first under-19s Merseyside derby of the season saw hundreds of fans descending on Bellefield and Liverpool sitting comfortably on a 2–1 lead with just fifteen minutes to go. Then, as the Reds prepared to defend a corner, Harvey made a substitution, rolled his final throw of the dice and on trotted Rooney.

David Carney's corner caused panic in the Liverpool defence, and who should pop up to stab home the equaliser but you-know-who with his first touch of the game. There was more in injury time when the Reds only half-cleared another corner to the waiting Rooney who, from the edge of the penalty area, unleashed a venomous volley past the Liverpool keeper. It was the final kick of the game and the transformation was complete: 3–2 Everton.

Academy director Ray Hall was forced to admit afterwards: 'I'm not one for singling out players, because it was a team effort, but Wayne Rooney, when he came on, did particularly well. Considering he is giving three years away, when he came on his impact was immediate.'

Their derby dismay only made Liverpool even more determined to prise Everton's star asset away from Goodison Park. Later that week they made another attempt to get him to sign schoolboy forms, but it was to no avail.

Rooney pledged his future to the Everton Academy instead, and was paraded in front of 38,615 fans during the half-time interval of a dour Premiership game with Derby County on 15 December. Wayne said at the time: 'Everton are the team I have supported all my life and I'm delighted to have finally signed on the dotted line. The next few years are important ones for me if I am to reach my goal of playing professionally and hopefully I can make a few more appearances for the under-19s this season and maybe get a chance in the reserves.'

Also in attendance as Wayne pledged his future to the club were his parents, Wayne senior and Jeanette, Keith Tamlin, the Everton director responsible for youth development, and Academy director Ray Hall. Hall said: 'Everybody at the club is delighted Wayne has decided to sign with us. Hopefully there will be many successful years ahead for both him and the club.' The signing was watched by then manager Walter Smith, and former teenage prodigy Francis Jeffers was in the stands watching on.

His future was secured and the confidence that would lead him to always attempt the audacious soared. When the Academy season resumed after the winter's break in January, another 3–0 defeat of Bolton provided one world-class moment when Rooney tried one straight from the David Beckham school of finishing. Spotting the Bolton keeper standing too far off his line, the Blues striker launched a shot from the halfway line. The keeper looked on in horror as the ball sailed overhead, but sadly for Rooney it cannoned clear off the crossbar.

The striker, however, could rarely be stopped. By the end of a season that should have been the first of three at Academy level, but proved to be the last before Everton could hold him back no longer, Rooney's tally had reached 25.

He tormented Manchester City both in the league and the FA Youth Cup, scoring a fabulous winner within five minutes of coming on as a substitute in the league game and netting twice in

the 4–2 cup triumph. It was Rooney, who else, who inspired
Everton's run to the final of the Youth Cup that season, their
second appearance in four years.

The Evertonians who gave him a rousing reception in the Derby
County game had obviously heard of his blossoming reputation by
then, and even those oblivious to his rise would soon find him
impossible to ignore as the youngsters' cup run gathered momentum.

A stunning double at Goodison against West Brom sent the Blues
into the fifth round in January. Everton were on top but finding it
increasingly difficult to break down the Baggies defence. Then, four
minutes before half-time, the new Blue sensation collected the ball
deep in his own half. He slalomed his way past three West Brom
players and, with the last beaten on the edge of the area, he unleashed
a ferocious low shot to put his side ahead.

With one minute remaining and the visitors looking more and
more likely to force a draw, Rooney pulled another stunning solo
effort out of his growing box of tricks. With his back to goal and two
defenders closing down, Rooney controlled a long clearance by the
Everton keeper, turned and flicked it between his markers, then
lobbed the Albion keeper from twenty yards.

Ray Hall said: 'Just when we were getting nervous towards the
end, thinking if we let a goal in you don't know what will happen,
young Wayne pops up again and scores a goal as good as you will
see at youth level.'

In the fifth round Man City were again put to the sword as Rooney
scored two and made two in a superb 4–2 win. Rooney, by now an
England under-17 international, needed just four minutes to add to
his double over West Brom in the last round, latching on to
midfielder Scott Brown's lofted pass, bursting his way past the last
defender and dispatching a cool finish into the bottom corner. The
striker then forced an own goal with a vicious cross, then saw
another delivery dropped by the City keeper, Steven Beck eventually
forcing in the loose ball.

City hit back, however, to produce a nervous finale for the Blues,
only for Rooney to settle nerves and the contest two minutes from
time with another sensational goal. He gathered a long clearance out
on the left, and with his team-mates just hoping he'd buy them some

valuable time, instead set off for goal, ghosting past two defenders, before turning the ball on to his right and curling his effort around the City keeper.

Rooney was seemingly on a one-man mission to ensure Everton reached the final. In the quarterfinal against Nottingham Forest at Goodison Park he again stole the show as the Blues came from behind thanks to two moments of Rooney magic in their 2–1 win.

Trailing to an early own goal, the Blues were back on level terms when the youngster produced a stunning overhead kick inside a crowded area after team-mate Alan Moogan's header had crashed down off the bar. Rooney then hit the bar with a fabulous strike from 35 yards, and when he repeated the trick a minute later the Forest keeper could only parry his shot into the path of Australian defender David Carney, who fired home the winner.

In his first full season in the Premiership Rooney never scored a scrappy goal – all were strikes of the highest quality. None, however, compare with the goal he scored in the FA Youth Cup semifinal second leg at Spurs.

After his performance at White Hart Lane saw the Blues triumph 4–2 on aggregate, the former Tottenham manager Glenn Hoddle raced from his seat to seek out youth coach Colin Harvey. Hoddle, in no uncertain terms, told Harvey that Rooney was the best youngster he had ever seen at youth level and asked if there was any chance Everton would sell him. The answer was obvious. As was the reason why.

Rooney sent the visitors into a 3–1 aggregate lead on ten minutes when he sidestepped a defender and unleashed a pile-driver from 25 yards that flew past the Tottenham keeper Rob Burch. But his best was to come in the 37th minute with a goal worth repeating over and over again.

Everton were awarded a free kick thirty yards from goal that Rooney, as only he could, believed was a possibility. He stepped up and curled a shot with his right foot straight into the Spurs wall. The chance, so it seemed by the cries of the home supporters, had gone. It hadn't. The ball spun into the air back to Rooney, and before it had even touched the ground he controlled it on his chest and sent in a first-time volley, this time with his left foot, into the top corner.

A moment of true genius, and one that no one who was fortunate enough to witness it will ever forget. Yet for Rooney, it was just the start.

Yet it was not only the Everton youth team that Rooney set alight. At the moment he has every right to be pulling on an England shirt, though it could still be for the youth team. The teenage Everton striker did have a youth-team career with the young lions, but it was certainly a brief one considering the phenomenal progress he has made.

His first inclusion in an under-15 side came in the Victory Shield against Scotland in November 2000 when he was included alongside his Everton academy mates Scott Brown and Sean Doherty (who now plays for Fulham). Only a year later, though, he had been fast-tracked into the England under-17s set-up – while still a fifteen-year-old playing for Everton's under-19s. Put it this way: he was a child prodigy. The main impact that he had for the England youth side was in the under-17s European Championship held in Denmark in April and May 2002.

Everton were without Rooney for three weeks, but considering he had only become eligible to play for the Premiership side at the Easter when he left school, England won out when the call was made. Once again he was set to make an impact.

In England's group were Holland, Denmark and Finland, and Rooney's scoring prowess was soon setting England on the road to the quarterfinals. He scored the first in a 2–0 victory against Holland in Gladsaxe, Denmark, with a typically superb individual goal. The sixteen-year-old striker also had a hand in England's second strike. His clever ball put in Manchester City's Lee Croft on the right of the box and his low cross was smashed home by Charlton's Stacey Long after the ball had been deflected into his path.

England coach Dick Bates was impressed with Rooney, saying: 'Of course he is just one member of the team, but with the rapid progress that he has made this season, it might have been easy for him to become a little distracted. However, he has shown an excellent attitude since he has been out here, as have the whole squad.'

Rooney could not keep out of the headlines even then, so it was no surprise when he scored again to send England into the semifinals in

Hvidovre, Denmark. He scored the only goal of the game, his second of the tournament as Dick Bates's side beat Yugoslavia to set up a semifinal clash with Switzerland, who beat Georgia 3–0.

Rooney continued the sparkling form that had helped take Everton to the FA Youth Cup final with another man-of-the-match display. He glanced in Stacey Long's left-wing cross past Yugoslavia keeper Igor Baletic after seven minutes, which proved enough to seal the quarterfinal victory.

Disappointing defeat at the hands of Switzerland meant England faced a third-place play-off, but Rooney was not to be denied some glory. He grabbed a stunning hat trick to give England third place in the UEFA Under-17 European Championships.

The Everton youngster made it five goals in five games in the championships as England's youngsters beat pre-tournament favourites, and the previous year's winners, Spain 4–1 to earn bronze medals. Rooney may have missed out on becoming the youngest-ever player to appear in an Everton shirt by playing in this international event, but he showed why he did not have to wait too long for his Blues debut.

After his strike partner, Crystal Palace's Wayne Routledge, had opened the scoring after 37 minutes, Rooney showed his unerring ability to find the net. Two minutes later he scored his first of the match to put England 2–0 ahead, sliding in to force Routledge's cross past Spanish keeper Roberto Santamaria from close range, and in the second half Rooney ran riot to round off an exceptional tournament for Dick Bates's side.

Spain's skipper Jaime Gavilan Martinez pulled one back just before the break, but it took Rooney, still aged sixteen, just six minutes after the restart to strike back and score his second, diving in to head home another Routledge cross. And he completed his hat trick six minutes from the end when Liverpool's Mark Smyth, on as a second-half substitute, played him in on goal and the teenage scoring sensation scored with a typically cool finish.

The England shirt certainly suited him, as he was to find out only ten months later when England played against Australia at Upton Park.

4

Early Stages

'One player cannot win the games on his own and without the efforts of everyone involved we wouldn't have achieved what we have done so far.'

    – Wayne Rooney talking about Everton's FA Youth Cup in May

It may have only been an FA Youth Cup, but these matches supply the grounding of the home-grown Premiership superstars. Most of Manchester United's English stars were victorious in this competition, but it is one thing that went wrong for Rooney in his incredible build-up to his first Premiership season.

Typically, just as Everton were losing 4–2 to Aston Villa in the two-legged final in May 2002, Rooney was having a £15m transfer fee slapped on his head. But at this point for Rooney, football was all about playing with his young mates for the Everton youth team, and the Youth Cup was therefore the most important thing in the world. Rooney had almost single-handedly fired the Toffees youngsters into the final.

Even so, he was unsure he could do it all on his own, as he said: 'One player cannot win the games on his own and without the efforts of everyone involved we wouldn't have achieved what we have done so far.

'It's the biggest game I will have played in. I think we deserved to get there and hopefully we can get the result everyone wants. It's going to be a tough game but if we can get a lead at Goodison and take that to Villa Park we are capable of winning it.'

But the fairy-tale ending to his youth-team career did not come off. 'Once a Blue, Always a Blue' were the words printed on Rooney's

T-shirt as he celebrated the opening goal of the FA Youth Cup final first leg. But the four goals in reply from Villa's young starlets were not really in the script.

Nevertheless Rooney's talent shone out like a beacon in youth-team football, and in this game, prompting Villa coach Tony McAndrew to describe him as the best player he had ever seen at that level – incredibly, at this point he was still eligible for the youth team for two more years.

More than 15,000 Everton fans flocked to Goodison Park for a glimpse of the sixteen-year-old they had heard so much about. For those supporters who do not follow youth football, watching Rooney was an incredible sight and they were not disappointed, as the first half was dominated by Rooney, his one goal – inching him to within touching distance of Michael Owen's all-time Youth Cup record – scant reward for his efforts. Six times he peppered shots at the Villa goal, not to mention a cunningly crafted pass which gave Scott Brown an opening he should have done better with than side-foot over the bar.

There was an air of expectancy around Goodison every time the teenager got the ball, and he rarely disappointed. One long-range volley was deflected over, while another was blocked by goal-keeper Henderson. In the fourteenth minute he muscled out the taller O'Connor in a chase for a long ball and slid a left-footed shot wide, then came the dynamic burst of pace that marked him out as a special talent. Michael Symes, a willing and effective strike partner, played in an inviting pass. Rooney controlled the ball deftly, produced a dramatic change of pace to charge past his covering defender and crashed in an angled shot at the target. Henderson blocked that effort, then recovered superbly to parry the follow-up and push the ball behind for a corner. But Rooney would not be denied. Carney's corner was headed on by Garside and Rooney steered in a far-post header.

For the record, Villa striker Stefan Moore, who made his own Premiership breakthrough under former Villa manager Graham Taylor in the 2002–03 season, scored a double in reply and, after another Villa goal, Moore completed his hat trick to somewhat overshadow Rooney. But of course it was Rooney still making the headlines, as McAndrew said: 'There's no way we can say this tie is over, not with two players like they have up front. Rooney is the best I've ever seen at that age and in that position, and if we think we've already won we could have problems.'

But Blues counterpart Colin Harvey was less hopeful. 'Tony's a good judge of a footballer,' he said, 'but we've got a mountain to climb. I think Wayne tired a little because he's just played five games for England over in Denmark. He showed a lot in the first half of what he is capable of and hopefully he will continue to improve and who knows what we'll see from him in the future.'

Harvey has been like a mentor to Rooney and the boyhood Blue paid special tribute to the Goodison legend who had guided Everton's youth team to their second final in four years. 'I have improved since I started working with Colin,' said Rooney. 'He's an excellent coach and playing with the older lads has also helped me. Colin pushes me and is the first one to say if you need to do something right and he makes sure you do it right next time.'

Whatever Harvey's powers, overcoming a 4–1 deficit was always going to be tough but, nevertheless, for the second leg at Villa Park five days later almost 20,000 fans flocked into the ground to watch Wayne's World – the sequel.

They left safe in the knowledge that the blockbuster has the potential to run and run and run. Villa's eighteen-year-old goalkeeper, Wayne Henderson, and sixteen-year-old Rooney continued the personal duel that had started during Tuesday's first leg.

Rooney produced another compelling performance, including an incredible eight shots that either threatened or flashed narrowly by the Aston Villa goal. But while his efforts earned him the Player of the Final trophy, it was the guardian of that goalmouth, goalkeeper Wayne Henderson, who was Man of this Match. His obstinate display ensured that, while Everton regained their pride with a 1–0 win, Aston Villa captured the cup as they professionally completed the job.

Henderson was finally beaten fifteen minutes from time by Scott Brown's ruthlessly dispatched strike but, whatever anyone else did in those two games, Rooney, just as now, was the centre of attention. It has been down to people like Harvey to keep the young footballer's feet on the ground and make sure he does not get carried away.

So he was the right man in the right place to issue a warning at the end of the Youth Cup. Talking about Rooney, Harvey said:

> There has been an awful lot of hype about him. It is now up to the coaches and the people who deal with him to see that this talent comes to fruition. Obviously we don't want him to fall by the wayside in any way. We've just got to make sure he gets to play in Everton's first team and we see the fruits of that.
>
> He's a level-headed lad and to play in the team he knows he has to play as a team member, which he does. It's up to him how far he goes. He's got a special talent but he's got a long, long way to go.

With Wayne hitting the headlines for the youth sides, there was a massive temptation to throw him into the Everton first team, especially when young former Preston boss David Moyes took over from Walter Smith. Rooney's Everton elevation could have reached new heights at Southampton at the end of the season. He was included in the Blues squad to travel to St Mary's Stadium and if he had gone on he would have become the youngest player in the club's history, breaking Joe Royle's 36-year record.

Moyes, though, was anxious to protect Rooney, who had continued the form that had helped Everton reach the FA Youth Cup final in two impressive reserve run-outs. But, as Moyes vowed to be as careful as Sir Alex Ferguson was with the teenage Ryan Giggs, the new Blues boss admitted that the time and place were right for the prodigy to gain Premiership experience.

He said: 'He scored another great goal this week and was unlucky not to score against Manchester United in the reserves. This experience will help him but we will continue to be careful with him. We've been playing him for forty-five minutes or so for the reserves. We can't just throw him in and we are trying to look after him in the same way that Sir Alex handled Giggs.

'It's a new experience for me, too, and you've got to be careful with young players that you don't place too much expectation on their shoulders.'

Moyes kept Rooney on the bench and, a week later in April 2002, Rooney was again foiled in his record-breaking bid by an international call-up. When Everton entertained Blackburn, Rooney was with the England under-17s in Denmark competing in the European Championship Finals for that age group.

Ironically, there was already a hint of the club-versus-country row that would blow up so massively a year later as Moyes said:

I would have liked to have Wayne Rooney involved on Sunday. It would have been nice for him to be involved in our last home game, but I can also see reasons why perhaps it's a good thing for him to wait a little longer. It will keep expectation levels down. People must realise he is still only a baby in football terms.

The fans showed on Saturday they are already aware of him, although I think most people in football are already aware of him. Wayne has the ability to be involved in the first team now, but we have to be mindful of his age and monitor his progress accordingly.

He is a fine talent, and like most people I would like to see him included in the senior side, but you also have to ask when is the right time for the boy. Wayne Rooney has a long-term future here and we have to protect that. He will definitely be involved with us during our pre-season preparations, but we will have to wait and see about the first team before then.

Rooney may have missed the chance to become the youngest player to appear in an official game for Everton, but he admitted the 2001–02 season still exceeded all expectations. The striker, an unused substitute at Southampton, added:

I didn't set out to make the first team this season. I just wanted to play in a few reserve games before the end of the season but it is what I have always wanted to do.

I want to play in Everton's first team because I've supported them all my life. It doesn't really bother me about breaking the record. The priority for me is taking my chance and hopefully staying in the team. They don't want to put me in too early and play me in too many games because that will have a detrimental effect in the long term.

The games at that level are much more physical and I will probably be introduced for twenty-minute spells. That will give me a chance to get used to the pace and the style. The last few weeks have been a good experience. I've just got to keep my head down, hopefully get picked again and when my chance comes I will have to take it.

Of course, one man had been dreading this moment more than any. Colin Harvey.

Ever since he handed Wayne Rooney his Under-19 Youth Academy debut – at fourteen – and watched him score a stunning goal, he knew the young forward had the potential to explode into the nation's footballing consciousness one day. He merely hoped to delay the inevitable – and when that day came make the transition as smooth as possible.

As one who made his own first-team debut in the cacophonic cauldron of the San Siro aged just eighteen, Harvey understands the pressures of teenage stardom more than most. He was insulated by Harry Catterick up until that point, but while he quickly became public property afterwards, the 1963 press focus was just a fraction of today's, where Sky is not the limit but just one arm of an increasingly intrusive media. 'With the best will in the world, Wayne won't be playing in the European Cup at eighteen for Everton,' said Harvey, 'but he is already attracting media attention . . . too much really.'

And this was the summer of 2002.

Harvey watched the excitement rise to fever pitch around young Rooney as he went from youth team to reserves to the subs' bench for the first team. But after working with him right through his school days, if there is one man who knows how good Rooney is, it is Harvey. And in June 2002 he set out his vision for young Wayne:

If it all pans out, he has an unbelievable future. He has got a very special talent. If I didn't work for Everton he's the kind of player I would pay to go and watch.

But life can be fraught with obstacles when you're that age. He has to realise that, people around him have to realise that; his friends, his family, his agent – so that we can hopefully enjoy his talent at the highest level. Part of that talent is that he is an incredibly hard worker and he has to carry on doing that.

He will have to be protected by the manager and staff in the years ahead. There's so much that can go wrong. But he definitely has a special talent. He isn't just a goalscorer. He can make goals, he tackles back and he forages constantly. Much will depend on how he handles himself when he does make the breakthrough.

For Harvey, the original breakthrough had come when Rooney was just fourteen. With Everton losing an Under-19 Youth Academy match 2–0, he decided to introduce his young substitute.

'Physically he was ready,' said Harvey. 'I put him on, I think it was for Nick Chadwick, and within minutes he had made a couple of chances. He then picked the ball up on the left, went past a couple of players and bent one into the top corner from twenty yards. He was only fourteen and he was playing against men, but nothing fazes him football-wise. We already knew all about him, but that just confirmed what we'd hoped really.'

5

Rooney Unleashed

'We need to make sure that we protect him in the right way and don't overuse him as he is definitely one for the future.'
— Understatement of the year from David Moyes on Wayne Rooney before the start of the 2002–03 season

The time had come, and there was just no holding Wayne Rooney back. David Moyes had desperately tried to resist the temptation of fast-tracking Rooney into the first-team set-up at the end of the 2001–02 season. But things were now different, and with Everton going through a transformation of their own, new blood was needed, and there was nothing better at Goodison Park than a new kid on the block. Nobody, but nobody could have predicted, however, as an Everton squad including young Rooney – who had been given the No 18 shirt – departed for a pre-season tour of Austria quite how the season would pan out.

The fact was that despite only being sixteen, Rooney was a revelation. Having been on the bench the previous season and scoring eight goals in eight games in Everton's FA Youth Cup run he simply had to be included in the senior squad, where he was up against strikers like club captain Kevin Campbell and Tomasz Radzinski for a place in the first team.

There was no way that Rooney was going to arrive quietly, however, so of course he did what he does best – scored goals. On the tour to Austria he netted a hat trick against SC Weiz. He scored another pre-season hat trick against Queen's Park less than a week later. By this time Rooney had only four reserve-team games under his belt, a measure of what was set to be a meteoric rise for the young forward.

His first senior strike for his club came against Austrian lower league side SC Bruck. Young defender Sean O'Hanlon and Tomasz Radzinski were also on the score sheet for the Blues. But it was the prodigious Rooney who was centre of attention following his impressive senior bow.

Moyes said: 'It was nice to see Wayne get his goal. I'm sure the Evertonians here are delighted to have been here for it and, but for a great save from their keeper, he could have had another. It is his first goal as a professional for Everton, and hopefully it will be the first of many from him.'

At that point the Blues boss had vowed to shield Rooney from the glare of publicity as he embarked on his fledgling professional career. He said: 'We need to make sure that we protect him in the right way and don't overuse him as he is definitely one for the future.

'The situation we have with Wayne means we are not going to build him up and put any more pressure on him than there is already. We are going to take it step by step and use him as carefully as we can.'

Rooney had set pulses racing during pre-season with a string of impressive displays, goals and assists, and expectations were sky high around Goodison Park. It may have been Moyes's first start to a season in charge at Everton, and his first full season in the Premiership, but all anybody was talking about was Rooney, the wonder kid with fire in his boots. However much Everton tried, they could not suppress such a fantastic talent, or the hype surrounding him. Try as they might, the club were finding it increasingly difficult to play his talents down.

Deputy chairman Bill Kenwright joked: 'We've all decided at Everton we've got to play down the fact that Wayne Rooney is probably going to be the greatest goalscorer in England. He's awesome. Walter Smith said to me two years ago that he'd seen something he'd never seen before on a football pitch. He's just got everything. He's by far and away the best I've ever seen.'

Cotton wool, at this point however, was still being shipped in to Goodison Park as the Blues desperately tried to protect their prize asset.

Rooney was still only sixteen, after all, and would ordinarily just be entering his third year at YTS level. Moyes's decision not to play him down at Southampton the previous season had deprived the youngster of the accolade of being the club's youngest ever player, but Moyes could never allow sentiment to enter into his head as he grappled with the idea of it being too early to throw Rooney into the Premiership lions' den. He said in August 2002: 'I'm not that worried if he becomes the youngest player in the club's history. I'm more concerned that he becomes the best player in the club's history. That's my aim and that's what I'm looking at more than anything.'

After mulling over the pros and cons of using a boy, who was admittedly as powerful as a silverback gorilla, Moyes eventually conceded that he had no choice but to give youth its head. It was a bold move at the time.

Moyes said, before a Premiership ball was kicked that season:

Wayne is incredibly quick in training, he is very strong for his age, he has great awareness and a footballing brain which normally doesn't come until later on in years.

He has got that at present, so from that point of view it is going to be difficult not to play him. But people have to realise that, with sixteen-year-old boys, mentally they are not fully developed and they will need to be taken out of the team at regular intervals and sometimes maybe even put back into the youth team, because really this should only be his first year at the club as a YTS.

Supporters have to remember that. There will be lulls in his game at times, big lulls, and we will have to know when the time is right to pull him out for his own benefit.

Wise words, and ones that bore some truth as the season and the controversy surrounding Rooney raged on. Yet it was almost impossible for Evertonians not to get excited on the basis of what they'd seen. How could they not be enthralled by the prospect of having a real star of their own on their hands? Francis Jeffers had promised so much, but had left the club for Arsenal with cries of 'Judas' ringing in his ears.

Of course, once people outside the cosseted world of youth football realised how good Rooney was they would be trying to snatch him from Everton's grasp. Thankfully, assurance to the fans that the youngster would not be sacrificed immediately to satisfy the bank manager came in early summer 2002 when Moyes said:

> I've heard some fans say that, but there's not a chance of that happening. When I came to take the job at Everton I was told about Wayne Rooney, but one of the things I said was if I come here I don't want to have to sell my best players. If players have to go it will be because I don't want them or because I think I can get a better player, so that certainly won't be the case with Wayne Rooney.
>
> He's got games to play and we don't want him to get above his station. He's only just left school two months ago so we have to be very careful . . . He is a special case and we need to deal with him that way and look after him as best we can.
>
> Obviously we will try if we can to protect him as much as we can by keeping the media spotlight off him. At times that might be annoying to the press but it is something I am quite determined to do. There will be times during the year when he will get opportunities to deal with the press but he is such a great prospect we are going to try and do everything we can to keep him right.
>
> He's sixteen years old so we don't know if he's going to be that good yet, but what we can see and what we're working with just now there's no question he's got as much ability as anybody I've ever seen at that age.

Rooney was as good as *anybody* had seen at his age. By the time his league debut arrived on the opening day of the season against Spurs he was a fortnight older than Joe Royle had been in setting a club record of 16 years and 282 days.

Unbelievably, in the 2–2 draw against Tottenham Rooney did not score, which considering how he had turned everything else he had touched so far in his career to gold, must have been a major surprise.

Another record was not far away though. Eight games came and went as Everton failed to make a particularly remarkable start to the season, and Rooney was used as a sub at times as Moyes kept to his word. But when the Worthington Cup came around and Everton were drawn against Wrexham, then Rooney was given another chance, and this time he made the most of it.

In fact, Rooney became the youngest goalscorer in Everton history as he smashed two goals and the Blues' Worthington Cup curse at Wrexham on 1 October 2002. Kevin Campbell opened the scoring with his sixth goal of the season, and Everton reached the third round for the first time in four years thanks to a 3–0 win at The Racecourse – but it was Rooney who took centre stage as he wrote his way into the history books.

The striker, 23 days short of his seventeenth birthday, sealed victory over the Third Division pacesetters with two goals in seven minutes after coming on as a 64th-minute substitute. His feat broke the 65-year record set by the legendary Tommy Lawton in 1937.

David Moyes said: 'Wayne is delighted to have got his goals. He's been a bit anxious over not scoring so far but you expect that of a sixteen-year-old. He took his goals well, showed what he is capable of and hopefully there is a lot more to come in the future.'

The Blues boss added: 'We know what a talent we've got here and we will keep using him carefully until he's ready to play regularly.'

It was not long, however, before he was making the headlines all over the world.

6

Wonder Strike

'We were beaten by a special goal and a special talent. He has intelligence, pace, quick reactions, accuracy in front of goal, a low centre of gravity. He's a big prospect for English football.'

– Arsène Wenger, in raptures despite his team's defeat

If the world did not already know about Wayne Rooney, his last-minute goal against Arsenal on 19 October 2002 announced him on the Premiership – and ultimately world – stage. Beating David Seaman from thirty yards has not proved that difficult in recent months after the goal he conceded against Ronaldinho in the World Cup, but it was Arsenal's first defeat of the season and Rooney was still only sixteen. Commentator Clive Tyldesley said over the roar of the Goodison crowd: 'Remember the name – Wayne Rooney.'

Everton have watched with mounting frustration as young talent has rolled off the Liverpool production line with monotonous regularity. Anfield's academy delivered Steve McManaman and Robbie Fowler, swiftly followed by Michael Owen, Jamie Carragher and Steven Gerrard. Everton's anxiety at this list of high-class talent was made even more acute by the fact that they were all – Gerrard apart – unashamed boyhood Everton fans. At long last there were envious glances across Stanley Park at the emergence of a new talent who was already earning plaudits from the game's biggest names.

Rooney's astonishing winning goal against Arsenal confirmed him as one of the brightest talents in the English game – a view backed by no less an authority than Gunners boss Arsène Wenger. He had to sit on the bench and watch as the ball fell to Rooney about thirty yards out. The youngster just looked up and, with incredible audacity, he took aim and the ball just flew in a wonderful majestic arc over the top of Seaman. To tell you the truth, any goalkeeper in the world would have struggled to save it, let alone 'Safe Hands', as Seaman likes to call himself.

Wenger just could not believe it. 'He is the biggest English talent I've seen since I arrived in England,' the Frenchman said after the teenager's goal. 'There has certainly not been an under-twenty player as good as him since I became a manager here. We were beaten by a special goal from a very special talent – you do not need to be an expert to see that he is a special talent, very special.'

From that moment onwards Wayne's world would never be the same. For starters, in scoring he became the youngest ever player to grab a goal in the Premiership – that is until he was unbelievably beaten a few weeks later by Leeds United's James Milner. In Euro 2004 he also became the youngest ever goalscorer, but again only for a few days, until a young Swiss player scored.

But it all went further than that. For the first time Rooney seemed to register on the nation's psyche. Of course by the previous summer most people knew him. But before this goal he was just a very promising kid at Everton who everybody was talking about. One swish of his right boot, however, and all that changed. To score a goal like that at his age was incredible.

But to do it against the reigning Premiership champions when they were unbeaten so far in the season, and for it to be the winner, was simply mind-blowing. The whole of Goodison Park went mad. But up in the stands sat two very proud parents who knew it was what their son had been born to do.

As Rooney struck his career-determining goal, like the rest of the Everton fans his parents exploded from their seats and screamed with delight. But, in true blue fashion, it was not only because Wayne had scored, but also because they had won the game.

Jeanette and Wayne senior were in the Main Stand with their two other sons. And it was to his family that Wayne ran when he scored in the last minute to open his Premiership account. Jeanette told the *Liverpool Echo*: 'We've been celebrating ever since the final whistle!'

It was a breathtaking moment for his parents, and a day after Rooney's wonder strike they had some time to sit back and reflect on what had happened. At the family home in Croxteth, Jeanette said: 'It was a very emotional day. I had tears in my eyes when Wayne scored. And we've been celebrating ever since, that's why I've almost lost my voice!'

With such a short career in top-flight football, Rooney was bound to pick this strike out as the one that meant most to him. When asked the question at the end of the 2002–03 season, he said: 'It would have to be my first Premiership goal against Arsenal. At the time I needed a goal to build my confidence, as I hadn't scored since the Wrexham game in the League Cup. It was the beginning of that great run in the league the club had last season and I like to think I have played my part.'

But did he know exactly what he was doing when he scored against Arsenal? He says: 'I knew that I was aiming for the top corner but I didn't think it would go in. When it beat Seaman I didn't know what to do, in fact I don't know why I ran over to where I did, but it was a great feeling and it was made even more special because it was against the then champions who had been having an unbelievable run.

'My mum started crying and my dad hugged me after the game. But that was just part of it. The dressing room was bedlam. The lads were all leaping about celebrating and we could still hear the crowd singing and cheering outside. It was five days before my birthday – a nice time to score. I knew it was going in because I'd caught it spot-on.'

Jeanette knows Wayne better than anyone in the world and, just 24 hours after that incredible goal, she was adamant he would be able to cope with the media attention. She insisted: 'He's level-headed and I think he'll be able to keep his feet on the ground.' Asked if Wayne might be leaving Goodison Park for another club, she added defiantly: 'No, he is not!'

Rooney's father said in the aftermath of the Arsenal strike that he hoped his son would go on to score many more goals for Everton. Wayne Rooney senior could not quite believe what had happened. But he said: 'Saturday was the proudest day of my life. I am a lifelong Everton fan and to see my son score for my team was out of this world. I'm sure it's the first of many goals – I hope I get to see them all.'

Another person who wept tears of joy in the Main Stand on that memorable Saturday was retired train driver Bob Pendleton, the scout who recommended Wayne to the Blues. Bob said:

> Wayne has set the city on fire. And the good news is this is just the start, there's so much more to come from him. He was born to score goals.
>
> As soon as he took the ball down and faced the goal I knew he was going to hit it. I'm not afraid to admit that, like Wayne's mum, I had tears in my eyes. And the crowd's reaction to the goal just made it even more emotional, they went berserk!
>
> Like everybody else, I found myself chanting 'ROONEY! ROONEY! ROONEY!' I know there's already been talk about Wayne going to another club, perhaps Manchester United, Arsenal or even Liverpool, but I honestly can't see it happening.

This was the news every Blue fan was just desperate to hear at the time. As already mentioned, Wayne turned down the chance of joining Liverpool as a nine-year-old, and Bob added: 'I can't see him going anywhere. Wayne and all his family are Everton, Everton, Everton!'

The reason Gary Lineker rarely talks about his former Everton employers is that no one ever asks him about them. But the Rooney rocket that exploded past David Seaman was a talking point for everyone in football, Lineker included. Everton's one-season wonder suggested Rooney could forge an international strike force with another boy wonder, one who swapped an Everton shirt for a Liverpool jersey long before he grew up. He did not have long to wait to be proved right. Shortly after the Arsenal game and Rooney's seventeenth birthday, Lineker said:

> Wayne Rooney reminds me a lot of the way Michael Owen broke through a few years ago when he was a similar age. Michael is a fantastic young player but, when you look at the England team at the moment, it's obvious we need someone alongside him on a regular basis. You're looking at a few players – Emile Heskey, Alan Smith, Robbie Fowler, Darius Vassell –

who might come on and do it, but none of them have proved themselves in that position.

There is a vacuum there . . . as we saw with Michael, when he was eighteen, he was in. Rooney looks a fantastic talent. I haven't even seen him play in the flesh but he excites me and he must excite every fan in the country.

The goal against Arsenal was out of this world, but the next bit of skill he showed was even better when he had the audacity to try and chip David Seaman. He might be seventeen, but he looks twenty-five, not just in his build and appearance but in the way he plays.

He's so confident and it doesn't look as if anything fazes him. We need to see him over a period of time before we can be certain, but to do that sort of thing at his age is unbelievable. Let's just hope we've really found one here.

Lineker added: 'I do still have an affinity for the club and it would be fantastic if they were to produce one of the great talents in Rooney.

'Everton have struggled more or less ever since I left. They gradually drifted away. But Rooney is exciting to see and in David Moyes he has a manager who will help him come along.'

Former Everton boss Howard Kendall – Everton's most successful manager, winning the League twice, FA Cup and European Cup Winners Cup – urged Wayne Rooney not to get caught up in the hype and instead take his career 'one step at a time'. Kendall was once, at the age of seventeen, the youngest footballer to play in an FA Cup final. Now he was giving the benefit of his own experience and advising Rooney he should not get carried away with things, but must concentrate on becoming an Everton regular.

Kendall said:

Wayne was always going to get a first-team chance this season and score when he did. The manner in which he achieved that against Arsenal was fantastic and there is no doubt he is one of the most exciting prospects around.

But he is not an established player yet and must take one step at a time. He should now work hard and show the manager he deserves to play every week. I was just a little bit older than Wayne when I played in the cup final for Preston, so I can imagine the pressure he feels.

But football is a lot different now and I did not have to contend with what Wayne has to in terms of the media and other commercial demands. The club will protect him and the spotlight will move away. It is up to Wayne to be responsible and if he does he will be a huge success.

Wayne will continue to score goals out of the ordinary and that will make him a media star like Michael Owen. There will be a lot of hype this season and for years to come. Wayne must keep his feet on the ground and stay focused. What he does on the pitch is the main thing and the rest will come if he carries on in the same way he did against Arsenal.

Typically the whole Blue half of Merseyside went mad after the goal. They had their hero and they wanted everybody in the world to know about it. The fact that he was home-grown and an Everton fan made it even better.

The football club made a sharp about-turn in their policy of protecting their teenage prodigy from too much publicity within days of the goal, although they did not put him in front of the press.

Until then the club had carefully protected Rooney from media exposure, but it emerged quickly that the Blues planned to fully exploit the new merchandising opportunities following Rooney's stunning last-minute winner. The strike made him the youngest goalscorer in Premiership history and left him negotiating a lucrative contract. His was already the most popular name printed on replica shirts sold at the club shop in the first part of the season. Club marketing manager Tracy Weston said nine out of ten shirts were printed with Rooney's name and number:

There is no doubt that Saturday's result [against Arsenal] combined with the school's half-term has sparked a flurry of activity in the megastore. The store has been busy all day with people queuing to have Wayne's name printed on their shirts.

Some customers who have already purchased their shirts were bringing them back to have Rooney's name inscribed on the back. Evertonians have been longing for a new hero and there is no doubt that

Saturday's result and Rooney's performance have renewed enthusiasm for the team and all associated merchandise.

The club has tried to carefully protect Wayne from the media. During this time, Everton has made a conscious decision not to capitalise on his popularity and jeopardise his development. However, fans will expect to obtain Rooney merchandise and will expect official merchandise through the club.

(New Rooney merchandise that the club hoped to swiftly get on to the shelves included a video of the thirty-yard strike that had stunned soccer.)

Rooney's popularity had knocked Duncan Ferguson from the top slot of most-wanted name for shirts sold at the club shop, the next most popular name being Chinese signing Li Tie (no real surprise with the obsession with the sport in the Far East). But within days a Rooney fan club had started up in Beijing. As a result of his goal, Rooney-mania swept the world as Everton's wonder kid made headlines around the planet. The youngster's last-minute strike that had ended Arsenal's thirty-match unbeaten run caused shockwaves worldwide.

Liverpool landed in Russia for a Champions League match to be greeted by *Moscow Times* headlines hailing 'Everton Kid Ends Arsenal Unbeaten Run!' Incredibly, the Reds' match with Spartak Moscow was a secondary story, much to the annoyance of Gerard Houllier and his boys.

Italian news agencies claimed that Milan had already offered Everton Brazilian defender Roque Junior, just for first refusal on any future transfer.

And influential Italian newspaper *Gazzetta dello Sport* carried a major feature on the youngster.

But beaming Blues boss David Moyes reiterated that, despite everybody going mad over his youngster, Rooney would remain at Goodison. 'When I arrived here I told the board I wanted to build a younger team. Now we have Wayne, Tony Hibbert, Joseph Yobo, Richard Wright and Li Tie all doing well and I don't want players like that leaving.

'Wayne's contract is done and dusted. He will sign a three-year deal with a two-year option. But he is not particularly mature yet on or off the pitch. We need to protect him and I hope our fans understand that.'

Rooney was due to celebrate his seventeenth birthday just days after his stunning goal. It was widely expected that that would be the date he would put pen to paper on his first professional contract. But despite Rooney being so young, agents are still a massively important part of the make-up of the sport and, just like the film *Jerry Maguire* with Tom Cruise, there is not always loyalty when it comes down to the nitty-gritty of committing yourself. Moyes, on the other hand, was not concerned about all this, and just wanted to get on with the job of protecting his new star. Little did he know at this point the battle that lay ahead.

Typically, the Scot insisted that, despite Rooney's stunning strike, all of his players deserved credit for ending Arsenal's unbeaten run. 'We were in the dressing room fifteen minutes after the match had ended and we could hear supporters still singing in the streets outside. It was a great experience and we told the players they were all responsible.'

Moyes pointed out that Rooney's strike was his first of the week. 'Wayne's goal was a great one,' he said. 'He hadn't scored all week in training and sometimes we have criticised him for shooting when it's unrealistic. But his position gave him a great chance to score and fortunately he did.'

Tomasz Radzinski, the striker Rooney replaced in the Arsenal game, added: 'I've been waiting my entire career to score a goal like that and he scores it at the age of sixteen against Arsenal to become a record-breaker! It's amazing!'

But however young and fresh Rooney seemed, and even non-chalant at what he had achieved, football experts had been preparing the Everton star for the limelight for two years. Everybody connected with Everton just knew the type of sensation that they had on their hands and did not want him to be thrown into the deep end.

The player was told by coaches at Everton's youth academy in Netherton to expect a spectacular break into Premiership football and to 'keep his feet on the ground'. Perhaps they did not expect it to come with such a brilliant goal.

FA football science advisor Professor Tom Reilly said after his goal against Arsenal that Everton coaches had carefully nurtured their young star. 'Rooney's mentors will have been saying to him that this will happen over the last twenty-four months. You can talk young talented people through the future and give them a clear picture about the exposure they will receive so they know what to expect when it happens.'

Prof. Reilly, who is based at Liverpool John Moores University, has published research on why some talented young players break into top-flight football and others fail. He said: 'Physical and genetic factors are very important in explaining why Rooney has such talent, but the key factor is the tuition he has received. The academy coaches will have concentrated on his joints, muscles and heart fitness. Compared with twenty or thirty years ago, young players have a lot more protection and play fewer games.'

Former Everton manager Howard Kendall, who nurtured Everton's last wonder kid Francis Jeffers, said Rooney's coaches would try to treat him like any other player.

'His challenge is to be a regular in the team. The manager will probably point out that other players are scoring goals at the moment and that he has to do the same. Physically he is capable of coping at the top level and if he is the best you have, you put him in the team. I fully expect to see him scoring a winner in the derby.'

Former cup-winning Everton captain Kevin Ratcliffe said: 'When I played there wasn't the massive exposure and you could probably go down south and not be recognised. Now clubs do try and limit access to their young players. As part of their scholarship I am sure they learn how to do TV interviews. We used to learn how to perform in interviews from the older players in the team.'

But there was no way that Rooney's advisors, mainly his mum and dad, were going to let their now-famous son get carried away with everything. So, as a result, Wayne celebrated his seventeenth birthday on 24 October 2002 with a Goodison giveaway that left other youngsters celebrating too.

The kind-hearted Everton star donated his record-breaking boots to Alder Hey Hospital's Rocking Horse Appeal. The boots he wore to become the Premiership's youngest goalscorer against Arsenal were handed over to the UK's first ever integrated cancer unit for children, to be auctioned off at the appeal's tiara ball the following month. As part of the visit Wayne was given a special birthday card made by an Everton fan who is at Alder Hey.

Professional Footballers' Association deputy chief executive Mick McGuire praised Everton's protective handling of Rooney. 'Wayne is a phenomenon who has come through so quickly he still has a year of his PFA scholarship to go,' he said. People seemed to forget that.

It was not long, however, before he was at it again and Rooney-mania again took hold as Everton's young striker, now all of seventeen, hit another memorable winner to give David Moyes's side their first league win at Elland Road since 1951. If there had been any doubt as to whether Wayne Rooney was all hype following his remarkable goal-of-the-season contender against Arsenal, then the Croxteth-born youngster blew them away in early November.

Just five minutes after his second-half introduction for Tomasz Radzinski, Rooney underlined just what an outstanding talent he is. There appeared to be little danger for Leeds when he picked up an 80th-minute through ball from Li Tie around 35 yards from goal. But first he showed a superb turn of speed as he left Eirik Bakke flat on his back, before powering his way into the area, evading the challenge of Leeds skipper Lucas Radebe and then firing an angled twelve-yard shot beyond the previously exceptional Paul Robinson.

He had scored directly in front of the travelling Everton fans, many of whom could not help but mob their hero as a mini-pitch invasion took hold, one that was soon dispersed.

Rooney's strike gave Everton a third successive Premier-ship victory, leaving Leeds with a miserly two points from their last six league games, and now firmly entrenched in the bottom half of the table.

After his strike at Elland Road after coming on from the subs' bench, Lucas Radebe said, 'I'm still banging my head against a wall to explain how Wayne Rooney scored that goal.' That just about sums the wonder kid up. He does things others can only dream about.

So what did Rooney feel like scoring the winning goal against Leeds United after the club hadn't won there for 51 years? He said: 'It felt fantastic because we had been on a great run and had enjoyed a few back-to-back wins. I was only on for about ten minutes and scoring the winning goal in front of the Everton fans is a moment that will live with me for a very long time to come. It is definitely up there with the Arsenal goal.'

From earning £80 a week, after signing scholarship forms at half-time against Derby in March 2002, to being on the verge of signing professional terms worth £13,000 a week by December – not bad for a seventeen-year-old who still played footie in the streets.

After the Leeds game he was spotted playing football in the road with his mates. Concerned Evertonians phoned the club to report him to his manager. David Moyes smiled. Playing with the ball was fine according to the Scot, but if anybody saw him doing something he shouldn't they should send him home. It seemed the whole Blue side of Merseyside had taken on the role of surrogate parents.

Three days after the Leeds win and Everton were playing Newcastle in the Worthington Cup at St James' Park. It was 3–3 after extra-time, so the game went to penalties. David Unsworth's was saved, Dave Watson put his away and Rooney scored the third, despite missing two the day before in training.

Kevin Campbell finished the job off. It was the first time Everton had won a penalty shoot-out since beating Borussia Mönchengladbach at Goodison Park back in 1971. The lad Rooney was becoming not just a phenomenon, but a lucky charm. It was a pity he wasn't still on the pitch for the shoot-out against Portugal in Euro 2004.

At this point Rooney could do no wrong as he was the rising star and everything he touched seemed to turn to gold. He took centre stage against Blackburn in mid-December and stepped into the spotlight again with an air of audacious authority to end Everton's three-match losing streak. As a player with the world at his feet he again showed just why he was held in such high esteem.

Following the successive defeats, Moyes decided it was time to call upon Rooney in a bid to stop the rot, with Tomasz Radzinski perhaps feeling aggrieved as he was the player to make way – and on his 29th birthday to boot. But Moyes's decision was perfectly justified as Rooney captivated an expectant crowd at Goodison Park, playing his part in the equaliser before scoring a sublime second.

After the Blues had gone behind, former Blackburn midfielder Lee Carsley, who scored twelve goals in his 54 appearances during his time at Ewood Park, started and finished a move leading to Everton getting back on track. It was his initial header that set Campbell free down the right, enabling him to turn in a low cross through the area, which Rooney struck first time from fifteen yards. Although the ball hit the base of the post, it fortuitously rebounded behind a diving Brad Friedel for Carsley to tap home from two yards.

Everton grabbed the lead straight from a goal kick and, although it might have been route one football, the finish was ten out of ten from Rooney. Richard Wright's punt bounced once deep in the Blackburn half, with Rooney's initial flick-on allowing him to pierce the defensive cover of Craig Short and James McEveley, who spent six years in Everton's juniors alongside the teenage star prior to his release. Rooney then produced a superb right-foot finish beyond Friedel for his fifth goal of the season and his third in the league.

Cries of 'Rooney, Rooney' echoed around Goodison Park again as it seemed there was nothing this lad could not do.

When the spotlight on such a young player is so massive, then of course as soon as he steps out of line in any way, the football world goes mad.

Up until Boxing Day 2002 everything was going like a dream for Wayne Rooney. His start to the season had been outstanding. He had scored one of the most memorable Premiership goals ever in beating David Seaman and he was playing regularly for Everton. Then came the Toffees' Boxing Day game against Birmingham City.

Rooney was again on the bench for this game and came on in the second half in their 1–1 draw. After being on the pitch for fifteen minutes the ball ran away from him close to the Birmingham City penalty box and he seemed to lunge in with a tackle on defender Steve Vickers. It was unclear how harsh a tackle it was and it did seem that he was going for the ball.

But, already in his brief Premiership career, Rooney had been booked four times and shown a hot-headed streak. David Elleray, in his last season as a top-flight ref, made a quick decision and gave him a straight red card, which was the first sending off of his career. The young Rooney could not quite believe what had happened and was distraught.

This, though, was where Moyes was at his best. Instead of criticising his young star, which would have been so easy, especially considering his lack of experience, he decided instead to defend him.

Vickers needed eight stitches in the gash on the top of his foot and was out of action for three weeks. But Moyes immediately asked the Middlesex official to review the incident. Elleray agreed, but then refused to make any further comment on the matter.

Moyes claimed Rooney was the victim of a bad decision by Elleray and turned his fire on the referee. 'I asked the ref to look at a replay of the incident on our TV monitor. Reluctantly, he did, but he wouldn't comment,' revealed Moyes. 'As far as I can see, it would be useless for us to appeal against the automatic three-match ban Wayne will now receive.

'As usual, the referees will get their stories straight and close ranks against us. At Everton, we feel they are too keen to act against us. We put forward a good case on David Unsworth's behalf when he was dismissed, with no effect. If we try again, it will only be the same result.'

Following Everton's attempt to have David Unsworth's sending off against Chelsea overturned, and after officials missed Steven Gerrard's challenge on Gary Naysmith in the Merseyside derby just before Christmas, evidence was mounting in Moyes's mind that his club was being unfairly treated. He said: 'It's a decision that could be construed in either way. In some people's eyes it could be seen as a sending off, in others' it wouldn't be.'

He also blamed Elleray for sending Rooney off because of his reputation. The kid now faced a three-match ban, which some might have said was a blessing in disguise and would give him a natural rest. Moyes said:

> Maybe a little bit of reputation has gone before him and maybe the referee has been looking at that. We have to tell him that he has to be a little bit more careful. We have told Wayne already this year and we'll tell him again.
>
> I honestly don't believe we are getting a fair crack of the whip from referees in general. Apart from Wayne's red card Mr Elleray got it wrong with his use of the advantage law. In that respect, his decisions were diabolical, absolutely scandalous. But I won't let the sending off affect my handling of Wayne. I repeat, it was a good, honest challenge. I'm delighted with the way Wayne is progressing.
>
> It was a decent attempt at a challenge by Wayne which possibly deserved no more than a yellow card. One thing is certain, I'm not going to ask Wayne to change his style, because aggression and strength are big qualities, together with the boy's obvious ability.

There was no way that Moyes was going to back down or allow his young lad to be criticised in any way.

In being sent off, of course, Rooney broke another record by becoming the youngest player ever to be shown a red card in the Premiership. He also *lost* his record as the youngest goalscorer, an honour taken on the same day by Leeds trainee James Milner at Sunderland, aged 16 years and 357 days.

With the New Year out of the way, what could be one of the most important days in Everton Football Club's history arrived when Rooney put pen to paper on his first ever professional deal. It was 18 January 2003, and it was the start of what promised to be an extraordinary multi-million-pound career. Rooney's response to signing the deal was music to the ears of Everton fans, as he said: 'There was never any doubt I would sign.'

The Blues hero signed a three-and-a-half year deal with his boy-hood club to instantly become one of the highest paid teenagers in world football. Rooney's first professional contract was the maximum a seventeen-year-old could sign under FA rules and

Everton are hoping he will sign an extended five-year deal now that he has turned eighteen.

On a hectic day of negotiations, Everton also secured the services of emerging fullback Tony Hibbert, who committed himself to a new four-year contract. But it was Rooney, in his first public appearance, who dominated the packed late-night press conference at Goodison and finally allayed any fears over his delayed deal – a deal that many believed was going to be settled on his seventeenth birthday the previous October.

It was incredible for the fans just to hear Rooney speak and the press conference was beamed live on Sky Sports to the nation, and then around the world. Rooney said: 'I am delighted everything has been sorted out. It means everything for me to play for Everton so this is a dream come true. I can't really explain what it means to me to sign. It is the best feeling in my life. Just playing for Everton gives me a buzz. It's a bit weird because I used to look up to players like Duncan [Ferguson] and now I am playing alongside them every day.

'I have been watching Everton since I was a kid so there was never any doubt I would sign. It was very important for me and my family that I stayed here.'

The contract had been held up by the issue of Rooney's projected image rights, raising fears Everton would lose a player his agent, Paul Stretford, described as 'the hottest property in English football' to one of Europe's heavyweights. The money-men from Madrid and Milan were all being linked with Rooney's signature as his first Goodison contract hit several delays and Evertonian nerves frayed with every one. But Everton and Rooney's ProActive Sports management team finally struck a joint image-rights deal whereby both the club and the player benefit. Such deals are commonplace in mainland Europe but unusual in the Premiership, although the likes of David Beckham and Michael Owen now have such arrangements.

Paul Stretford explained: 'Wayne's fame goes beyond these shores and it was important we got the structure of the contract right. The image rights were complicated but we have found a joint alliance where both Everton and Wayne are marketed by a joint marketing operation. It is not normal in this country or for a player of Wayne's age but it reflects the status of the player. This is a massive signing for Everton Football Club.'

The clues were fairly obvious on the T-shirt upon which he'd scribbled 'Once a Blue, Always a Blue' that he would sign this deal. But just in case protracted contract negotiations had raised any doubts about Wayne Rooney's allegiance, he was more than happy to set the record straight at the press conference. 'If people asked me, "Real Madrid, Inter Milan or Everton?" it would be Everton every time,' he said. That ought to do it.

It was now eight months since the new Goodison hero had begun his own fashion range after scoring in the FA Youth Cup final against Aston Villa but, in terms of attention, adulation and now financial security, it must surely have felt like another lifetime for the entire Rooney clan.

Wayne senior and mum Jeanette were in proud attendance at Goodison Park as their teenage son signed his first professional contract and was then unveiled to the world's media for the first time. For anyone making their first appearance in front of a mass of TV cameras, reporters and photographers it would be a daunting experience – his dad was even sweating with nerves at the back of the Joe Mercer Suite! For a seventeen-year-old fresh out of school, though, it's safe to say no one knows what it must have felt like because so few have gone before him. His voice could barely be heard above the clamour for every word from the youngster.

But fresh from the grilling, in the safety of the Goodison boardroom where a few hours earlier he had signed the long-awaited deal, Rooney could finally start to relax and enjoy the moment. As David Moyes broke open a bottle of Diet Coke for his prodigious talent, the Everton sensation – still with his tie perfectly knotted just in case anyone in the English establishment is worrying – was anxious to stress what all this meant to him. Speaking to Andy Hunter of the *Daily Post* he said:

I never had any doubts during the talks. I never wanted to go to another club. It's as simple as that. Running out there at Goodison with 'Z-Cars' playing in the back-ground is one of the best feelings in my life. It's what I've always wanted to do.

Now my ambition is just to keep playing for Everton, to keep doing what I am doing now and hopefully get in the England squad. I really hope I can realise my ambitions with Everton. We have other good young players and hopefully we can continue what we have achieved this season and push even further up the table . . . The fact the team has done so well has made it even better and easier for me to come in.

The adulation he had received had knocked him sideways a little, but as Rooney added:

Sometimes it is hard dealing with all the attention, especially when people are sitting outside your house. That's the bit I don't like, that's the downside and I wish it would go away.

On the pitch I think maybe because of all the attention my card is being marked a bit more, like the sending off at Birmingham for example which was never a sending off. Maybe because of my style of play people have been looking out for me, but I've been booked a few times this season for silly things like kicking the ball away, so it is up to me as well to take it all on board and learn.

But I haven't changed a bit in the last six months. I am the same now as when I left school and I have all the same mates. The contract won't change that at all. The manager is keeping me in control so I don't think keeping my feet on the floor is going to be a problem. Besides, I am more interested in playing football than money.

Moyes, of course, stressed the need for hard work: 'His exceptional talent will go away if he doesn't keep hard at it. Young players have difficulties off the field just like young men have difficulties in life. Both Tony Hibbert and Wayne are reasonably level-headed but, like anyone else, they will make mistakes and we know that. We are trying to take away their adolescence. I don't believe that should be the case, but if they fall then we will try and pick them up.'

Rooney's agent, Paul Stretford, explained:

Wayne understands the media is part and parcel of the modern game. He has a God-given talent as a footballer, but he's not a natural public speaker. This is the most exciting time now because we will see Wayne develop as a footballer and a person, but we've all got to give him time to grow up. People forget. When they see him on the pitch he plays like a man, he is a man, but off the pitch these are fairly daunting times for him.

He would like to be like the other lads in the Academy and come up gradually, but he has exploded like a rocket and we just hope people can be forgiving. Supporters want heroes and, as David Moyes said, forty thousand people stand up as soon as he gets the ball. Wayne just blanks that out and gets on with it. The big question for David and the club and me is how to handle that. We want to help him grow as a person.

Talking about Rooney's image-rights deal, Stretford added:

There can be complications but Everton have acted in the manner befitting a club with the status they have. There was no negativity about it, if anything it's going to be something that's beneficial to Everton because they have got a very positive image to exploit. We hope that's how it will be. That was a difficulty but not as much as the fact it was Christmas, which meant it was hard getting everyone to sit down together.

Wayne is still an Academy player so can only sign an Academy contract. That means there is only a limited time it can be structured for. Because we are halfway through a season he's signed for three and a half years, but once he's eighteen it's a different situation.

He's signed for that much not because that's all he wants to, but because that's all he can do legally. We will be sitting down back here when things progress. Where Wayne has come in six months is unbelievable – but it's nowhere compared to where he can go.

As his proud father then said: 'This is great for Wayne and for us. He is a true Evertonian and all his family are true Evertonians so we are just delighted for him.'

But, of course, it would be remiss not to leave the final word on the contract with Bill Kenwright who, having secured two England hopefuls to the Everton cause in Rooney and Hibbert, admitted: 'It's just a pity a seventeen-year-old can only sign for three and a half years. We did try for thirty-three and a half, we really did.'

But even more typical of all this fuss and what the Rooneys are really about, Kenwright said about Wayne's family: 'They're a smashing sports-mad Liverpool family and their feet are on the ground. We had dinner and I asked them what was it like when Wayne came home after that goal against Arsenal. What did you all do? "Nuttin," they said.'

Playing for Everton was simply a dream come true for young Rooney. And he was happy to explain what it was that made him catch the Everton bug.

Rooney's inspiration as a youngster was the atmosphere generated inside Goodison Park. He said he will never forget the thrill of the day when he was a mascot for the club he supported as a boy. So what was the best game he watched as a fan? He said:

It would have to be the one against Coventry when Gareth Farrelly scored to keep us up in 1998. I didn't think we were down but I did have my doubts. It was a fantastic atmosphere inside Goodison and I'll always remember all the fans on the pitch at the end of the game.

When I walked out as a kid as a mascot in the Merseyside derby it was hard to imagine I would be playing for Everton one day. I always hoped I would. I wanted to play for Everton so badly that I just used to play football in the street all the time, reliving the games.

My first derby match as a player was at Anfield. I got a bit of stick that day and all I could think about on the bench was coming on and scoring so I could wind their fans up.

I'd love to captain Everton one day because it would mean so much to my family and me. We've supported the club all our lives. It psyches me up, it's as simple as that when I hear 'Z Cars' playing as I go down the tunnel on match days. As a kid I used to get shivers down my spine when I heard it and I still do today when I line up with the rest of the team. It makes me more focused on the game.

It was a weird feeling when I first played alongside Duncan Ferguson, though, when only a few years back I was watching him from the stands. I used to idolise him when I was a kid and then a few years later I'm in the same side partnering him.

Wayne explained the background to how he had developed so astonishingly quickly. 'I think last season in the Youth Cup and in the under-19s was the best season that I have had as a footballer so far. I have always wanted to play and I have worked hard to get myself where I am today. But I know I have to work even harder to stay there and make the necessary improvements.'

Rooney was delighted by the reaction from his colleagues in the youth team regarding his achievements. He is still a kid, and his natural friends at Everton are those that he grew up with in the Academy rather than the first-team squad. He said:

> They have been very helpful. They have supported me along the way by coming to the games and they have all offered me advice. They have played a major part in getting me where I am today and I am still mates with them all today.
>
> I don't know whether I could help them as such. But I would be able to give them advice as to what it is like playing at the next level. It is a lot faster, more physical and it is something that is a bit of a shock when you move up.
>
> You have to be on top of your game all the time, if you make a mistake in the Premiership you get punished straight away, it is not the same at youth level. I have played with the youth team and I know there are plenty of talented young players at Everton and hopefully you will see them playing in the team sooner rather than later.

And what about that speculation that he could join Real Madrid? He said: 'It didn't bother me and I took no notice. I am a hundred per cent focused on playing for Everton and hopefully it will stay like that for a long time to come. I know it is part and parcel of football life being linked with other clubs, but you have to remain focused on where you are and what you are doing. Anyway, I don't read the papers, I just look at the pictures!'

7

Youngest Lion Ever

– 'Wayne's only seventeen, but Pelé was seventeen when he won the
World Cup in 1958 in Sweden and he scored twice in the final.'
– Sven Goran Eriksson

'Wayne is going to be England's wild card for years to come. He has all
the attributes to be a world-class player. He will go on to become even
greater than Alan [Shearer].'
– Kieron Dyer

Sven Goran Eriksson caused one of the biggest controversies of his
reign as England coach the day he announced he planned to field the
youngest ever England side in the second half of the friendly with
Australia at Upton Park in early February 2003. What rocked the
country more, though, was that Wayne Rooney was going to be a
part of it. The clamour had grown throughout the Christmas and New
Year period as Rooney's impact on the Premiership just grew and
grew. The debate raged after England's disappointing draw against
Macedonia in October 2002 as to where the national team went from
there. Another disappointing start to a qualifying campaign for a
major tournament meant that, after the high of the World Cup,
England were again in the doldrums and people wanted new blood.
Eriksson himself was coming under increasing pressure as people
started to ask whether he was still the man for the job. His response
was as drastic as it could have been.

In the lead-up to the squad being announced it was believed that
Rooney, along with fellow youngster Jermaine Jenas, would go with
the under-21 side to Italy for a training camp. But slowly, after

speaking to all of his close advisers such as Tord Grip, Eriksson changed his mind to stun English football. When the squad was announced Rooney's name was in it, which meant he would be making history – assuming he played – by playing for England at the age of 17 years and 111 days, making him the youngest ever player to pull on the Three Lions shirt, beating the previous record of Clapham Rovers' James Prinsep, who was 17 years and 253 days old when he played against Scotland in 1879.

Eriksson planned to start with his strongest possible line-up, but promised leading clubs that he would use none of their players for more than 45 minutes. In the second half he intended to turn to an under-25 side, starring not only Rooney but also Jenas and Paul Robinson. 'Wayne's only seventeen, but Pelé was seventeen when he won the World Cup in 1958 in Sweden and he scored twice in the final,' said Eriksson when selecting Rooney for the squad for the first time. 'Everyone that I've talked to says he's a special talent, so why not look at him in a friendly game. I'm not afraid of the age of seventeen. It's more important to see whether he's ready and whether he's good enough. My hunch is that he is.'

Rooney was so staggered by his selection that he mistook the call-up for a place in the under-21 squad. Everton manager David Moyes told him the good news and Rooney admitted: 'When the gaffer told me I was in the squad I asked when the under-21s had to report. He just laughed, shook his head and said, "No, the full squad."

'I couldn't believe it. To have the chance to be around senior internationals is going to be a great experience and I can't wait.'

Eriksson's 'vision of the future' also saw call-ups for Francis Jeffers and Matthew Upson (a major surprise as neither had been Arsenal regulars), as well as Charlton duo Scott Parker and Paul Konchesky.

The emphasis on youth meant Gareth Southgate, Trevor Sinclair, Nicky Butt and Robbie Fowler were all left out. Emile Heskey was injured, while David Seaman was rested and Steven Gerrard ineligible. The England coach promised that he would keep faith with any youngster who made his mark at Upton Park, just as he had done previously with Darius Vassell and Ashley Cole.

For the record, the full 27-man England squad that Rooney was named in for the first time was:

Goalkeepers: David James (West Ham), Paul Robinson (Leeds), Richard Wright (Everton)

Defenders: Gary Neville (Man Utd), Ashley Cole (Arsenal), Danny Mills (Leeds), Paul Konchesky (Charlton), Rio Ferdinand (Man Utd), Sol Campbell (Arsenal), Ledley King (Tottenham), Wes Brown (Man Utd), Matthew Upson (Birmingham)

Midfielders: David Beckham (Man Utd), Paul Scholes (Man Utd), Frank Lampard (Chelsea), Owen Hargreaves (Bayern Munich), Kieron Dyer (Newcastle), Jermaine Jenas (Newcastle), Sean Davis (Fulham), Scott Parker (Charlton), Danny Murphy (Liverpool), Joe Cole (West Ham)

Forwards: Michael Owen (Liverpool), Wayne Rooney (Everton), James Beattie (Southampton), Darius Vassell (Aston Villa), Francis Jeffers (Arsenal)

When the squad assembled, England captain David Beckham acted as Rooney's personal minder. Eriksson revealed that Beckham would take Rooney under his wing to shield him from the huge publicity he was likely to face. Eriksson said: 'I don't think I even need to ask David, he will just do it naturally. He does that all the time when young players come in and is very, very good as a captain.'

Beckham was more than comfortable in the minder's role when asked about it. 'People tell me Wayne was ten when I made my England debut and that makes me feel old,' he said. 'But it was the same when I came into the England squad for the first time, and if I had a problem I would go to Alan Shearer and the older players.

'Wayne is a quiet lad who seems level-headed on and off the pitch, but I am sure if he wants to ask me about dealing with fame and things like that then he will. It's just a case of him listening to people and he's just got to enjoy his football and he seems to be doing that.'

Despite disposing of proposed 'meaningless' friendlies in August and November 2002 – in an attempt to appease club bosses – England manager Sven Goran Eriksson still faced a diplomatic minefield as he prepared for the Wednesday night international friendly with Australia.

Former Liverpool manager Gerard Houllier and Arsenal boss Arsène Wenger urged Eriksson to be 'sensible' and 'use common sense' when selecting his squad, implying that they would like him to limit the playing time of their star players. While it was understandable that club bosses wanted to keep their players fresh for a heavy fixture list, it was also clear that this was Eriksson's only chance to prepare his squad for a crucial Euro 2004 qualifying double-header against Liechtenstein on 29 March and group leaders Turkey on 2 April, with England's qualifying record in a far from healthy state.

The Three Lions' campaign had so far seen them make hard work of a 2–1 away win over Slovakia and then struggle to a diabolical 2–2 home draw with Macedonia. Those results left England five points behind World Cup semifinalists Turkey, who had played one game extra. Once again the traumatic prospect of having to play-off to qualify – their fate if they failed to win their group – confronted England.

However, club chiefs are understandably reluctant to commit to friendlies. Houllier's most outspoken gripe about the international against Australia was regarding his injury-prone midfielder Steven Gerrard – who has a history of back problems and had been receiving specialist treatment in Paris: 'You cannot have an agreement about how long he plays for, but you rely on the national coach being sensible.' The FA kindly removed the need for Eriksson to be sensible when they slapped an immediate three-match ban on Gerrard for his two-footed lunge on Everton's Gary Naysmith during the Merseyside derby. Under FA rules, the domestic suspension rendered him ineligible for the friendly against the Socceroos. The FA offered Houllier the chance to appeal against the player's ban – which would have left Gerrard free for England selection. While Houllier had insisted he would not prevent any of his players going on national duty, he rejected the opportunity on the grounds that his star would then miss the Worthington Cup final against Manchester United on 2 March, should the appeal fail.

Houllier did deliver one plus when he rested Michael Owen at Upton Park on the Sunday before the international – meaning the striker, who had only scored one goal in his previous thirteen Premiership outings, would be fresh for England duty – while beleaguered forward Emile Heskey also looked to be back to some sort of form.

So, there was no real requirement to rush the latest Boy Wonder, Wayne Rooney. Arsenal manager Wenger added to the fragile nature of relations between club and country by also urging Eriksson to err on the side of caution. The England manager had already said he would no longer select veteran, and still first-choice, goalkeeper David Seaman for friendlies and Wenger also wanted Ashley Cole and Sol Campbell to be used sparingly.

Such was the pressure on Sven that some sections of the media suggested the Swede would quit as England manager if he encountered further resistance. The club-versus-country row would blight the whole of the second half of the season, especially when it came to Wayne Rooney. At this stage the debate just raged about whether, at seventeen, he was too young to be involved in the England set-up, or should he join the squad and get experience now?

The most likely candidate to benefit from Owen, Heskey and Robbie Fowler's relatively poor form was Southampton's 24-year-old striker James Beattie, who was in the form of his life and second top scorer in the Premiership behind Thierry Henry at the time. Rooney was never considered to be a serious option by many at this stage because he had only started a handful of senior games for Everton.

Eriksson obviously felt differently, despite_Rooney's lack of experience. But his parents and family could not care less about whether Wayne was too young or not to be involved with the senior squad. The only thing they felt was incredible pride at the achievement of their son, who only nine months before had still been sat behind his desk at school.

It was an incredible turnaround and Rooney's father said: 'The whole family is absolutely delighted for Wayne and obviously I am a very, very proud dad. Playing for England has always been his dream. We all can't wait for Wednesday.'

His mum added: 'Since Wayne was a little boy he has only ever wanted to play for Everton and his country. I'm thrilled that he has a chance to achieve both ambitions so soon in his career.'

A certain Liverpool primary school was looking forward to claiming a slice of soccer history when two former pupils, Everton golden boy Wayne Rooney and former Goodison star Francis

Jeffers, were due to lead the line for England in the second half against Australia, with Jeffers also making his debut. Headmaster Tony McCaul, who taught both players PE, said he never had any doubt they could make it to the top:

Both Wayne and Francis were brilliant players when they were at the school. They are different. Wayne is very strong and was always a big lad but Francis relied more on speed.

I couldn't say who was better in those days as they were both so obviously talented with a football. It is a great honour for the school to have two old pupils playing for England and I cannot wait to watch them in action. There surely isn't another school around where two former schoolboys are playing in attack for their country.

They are both smashing lads who are really down to earth and they have great careers ahead of them. There are lots of good strikers around but Wayne and Francis are being given the chance to show what they can do. It would be amazing to see two of my old pupils playing up front for England in the World Cup.

In contrast to the England manager's woe, Socceroos boss Frank Farina had an unusually easy time in naming his squad. The Australia coach normally faces massive resistance and withdrawals from European clubs when he calls upon his players but, as this clash took place in England, Farina was able to announce an entire squad made up of Europe-based talent – probably his best players – without any problems.

Farina could call upon stars from around Europe's top leagues – La Liga, Serie A, Ligue 1 and the Dutch Eredivisie – and his side was always going to provide a tough test, especially with Premiership-based players such as Leeds duo Harry Kewell and Mark Viduka eager to put one over their club-mates. The Socceroos were not to be taken lightly; after all, they were ranked 36 places higher than Macedonia at the time, and only narrowly missed out on qualifying for the last two World Cup finals.

Nobody, though, could have quite prepared the East End crowd for what went on at the debacle at Upton Park. England may have had some embarrassing results through the years but this 3–1 home defeat to Australia comes close to being top of the pile – and that takes some doing.

At the 1950 World Cup, England's 1–0 defeat at the hands of a part-time USA team was such an upset that when the final score came through on the news wire many thought it a misprint. At least England dominated that match, even if they couldn't find the back of the net. In 1993 the USA were again responsible for another of the national team's lowest ebbs, when a ginger-bearded, wannabe rock star, by the name of Alexi Lalas, headed home the clincher as Team USA grabbed a 2–0 win at the Foxboro Stadium – but at least that was on foreign soil and it was under the tenure of Graham 'The Turnip' Taylor.

The Three Lions were odds-on favourites for victory. A win that would restore some pride in England's sporting rivalry with Australia after a tortuous Ashes loss in the cricket and a laughable Davis Cup defeat at tennis had already ensued in a fledgling 2003.

Instead, England completed a humiliating hat trick of defeats. There were few crumbs of comfort to be taken from it – but one was Wayne Rooney's England debut.

But the first half, when the so-called senior side was playing, was a complete disaster from Eriksson and England's point of view. Crystal Palace defender Tony Popovic shrugged off the Manchester United right back Gary Neville to meet Stan Lazaridis's free kick and head Australia's sixteenth-minute opener. After four minutes of gobsmacked disbelief at the one-goal deficit Paul Scholes appeared to equalise for England, but his close-range scrambled goal was ruled out for a dubious foul by Southampton striker James Beattie – who lacked service on his debut.

And that was pretty much that from a worryingly pathetic first-half performance from England's supposedly 'strong' side. Australia continued to make the most of England's inept defending and, after West Ham United keeper David James had been forced to make two good saves, and Chipperfield had flashed a ball past the post, Harry Kewell shrugged a below-par Rio Ferdinand off the ball, rounded James and put the visitors 2–0 up.

A lacklustre England were second-best all over the pitch and the side's abject display was epitomised by Michael Owen's poor finishing. The Liverpool hit-man, so often England's saviour, had three good chances to score but his inability to hit the back of the net just highlighted the lack of confidence of a striker who had only scored once in fourteen Premiership games going into the match.

The first eleven were booed off as they left the pitch at half-time to shouts of 'Are you West Ham in disguise?' The biggest cheer of the match ensued when the stadium's Tannoy announced that, despite being 2–0 down, Eriksson would still field a completely new side after the break.

England's Young XI took to the pitch in a no-lose situation and offered a slight glimmer of hope for those unfortunate enough to have bought a ticket for the game, with a more threatening 4–3–3 formation.

In doing so Rooney, very much the centre of attention before the start of the match, finally became the youngest player to represent England and made an immediate impact with his first touch – a cross-field ball to Aston Villa striker Darius Vassell, who shot straight at the keeper from a tight angle. Rooney then combined with Jermaine Jenas, another debutant who was head and shoulders above the majority of his colleagues, and the Newcastle midfielder delivered a perfect cross for under-21 graduate Francis Jeffers to head home and make the score a more respectable 2–1.

Just as fans began to entertain the thought that the new boys might rescue England from the bottomless crevasse the seniors had dumped them in, Feyenoord midfielder Brett Emerton, angling for a move to the Premiership, scuppered all hopes with Australia's third goal in the 83rd minute. The humiliation was complete. Well, nearly. The chants of 'We want four' from the Socceroos' contingent destroyed any remnant of an Englishman's pride.

England had thrown two different sides at Australia, who therefore had a ready-made excuse in case of defeat, and not even the faint silver lining of Rooney and Jenas's debut performances could hide England's glaringly obvious deficiencies against a side playing their first full match for fifteen months, when they lost a World Cup qualifying play-off against Uruguay.

The shambolic defeat left more questions than answers. In many ways the terrible display by the first eleven did in fact seem to overshadow Rooney's debut. This was probably the lowest point of Eriksson's England career, and it became apparent after the game that many of the senior players, like Rio Ferdinand, David Beckham and Michael Owen, wanted to go back out for the second half and play on to try to rescue a situation that they helped create.

The row over making eleven substitutions was now much bigger than whether or not Rooney should have played. But the words of Kieron Dyer were well worth remembering when it comes to the impact Rooney made:

Wayne is going to be England's wild card for years to come. He has all the attributes to be a world-class player. People always say kids have no fear but this boy really does have no fear.

He's strong, quick, powerful and can shoot with his left or right. He knows when to take a touch and turn with the ball and when to give it ... Wayne has a God-given talent. And in David Moyes, he has the ideal manager to help him and look after him at Everton.

He's already got some of Alan's game and he is quicker. Alan's got experience and knows how to get free kicks and back into defenders. Wayne hasn't got that yet, but he'll get it. He will go on to become even greater than Alan.

Rooney had suddenly had a taste of something very special. He was whisked away from Upton Park quickly by his family with the help of the FA press staff. But the wonder kid knew exactly what he wanted: 'My dream is to continue playing for and one day captaining an Everton side that is challenging for honours, as well as being the number one striker in England.'

Rooney may have looked cool, but he was nervous about what was going on and his parents were naturally highly emotional when he made his England bow. Wayne admitted:

My mum and dad were shocked at the call-up. There had been a lot of speculation and privately I did hope I would be named – but in all honesty, I didn't really think I would.

Wrighty [Richard Wright] helped me a lot when we were with England and so did Franny Jeffers. I've known him for years and he was there for me. David Beckham also spoke to me and gave me some good advice which was very much appreciated. He's a big, big name but I was a bit nervous about meeting them all. I wondered what they would think of me.

Sven helped me a lot to be fair. He pulled me to one side and had a little chat with me, which put me at ease. The Liverpool lads are also good. I speak with them and Franny more than anyone. Steven Gerrard has become a good friend off the pitch.

8

The Call-up

'He is a special talent. We said that after he scored the winner against us at Everton earlier this season and he has made a step forward since then. You can see he's more of a man now. He looks much more mature than when he came on against us in October last year. This boy is international class.'

— Arsène Wenger

Football is such a massive financial melting pot these days that life cannot just be easy for a talented seventeen-year-old. As a result Wayne Rooney became the central figure in the club-versus-country controversy that had previously been the domain of Sir Alex Ferguson, Arsène Wenger, and Gerard Houllier. Suddenly David Moyes was a key character as Sven Goran Eriksson weighed up whether or not to include Rooney in the back-to-back European Championship games with Liechtenstein and Turkey that would define England's European Championship campaign. It was a daunting enough assignment for the vastly experienced, let alone a kid who had only made a debut cameo appearance against the Aussies just a month before.

Moyes made an impassioned plea not to risk burnout for his kid who had managed just eighty minutes of Premiership action prior to the season's second encounter with Arsenal on the day Eriksson named his Euro squad. Moyes gave Rooney an hour-long run-out in the reserves against Bolton on the Wednesday night before the Sunday 23 March contest with the Gunners and, starved of footage of the youngster, as ITV and Sky hold the rights to footage of Premiership matches, a BBC camera crew were dispatched to the game. As the technician had no idea who Rooney was, one of the crew came up with the bright idea of asking a supporter standing next to him. Unfortunately, the fan had a wicked sense of humour and when the Beeb's sports journalists arrived the following day to study the shots they discovered 45 minutes of a bald 29-year-old Lee Carsley!

But the serious issue was that Eriksson expressed his wish for more games for Rooney so that he could judge how good he really was in the heat of the Premiership. The Everton manager responded:

> I can't do anything about that. If England are relying on a boy who has just turned seventeen they have problems to mend. I do what is right for Everton. I don't think anybody has influenced me how we play Wayne and how we use him. I think everybody would understand that Tomasz Radzinski has been in tremendous form and his goals have been good. Wayne has done a tremendous job coming off the bench. He has played in every Premiership game except one this season and for a boy... that's fantastic.
>
> I have not shown any reservations about Wayne and England. If they think Wayne is good enough at his age then he should be picked. That's it. They have to decide if they want to play him, it's their shout. I would never hold Wayne back from being an international player. Never. As a footballer he is ready. Mentally, I am not sure he is ready to go on to that level of spotlight.

So, should the kid play straight away in the European Championships, or not? That was the searching question at the time. Moyes was clearly of the opinion that Rooney had time on his side and shouldn't be rushed. The club-versus-country debate raged on with Alan Hansen fronting a documentary on the topic. As part of the programme Hansen said: 'Wayne Rooney became his country's youngest international. But the FA left him out of an England youth squad because Everton didn't want him to miss Premiership games. The country's call is not always one his manager wants to take.'

Another problem at this point was that there was an England under-20 youth team being put together for a tournament that clashed with the end of the Premiership season, and it had been discussed within the FA as to whether Rooney would be called up for that. His appearance in the England senior set-up pretty much ruled him out of it, but it still caused controversy. As Moyes said:

The thing is, you know, the FA want us to get the young players in the team and play them as soon as we can, yet we've put them in the first teams ... The boy at Leeds [Jamie Milner] is doing very well and you think of Defoe at West Ham and our boy Wayne Rooney. [But] we know the tournaments come along during the season and they want us to take them out of our teams.

Now I can understand the FA saying you know the experience these young players will gain from that and I can't argue with that point . . . But I do think it's a problem, and I for one would not have let Wayne Rooney go.

The FA's acting chief executive David Davies said:

Because the judgement has to be between the coach of the under-20 team, in this case Les Reed, and the club manager and there were players who were active ... we understand the clubs' position. We don't think that actually a tournament like the under-20 tournament should have been scheduled at that time of year, in March and April with the European season coming to a conclusion.

You have to understand the clubs' position, equally they have to understand the position that we are in. We are playing, as I say, in a world game and FIFA have a problem. Their answer to it is you can't run every tournament when it suits Europe and that's why the world calendar is so important.

Moving on from the under-20 tour, the big issue was Rooney's fast-tracking into the sphere of European Championship qualifiers. Moyes suggested that he would not allow Eriksson's desire to see Rooney play more club matches affect his handling of him. So the crunch came at Highbury in March on the Sunday the England squad was announced, with Eriksson sat in the directors' box hoping to see Rooney deliver.

Everton faced Arsenal with everyone aware that it was against the Gunners back in October that Rooney had launched himself on to the national scene with his memorable first ever league goal.

But whether Rooney would get any nearer than substitute at Highbury was very much open to question. Moyes's softly-softly approach left the England boss with a near impossible decision of whether to call up the youngster again.

Moyes defended his decision not to start him in a first-team game since early January. He said: 'If you look at Wayne's matches, he's been involved in every Premiership game he's been available for, and he's come on in every game bar one this season that he's been involved in. I'd not look at how much he's played recently, I'd look at the fact that he started the season as a sixteen-year-old and he has played in everything he's been available for.'

Everton's reluctance to give Rooney his head was a major problem for Eriksson. If he selected Rooney it would have nothing to do with current form – and that would not be Rooney's fault. The last time Eriksson had gone to watch Rooney, he chose to leave Charlton's Valley ground before the youngster got on for the final few minutes of Everton's 2–1 defeat in February. That did not stop Eriksson picking Rooney for his England debut a few days later.

Moyes was unsure about Rooney's exposure to the full England spotlight, although he made all the right noises when the situation eventually presented itself. Since the England game on 12 February, Rooney had played just 63 minutes of Premiership football in three substitute appearances over five and a half weeks. Since he played the full match at Shrewsbury in the shock FA Cup defeat on 4 January he had served a four-match ban for his red card at Birmingham and collected five cautions.

For all the fanfares, he had started only ten first-team matches and come on nineteen times as substitute. Whether that was enough for him – despite his obvious talent – to jump the England strikers' queue for a couple of internationals that really mattered was the big question mark. Moyes had firm opinions. It all seemed to come down to that one game at Highbury in the end, which in itself perhaps made a farce of Eriksson's selection policy.

At first Eriksson revealed to the media in a pre-selection briefing that he did not think Rooney was yet ready for the senior England team. This came as a welcome relief to Moyes, who believed the England coach would be 'desperate' if he was relying on the kid for back-to-back Euro 2004 qualifiers against Liechtenstein and Turkey. Eriksson said:

It is difficult to pick him for qualifying games because of the number of minutes of Premier League football he is playing. What I have seen of him I like. I had Rooney for two and a half days before we played Australia earlier this month and he also played forty-five minutes in that match, but he is not playing much Premier League football and it is difficult to pick a player who plays only for the last fifteen or twenty minutes of games for his club.

Desperation is a strong word and I am not desperate at all. I'm interested in Wayne Rooney because he is a very good football player, I think. If he is ready or not is a difficult question for me, but I am not 'desperate' and he may have to wait his time, although he is young, he is talented, his future will be bright. But right now, I have to pick a team to face Liechtenstein and Turkey, not for the future.

Eriksson was speaking from Upton Park, where he revealed that West Ham goalkeeper David James would replace David Seaman if, as expected, the Arsenal player failed to recover from a hamstring injury. Eriksson chose his press conference to take a swipe at his bosses at the Football Association. He believes English clubs play too much football, and that it is having a detrimental effect on the game as a whole:

I talked before and after the World Cup about too many games in this country and I would like to mention it once again. I am not talking only on behalf of the national team, I am trying to defend the clubs as well. There is only one English team playing in Europe before the end of March and I don't think that is because we don't have good clubs – it is because we play too much football and we pay very heavily. We play more football than any other country and we don't have any breaks at all.

I am sorry to say it once again but things will not change in the future if we don't change the number of games. I say it with my heart and I believe it strongly.

How do we change that? That is the big, big question, which I cannot answer, although I have some of my own suggestions. The people who govern English football have to sit down and think about it, because it is not fair for the clubs and it is not fair for the national team at the end of the season. I talk to the people at the FA about it every time I see them, and they think I am awful I guess.

Every time I say something I will be criticised, but it is bad for the players, bad for the clubs and bad for the fans – and it is bad for me as well. Take Arsenal as an example, although I am here to defend them; but if you talk to a sports doctor about the fact they played Valencia on Wednesday, face Everton on Sunday and Chelsea on Tuesday, then they will tell you that to play three games in six days, physically it is not possible – it is incredible, we don't give the players a fair chance. Italy and Spain both have three teams left in the Champions League and we have one, and I don't think we are worse than Italy or Spain.

Ironically, in the case of Rooney, he wanted him to play more games, while Moyes was worried about burnout for a player who had packed so much into such a short space of time! Once again the wishes of club and country managers failed to dovetail.

On the basis of what he saw of Rooney at Highbury, Eriksson then changed his mind about his England selection. Moyes gave little away before the game, but there was a feeling that Rooney would play against the Gunners. He said:

Wayne got a four-match suspension in January which was completely unjust. I think it affected the boy. He lost a little bit of confidence from it. There's still a lot to be asked about that decision.

I will take no notice of anyone else on how I do my job at Everton. I will use my players how I see fit. If I had said before the season started that all this would happen to a sixteen or seventeen-year-old boy you would have said 'what an achievement'. I think people should be applauding rather than looking at why he isn't playing more.

There's not another youngster in the country at his level. He's in the team and involved with the team because he's good enough. I hope that when he's twenty-four and playing regularly for England people will say we did a good job with him when he was younger.

The key to selection for Moyes was the goal in the corresponding game that had brought Rooney to the public's attention. He added: 'We needed him to score that goal in such a high-profile game because he had the ability and quality to do so. We realise the media exploded after that but it was also good for Everton because it brought us to everyone's attention.'

The scene was set in front of the watching England coach and Rooney delivered, even in defeat, with a goal that forced his way into the squad. It was a spellbinding display.

He was widely expected to be included in the under-21s rather than keep his place in the senior party for the back-to-back qualifiers. However, while John Terry also earned a first call-up, Eriksson named Rooney in the 25-man squad after watching him start and score in Everton's 2–1 defeat at Highbury.

Eriksson had completely changed his tune from what he had said the day before. His ensuing call-up came at the expense of Alan Smith, who was suspended for the first qualifier in Liechtenstein, and James Beattie, who had reached the mark of twenty Premiership goals.

Rooney was joined in the squad by another young talent, twenty-year-old Jermaine Jenas, while Francis Jeffers also kept his place among the forwards, with Emile Heskey returning after injury. Amid Rooney's understandable joy, Beattie was entitled to feel aggrieved at being dropped after just 45 minutes' action against Australia.

Moyes consistently called for a cautious attitude towards the teenager's development, and after the game at Highbury, while talking to the press and waiting to see if Rooney would be in the squad, he was clearly angered by all that was going on. He felt that Rooney should be given time to develop rather than being relied upon to come up trumps. He declared, in a veiled criticism of Eriksson: 'We are trying to nurture him and not give him too much, too soon. His ability isn't in question but he's not ready to do it all the time.

'Seven months ago, he was still sitting at a school desk so let's put it in perspective. I think that he needs to be developed. I'd never stop anyone playing for their country as it's a great honour for them and I wouldn't try to put Sven off. I have spoken to him many times and I think he understands the situation.'

When Eriksson named his squad, Moyes acknowledged that it did at least give Rooney a degree of stability rather than being 'dropped' down to the under-21s. Moyes said:

> I don't think that would damage his confidence but it's a difficult one to answer. It was good that he got recognised for the last squad but he's just got a lot more development to do. We're just trying to bring him on in the correct manner.
>
> He's got some fabulous pieces to his game but he still has a lot of parts to be worked on. You've got to say what's he going to be like when he's twenty-five or twenty-six, the same age as Thierry Henry?
>
> Sometimes because it feels like he's been in the Premier League so long – a year – everyone thinks that he's ready. But there are too many players who were raved about when they came into the game but then fell away. I'm just trying to do the right thing for him.

The full squad to face Liechtenstein and Turkey in the Euro 2004 qualifiers was:

> Goalkeepers: David James (West Ham), Paul Robinson (Leeds), Richard Wright (Everton)
> Defenders: Gary Neville (Man Utd), Danny Mills (Leeds), Wayne Bridge (Southampton), Rio Ferdinand (Man Utd), Sol Campbell (Arsenal), Gareth Southgate (Middlesbrough), Jonathan Woodgate (Newcastle), John Terry (Chelsea)
> Midfielders: David Beckham (Man Utd), Pual Scholes (Man Utd), Nicky Butt (Man Utd), Steven Gerrard (Liverpool), Danny Murphy (Liverpool), Kieron Dyer (Newcastle), Jermaine Jenas (Newcastle), Owen Hargreaves (Bayern Munich), Frank Lampard (Chelsea)
> Forwards: Michael Owen (Liverpool), Emile Heskey (Liverpool), Darius Vassell (Aston Villa), Francis Jeffers (Arsenal), Wayne Rooney (Everton)

Eriksson's chief concern that Rooney was not playing regularly enough for Everton was answered by his ninety-minute involvement at Highbury, while his class was evident as he tormented the below-strength Arsenal defence, even though Everton eventually lost.

There was no doubt in Arsène Wenger's mind that Rooney was 'international class': 'He is a special talent. We said that after he scored the winner against us at Everton earlier this season and he has made a step forward since then. You can see he's more of a man now. He looks much more mature than when he came on against us in October last year.

'This boy is international class. Is he good enough to be in front of other players in the England squad? That's down to Sven to decide, but he will certainly one day be a regular international. What he makes of his career will be down to the mental aspect as the talent is clearly there.'

Eriksson dismissed Moyes's concerns that Rooney's long-term development could be harmed by his promotion for a competitive game at the age of seventeen. Attempting to defuse the expectations bearing down on the youngster by confirming he would not start against Liechtenstein, he claimed: 'I think it's good for him to be involved in international football, it can't harm him. He might be ready to start but I don't think he will do so. He's one of five forwards and I don't think you should expect him to start the game and score three goals. He might come on as a substitute, or he might not, but just to be there will be a huge experience for him. He has very little experience of international football, after all.'

Moyes repeated his worries that Rooney's career was being rushed along too quickly, even though he did not try to stand in the way of his second England call-up. Eriksson nevertheless insisted: 'I talked to David Moyes an hour after the game at Highbury to tell him that Richard Wright and Wayne Rooney were in the squad, and he was very happy about that. He had absolutely no opinion other than that. If he wanted to say something else, he should have done that then.'

Asked if he was worried about Rooney struggling to live up to overblown expectations or being deflated at being dropped in the future, Eriksson responded: 'I hope not, of course. He is a big talent, a very good player and that's the reason why he's picked. For him, it must just be a great experience to be there with the others.'

Emile Heskey was the man most under pressure from Rooney. But the former Liverpool striker, who recently joined Birmingham City, seemed unflustered by the threat of Sven Goran Eriksson's teenage wild card in the lead-up to the game against Liechtenstein.

It is no wonder his former club boss Gerard Houllier has described him as a sleeping giant, but it is that laid-back style which leads people to believe Heskey lacks confidence. As a result Heskey is easy to criticise, and the fact he had scored only four goals in 31 games for his country before this match did not help his cause as he had come under a barrage of criticism.

Heskey, though, was not bothered, and insisted that maybe he was a little misunderstood as a player:

> It is up to people to criticise. When you play for England you are there to be shot at but I am happy with my performances. Being a team player can be overlooked. I think I am one of those, but there are other players who perform for the team, like David Beckham for example.
>
> If the manager is happy with me, then I am happy as well. I hope Michael Owen likes playing alongside me. I think he does because he has not said anything yet. But the reason we are picked together for club and country is because I think our game complements each other. We have been playing together for a few years and it has worked out. In some respects half my job is done if I help Michael score goals. At least we are getting the points and the goals that we need.

At 25 Heskey was, incredibly, the oldest striker in the England squad. But it was ironic that it was the youngest, Rooney, who was looking to take advantage of any more slip-ups by the Liverpool man.

The sleepy town of Vaduz in Liechtenstein, which is surrounded on all four sides by the Swiss Alps, could have been the perfect place for the young Everton lad to make his competitive debut. Instead Eriksson went for experience in Heskey, although he suggested he might give the bull-like figure of Rooney a cameo role.

Heskey was adamant he could cope with all the pressure. He commented:

I think Rooney has been brilliant for a seventeen-year-old. He is full of self-confidence. You should see him in training because he is brilliant.

He really is that special, he is a very good player. I can't believe he has so much confidence and ability at such a young age. He can only go forward and has more talent than a lot of people have seen.

But all strikers are different. He is different to me and Michael, but he is a class player. Alan Shearer and Michael Owen have both been criticised during their England careers, but both are strong characters and came through their barren spells well. Michael is brilliant at it and you have to cope. There is always pressure for places, though, and with Wayne, Francis Jeffers and Darius Vassell around then there is bound to be pressure.

I don't lack confidence or rely on other people for it. I give it to myself. People have got me wrong when they think I lack confidence.

At the end of the day we owe England a performance and need to come good. The boss has said we have not played that well since the World Cup, but hopefully we can sort that out.

In the build-up to the game, fullback Gary Neville had suggested that if the current crop of England players didn't win a trophy in the next four years he would regard it as failure. The straight-talking Manchester United man meant either the European Championships or the World Cup. On the evidence of the first half in particular, it seemed a forlorn wish.

England struggled to stave off embarrassment in Vaduz against a team whose sum total of international wins can be counted on one finger and who could easily have grabbed an injury-time consolation when Martin Stocklasa smashed a shot against the post.

Not for the first time, Eriksson's star duo, Michael Owen and David Beckham, came to their country's rescue. With the expected breakthrough looking increasingly unlikely, Owen put England in front just before the half-hour when he rose to meet an Emile Heskey cross and arrowed home an excellent header. While Beckham is some way behind the Liverpool man's tally of twenty international strikes, the England captain can always be relied upon in free-kick situations. And yet again he thrived on the responsibility, firing home what proved to be the final goal of the night eight minutes after the break.

On his first competitive appearance for his country, David James was called into action on a more regular basis than he might have expected. Under-fire Heskey was one of the few visiting players to enhance their reputation in a listless display. The Liverpool striker strove tirelessly to improve his team's lot, running off an ankle knock that briefly threatened to bring Rooney into the game before half-time.

Quite what Group Seven favourites Turkey, watching on TV from their base in the northeast of England, made of the game can only be guessed at. Although if they concurred with the majority of a near 4,000 crowd at the game itself, the World Cup semifinalists would hardly be quaking at the prospect of facing England at the Stadium of Light.

However, they might have been worried about a different challenge in Rooney, whose ten-minute cameo at the end put him in line for a starting spot in Sunderland. It took the eventual introduction of Rooney to bring England back to life again.

At 17 years and 156 days, the kid had two chances to become the youngest goalscorer in England history. However, he could not convert one difficult header, then also failed to slot home a better opportunity after Dyer had found him with a neat cut-back.

Former England caretaker-managers Howard Wilkinson and Peter Taylor acclaimed Rooney's cameo in Liechtenstein – but predicted that the reaction to England's disjointed victory would upset Eriksson. Wilkinson, unemployed after being sacked as Sunderland boss earlier in the month, had helped Rooney's development in his old position as the Football Association's technical director. 'I know Wayne very, very well as we watched him develop as he came through the England youth ranks,' he said. 'And when he walks on to a football field, he goes from an adolescent to a man. He's ten or fifteen years ahead of his time as far as his football development is concerned. Physically and mentally, that boy has a man's head on a boy's body.'

Wilkinson also praised the professional attitude of Eriksson's men. He added: 'England wanted to come away with a clean sheet and a victory. They got that and what matters now is preparation for what will be a very hard game against Turkey. There'll be a press reaction about the performance but the players will be well focused on Turkey by Wednesday morning.'

Taylor, now manager of Third Division Hull, believed the media criticism of Eriksson's team would sting the Swede. 'I'd say Sven's probably not enjoying the job as much and he's probably surprised by the amount of criticism he's getting,' he said. 'But he's a cool man, understands the job and I'm sure he'll get on with it.

'If I was manager, I'd have been saying get a result and make sure you're right for Turkey. With that game coming up, when the players knew they would win – which I think was when Michael Owen scored the first goal – they were making sure they didn't get injured.'

Not everyone within the England camp was overjoyed to witness a profusion of youngsters taking over. Middlesbrough defender Gareth Southgate, who made his 52nd appearance against Liechtenstein, then aged 32, believes that Eriksson picks too many young players who lack international experience. Southgate made his views public and they were given a wide airing in the weekend press: 'I feel we are going into games with lads who haven't got the experience for the huge matches they are about to face. You have to have a balance of both experience and exciting young talent. The lads coming through have given England a breath of fresh air, but if you want to win things, you need a lot of players who are 27, 28 or 29. We are looking for the next bright young thing right now – but that can be dangerous.'

Southgate continued by saying that he feels the England coach fails to select his players on current form. 'It's picked on who has done well for him in the past. The manager has his pecking order and it's obvious to me the way it's going. All players like to know exactly where they stand, but I don't think the manager works in that way.'

The only place that Rooney stood was on the edge of a wonderful England career that was just kicking off. Bring on the Turks.

9

Triumph Over Turkey

'You look into his eyes and he is seventeen. But then you watch him play and it is as if he is thirty-two. I was watching him on the bus heading to the match and he didn't seem to have any nerves at all. He was just having a laugh with Rio Ferdinand and, if I hadn't known better, I would have sworn he was just one of the experienced players.'

— David James

Depression over the war in Iraq, the SARS virus from China, anxiety over the impending Budget . . . but here comes Wayne Rooney to brighten the day. The feel-good factor could not have been better timed for the FA ahead of sending out their tender documents to the TV companies for their next round of contract negotiations, and with 20 per cent redundancies looming inside Soho Square on the back of the excesses of the Adam Crozier regime.

Then along comes Wayne. Yet his arrival in the England team was shrouded in mystery as Sven Goran Eriksson made up his mind, so he claimed, immediately after Rooney's brief appearance as a late substitute for Emile Heskey in Liechtenstein, but kept the decision under wraps to avoid any pre-match tension for the youngster.

Eriksson began the build-up to the vital tie insisting he would resist the temptation to give Rooney his first England start against Turkey – even if Heskey was not fit. Heskey had been replaced by Rooney with eleven minutes remaining after injuring his knee against Liechtenstein. Eriksson publicly discussed his desire for the Liverpool forward to recover in time to face the Turks and, even if Heskey was ruled out, the England coach was still reluctant to press Rooney into the starting line-up. Or, at least, so he intimated.

Eriksson, who also resisted calling up Alan Smith, would instead turn to Darius Vassell or Francis Jeffers, or ask Paul Scholes to push further forward – the usual spin from the Swede to deflect attention from Rooney.

Outside the press marquee in Vaduz as he came under fire for England's lacklustre display against Liechtenstein (and as the local press co-ordinator poured a glass of water over his Italian suit by accident – Eriksson did not see the funny side of it), he explained: 'I think Wayne Rooney is ready but only part-time. I don't think we should expect him to come in and resolve a game against Turkey . . . It could happen – who knows – if he comes on, as he's physically strong, good on the ball, quick and he scores goals . . . Let me think about it but maybe starting him isn't fair on him.'

Despite repeated criticism of his lack of goals, Heskey, whose team-mates stress the importance of his all-round play, set up Owen for the opener in Vaduz and won the free-kick from which Beckham struck. 'Emile didn't seem too bad at half-time, he said it was no problem to go on. But he started limping after a while in the second half and so we took him off,' said Eriksson. 'We will see if it's only a knock or not. I think Heskey will be OK for Wednesday, I hope so.'

In training Rooney was performing tricks that had the seasoned pros admiring, and Eriksson tried both Heskey and Rooney at various stages. But nobody who was in and around the England squad at the time, including the press, could quite believe that Eriksson would take such a risk with Rooney on such an important game.

Gary Neville observed: 'He is built like a man, not a boy, he has strength, pace and his one-touch is excellent. Sometimes you just have to give players their head and put them in and Wayne is in that category. Sometimes you have to forget the player's age. It was difficult for him getting only fifteen minutes [against Liechtenstein], the team had eased off but even in that short space of time he showed great touches, that he can link up play, that he belongs.'

But not everyone within the camp agreed. England have to hold back Rooney or risk burning out their country's brightest young footballer, argued team-mates Sol Campbell and Michael Owen. As England faced a much tougher qualifier against the Group Seven leaders, expectations were raised that Rooney should be blooded again in the international arena. But Campbell and Owen both believed that Eriksson needed to take his time with a player who had spent most of the season warming the Everton bench.

Campbell, against whose Arsenal side Rooney had scored twice already, believed Moyes had so far adopted a sensibly cautious attitude to the emerging striker. He told a news conference:

> You've got to look at his age. You can't keep thrusting a young lad in all the time. Being in the squad, and coming on and doing a bit, will build his confidence and he'll get better and better. He's a fantastic prospect – don't kill him . . .
>
> He's learning all the time [so] don't overrun him. When someone like him comes along don't destroy him. But while Michael Owen just came on the scene and destroyed everybody, Wayne has got time on his side and he can only get better and better.
>
> He'll do the business, no doubt about it. Wayne's come on and won a few games and will do that even more next season and in the seasons to come. He's a fantastic prospect.

But Campbell was impressed with the boy in training, and it was at one of these limited sessions that Eriksson was as stunned by his brilliance as his players. He observed: 'Wayne's an all-round centre forward. He will come and go, come and go again to make a bit of space for himself, and his brain's ticking all the time.

'He comes off to create situations, crosses great balls for other people and comes on and scores goals. Wayne's a good player and gets in some great positions to shoot from. If you're not ready for that he'll get a shot on target. Whenever he's come on he's done something on the pitch.'

Owen also paid tribute to Rooney's skills. It was Owen's record as England's youngest international of the modern era that Rooney broke in February against Australia. The Liverpool striker had just turned eighteen when he made his international debut against Chile in a friendly in February 1998. Rooney was more than a year younger.

Owen was still a substitute at the start of the 1998 World Cup before Glenn Hoddle bowed to overwhelming pressure to start him against Colombia after he had come off the bench to score against Romania. The following game, only his ninth cap, saw his tremendous goal against Argentina.

But looking back to his own development as a player, the 23-year-old also argued for Rooney to spend more time as an England spectator:

Wayne Rooney could be an unbelievable player. He could be an England regular for the next decade, but no one knows yet. I think the way he's being handled at the moment is the right way. When I was coming through at Liverpool, I wasn't playing every single game. I was rested here and there and David Moyes at Everton looks to be doing the same – so I think it's only right that the same should be done at England.

At Everton, he probably sits on the bench and wants to play in every game because he feels he can – and I've no doubt he is good enough to play in every game in the Premiership.

But you've got to manage players at that age . . . I never wanted to sit on the bench or in the stands and I think that's the right attitude to have. But now you're older and wiser you think to yourself it certainly was the right way to do it. You think you can do anything when you're a kid. You think you can play in every game because you have been since you were seven years old and played about five times a week.

Owen did point out a couple of differences between the two strikers: 'I'd played a few more games for Liverpool and England before I burst on to the scene. When he came on against Australia he had a couple of half-chances that came to him a bit quick.

'Sometimes when you come on it's difficult to get into the game. But he had a couple of chances and that's a good sign. People think that if you have two players exactly the same they can't play together, but we're different. I think he's more developed as a man, physically,' Owen said, before quipping: 'I'm probably still not as developed as him!'

Sir Bobby Robson was foremost among those in favour of giving Rooney his first start against Turkey. Writing exclusively in his *Mail on Sunday* column, he said:

Sven Goran Eriksson is truly blessed by the emergence of the wonderfully talented Wayne Rooney. Now Sven must be brave enough to begin reaping the benefit immediately. England need Rooney on the pitch from the very start of the vital European Championship qualifier . . . His is a phenomenal talent that must not be denied or restricted . . .

Age is merely a number – whether it's seventeen or, as in my case, seventy . . . I have watched the boy play on several occasions. He takes my breath away – he is sensational.

He can do things which are way out of reach of any other player. And already he has the confidence to do them . . . Paul Gascoigne was twenty in 1990 when I, as England manager, had no hesitation in determining that I had a very special talent at my disposal . . . Sven urgently needs to inject a spark, to discover fresh impetus, to lift the mood and raise the optimism.

He needs a great player and Rooney, even if he is only seventeen, is already a great player.

Sir Bobby talked about how Eriksson had seriously thought about a comeback for Alan Shearer but he added that the 'future has to be Rooney. Shearer is the past, no matter how distinguished so far as England is concerned. The dawn of a new England great should be witnessed from the start . . . He is certainly capable of illuminating the Stadium of Light.'

The feeling was that to pick Rooney in such a vital game would nevertheless be something of a gamble for a cautious coach like Eriksson. Heskey's team-mates were sympathetic and felt he deserved to keep his role up front, despite their belief that Rooney could soon become an England regular for at least the next decade.

Owen, with more experience than Rooney at the same age, still felt ready to play for England when others prevaricated and suggested the Everton striker would feel the same way: 'When you're young, you are fearless.'

Owen – who suffers hamstring problems that could be linked to overplaying at a young age – thought that Rooney, who is more physically developed than he was, could ably partner him for England. However, that would overlook the case of Heskey and while many critics pointed to his poor return of goals, his team-mates have rushed to his defence.

Owen insisted: 'As a striker, you have to have an influence on the game, whether it's scoring or creating a goal. If we're judged on that, then he created two goals on Saturday [against Liechtenstein]. Wayne Rooney has got two caps now and not even played for ninety minutes. He's not been around for that long so it would be unfair to compare him and Emile.'

And Sol Campbell added: 'It may not always look pleasant to everyone but the players know what Emile is contributing to the team. He has seen it and done it and scored vital goals for us. A blend of youth and experience is the way forward for England and what counts sometimes is that the players and manager all respect him.'

Irrespective of Eriksson's decision to keep Rooney's selection under his hat, the media attention was relentless, with the *Sun* maintaining their opinion that their readers wanted him to start. In the more sedate *Daily Telegraph* the recently acclaimed Sports Columnist of the Year, Michael Parkinson wrote:

> The hysteria surrounding the ample figure of Wayne Rooney is more an indication of what we are missing than a celebration of what we have. In other words, in a game increasingly dominated by foreign players, the search for a home-grown star, particularly one with an aptitude for scoring goals, takes on an almost mythical significance.
>
> The young man will take a lot of careful counselling if he is to survive and David Moyes, his manager, is right to suggest that promise is what he has, not certainty. Will he make it? We won't know for a while yet, but on the evidence so far there is reason for optimism.

Even James Beattie, who lost his place in the squad to Rooney, couldn't help but admire The Kid. The Southampton striker said: 'Wayne is exceptional for a seventeen-year-old. In terms of natural skill he is as good as I have seen. He is quick and strong with a great shot. He also has the mental toughness to handle all the attention he will be getting.'

Former England coach Glenn Hoddle, who infamously suggested Owen was 'not a natural-born goalscorer' when in charge of the national side, felt it was too soon for Rooney. He said: 'I think Sven should resist calls to play him from the start. He is used to coming on as a substitute and he is still finding his feet as a Premiership player. He has turned games from the bench and could do the same for England. But Sven knows that to play him from the start would put too much pressure on him. He will cope with the pressure, eventually, but he doesn't need that pressure right now.'

The debate raged for several days, with World Cup winner Roger Hunt having his say: 'Sven never says much in public and, in this case, I can understand why. Imagine the reaction if he said Rooney was starting against Turkey. That would put the lad under immense pressure, but if it was all kept under wraps until just before kick-off, Rooney would have had twenty-four hours to prepare for the game. If anyone can produce a touch of the unexpected it is Rooney. I hope England don't waste the ace up their sleeve.'

The opposition feared his inclusion as Yildiray Basturk observed: 'We know Wayne Rooney will be a big threat if he plays. I am not saying Owen and Heskey aren't top strikers. But Rooney would give the crowd a lift and maybe give England that spark they have been missing recently. I watch the English league every week and have seen the goals he scores. He is incredibly quick and his finishing is excellent. It is unbelievable to think he is just seventeen. If he plays we know our defence and midfield could have problems.'

Basturk, who made his international debut at eighteen, said: 'When you are that old you play without fear and, while there is pressure on England, Rooney probably won't feel it.'

In the final practice match, Eriksson utilised Rooney alongside Owen almost as much as he did Heskey, and later at the England manager's final press briefing he confessed he was still undecided about whether to play the kid from the outset.

Eriksson was torn between his loyalty to the vastly more experienced Heskey or gambling on the youthful spark of Rooney in the must-win clash. Eriksson admitted that Rooney, who was not released to the under-21s with two other youngsters on the Monday following the Liechtenstein game, had a chance of making the starting eleven. 'Rooney is still here with us so he has a chance like everyone else in the squad,' Eriksson said.

The public craved to see the seventeen-year-old test his mettle against the Turks after the lacklustre performance in Vaduz, but a typically calm Eriksson insisted he would not bow to popular opinion. 'I will never think of public opinion when picking my team,' Eriksson told the BBC. 'I have to be convinced that it is the right thing, whether it is naming a squad or a side. If I am convinced I do it. But I couldn't listen to public opinion before making my decision.'

Eriksson's position as England manager was going to be under scrutiny if he failed to get a result, but the Swede left his decision until the last minute – remaining unswayed by a *Sun* poll that suggested 83% of voters wanted to see Rooney start. England fans told Sven Goran Eriksson in no uncertain terms: 'It's time to unleash Roonaldo,' blasted the *Sun* in typical fashion.

'Let's wait until Wednesday night to find out whether I am in that 83% or part of the 17% who disagree,' Eriksson concluded as he left the door firmly ajar for Rooney.

The manager insisted he felt no pressure over his future and dismissed notions that he should change his laid-back character by reinventing himself as a motivational expert and shouting more at his players. Instead, he accepted his fate would be governed – as ever – by results and therefore urged a positive attitude. Eriksson said: 'Do I feel under pressure? Absolutely not. In life, we are often pessimistic. We always talk about "what happens if". But why worry about things that might never happen. I never think about what happens if we lose. I refuse to think that way. Why should we lose?'

One of the main accusations levelled at Eriksson was that he is not passionate enough and is too detached to rally his team; exactly the qualities he was praised for when he took over from Kevin Keegan, who was overly reliant on his motivational skills.

History was rapidly being rewritten, chiefly because England had faltered since their World Cup quarterfinal defeat by Brazil, when one squad member – who remained anonymous – insisted the Swede should have been 'more like Winston Churchill and less like Iain Duncan Smith' at half-time against Brazil. A far more valid charge was that Eriksson did not change the shape of his side when Brazil were reduced to ten men, while he had still not resolved questions over the left flank or Michael Owen's strike partner.

However, the Swede made it clear he was not about to start impersonating Keegan or, indeed, Sir Alex Ferguson just to keep his critics happy. He declared: 'If you want someone shouting then you will have to change [the manager] as I will never do that. It has never been my style and I have no intention of changing my character at my age. You are always criticised if you don't win matches – whether you are shouting or not shouting, whatever you do. So the best answer is to win football games.'

Eriksson canvassed the opinion of his coaching staff to see what they thought about Rooney playing, and they were fifty-fifty over the youngster's inclusion. What might have helped sway Eriksson's mind was when in training Rooney beat a couple of players and then lifted the ball over one of the goalkeepers. The rest of the players just stood and applauded while Rooney jogged back to the halfway line.

The national press were undecided until late into the Tuesday evening before the game on the Wednesday, 2 April. Slowly but surely the news leaked out that Rooney would start. It went from a maybe to a definite yes and plenty of stories and headlines were changed as quick as a flash as everybody battled to get the story into print. When the decision was announced, in a pre-recorded interview with Beckham, the England captain said: 'If he is given his chance he is up to it.'

Garth Crooks interviewed David Moyes prior to the TV coverage and the Everton manager said: 'I have spoken to Sven and just after lunch time he told me he may be playing. I'm delighted for Wayne, it is a great honour.' However, Moyes added some caution amid all the euphoria. 'Don't expect him to carry England through, don't be too disappointed if he cannot do that.'

Rooney himself praised David Beckham for helping him before he made his first start for England against Turkey. He said:

Most of the players were quiet in the dressing room before the game but I spoke to the captain and he helped me along. He just told me to keep focused and go out there and play my normal game. Most importantly he told me to enjoy myself. All I was thinking about on the pitch was winning the game for England.

It was a massive qualifier and I wanted to make sure I performed to the best of my ability, not only for myself but for club and country. The England players are all good lads and have made me feel welcome whenever I join up with the squad. I keep in touch with Steven Gerrard off the field and that helps when England get together as it is good to have a familiar face around.

The Stadium of Light fans could not believe it, and all the violence that went on outside seemed to disappear inside the ground as the crowd went mad about Rooney's inclusion.

There were a few stunned faces in the press room before the game, with many of the journalists already starting to write that this was the biggest risk of Eriksson's England career. The record books were opened as writers got the necessary background information ready to go for the next morning. What must Emile Heskey have thought?

Eriksson's side might have laboured against Liechtenstein on Saturday, but by Wednesday, with Rooney proudly wearing the No 9 shirt, they tore into Turkey as they secured the all-important win courtesy of Darius Vassell and a late penalty by Beckham.

Eriksson's calculated gamble on Rooney paid off spectacularly. Apart from one impudent back-flick, the game had largely passed the teenager by until the final fifteen minutes of the first half when he started to come into his own. One acrobatic juggle of the ball saw him switch play out to the right flank, from where Beckham crossed only for Owen to miskick on the turn. Rooney was not finished there, though. He promptly opened up the Turkish defence with a through ball that saw Owen just denied by Rustu.

At half-time, the studio discussion between Gary Lineker and Alan Hansen on the BBC focused on Rooney or, as Hansen put it: 'The Wayne Rooney Show.' Hansen said: 'Wayne Rooney showed what he is all about with his touch, his strength and his technique and he gave England a real boost going into half-time.'

He looked over to former Arsenal and England striker Ian Wright and added: 'He has Ian Wright's effervescence. He is not afraid to work, his display was awesome.'

Rooney displayed the confidence to take on opponents, although he was left with a new strike partner on 57 minutes when Owen went off clutching his back after a hefty challenge by Alpay. Vassell, on the pitch as a substitute for Owen, drew inspiration from Rooney and had an effort tipped over the bar by Rustu, who also kept out another dangerous Beckham free kick. Rooney was a revelation on a memorable full debut. He was full of aggressive running and showed a few tricks, too, juggling the ball to beat two defenders, and giving one exhilarating back-heel into the path of his skipper.

The Turkey goalkeeper managed to deny Vassell again at the near post, but England's pressure finally told on 75 minutes. Bridge's cross left Rio Ferdinand in the clear only for Rustu to prove equal to his volley. But Vassell was on hand to provide the calm finish, before being besieged under celebrating England fans.

England were still indebted to James for an acrobatic save to deny Kahveci Nihat's header, but it was Rooney who drew the standing ovation as he made way for another substitute, Kieron Dyer, with two minutes left. There was still time for Dyer to go down under a challenge from Penbe Ergun and for Beckham to convert the penalty with aplomb. Beckham duly made certain of victory from the penalty spot in the final stages. But the captain would now have to miss the next qualifier against Slovakia after picking up a booking.

The two pitch invasions which accompanied England's goals were unsavoury and would get the national team in a lot of trouble, especially as Aston Villa and Turkey defender Alpay was kicked. The two sets of players squared up to each other at the final whistle, and there was even talk of a major fracas in the tunnel as tempers boiled over. It was one hell of a night.

This, though, was when Rooney came of age. After all the talk of a 'diamond' midfield formation, the teenage Everton striker was England's real gem. Fielding a strike duo with a combined age of 39 – less than David Seaman – Eriksson could finally look forward with renewed heart for the first time since the World Cup. England would still need to secure at least a draw in their final qualifying game in Istanbul, but automatic qualification was now a realistic goal once again.

Hope had duly returned to the England side and, for that, a seventeen-year-old with just a handful of Premiership starts behind him was as responsible as anyone else.

Rooney carried England through and the reaction was startling. From the front page of *The Times* – with the headline 'Wayne's

World' – to the front page of the *Mirror*, Wayne Rooney was headline news. England were inspired by Rooney as they rediscovered their passion, poise and promise to keep their Euro 2004 qualifying hopes high.

Euphoric England captain David Beckham dedicated the impressive win to Eriksson as the stirring victory took England to the top of Group Seven and answered the critics who claimed the national team and its manager were lacking the spirit necessary to take them to the finals in Portugal.

Eriksson left it late to tell Rooney he would be playing, and hinted that the Everton striker would hold on to his starting place for the next match. 'Wayne only knew about it at about four o'clock. To be fair to him he said, "Hmmm. OK" – it was a very good reaction,' Eriksson said. 'You can see that he's a football player and that he's ready, at least in training. You never know his reaction in a game but when I told him he was playing, you could see that he was focused and not that nervous. He is very mature to only be seventeen. He's a great talent, we knew that before.

'But now we know he's ready for the big matches. I can't see any reason why I should leave him out if he plays like that. But all the players played well. It was an extremely good effort all round and these are three very good points.'

Bill Kenwright is not prone to understatement, but his famous phrase uttered at the outset of Rooney-mania may yet underplay the Everton youngster's impact on the global game.

'How can you not get excited about the most exciting thing in world football?' the Everton deputy chairman said, *before* Rooney made his Premiership debut. After the Turkey game he was struggling to contain fresh eulogies after witnessing the seventeen-year-old's astonishing full international debut.

'It's difficult to put into words what it means to see a seventeen-year-old Blue wearing the England number nine jersey and getting a standing ovation. 'That ovation was mirrored in our house. Jenny [his wife] and I were standing cheering with tears in our eyes. It was another wonderful moment from what has been a wonderful season for Evertonians already.'

Kenwright revealed he knew Rooney was in line to make his full competitive debut – even before the player himself – and he struggled to contain his excitement:

> From the moment David Moyes told me he was playing shortly after lunch I couldn't wait for kick off. I spent most of the afternoon at the Gielgud Theatre where I'm working on Andrew Lloyd Webber's *Tell Me On A Sunday* starring Denise Van Outen, but all I could think of was Wayne.
>
> I am an Evertonian who got carried away with excitement when David Unsworth got his first cap against Japan in a friendly, so you can imagine how I felt as we approached Wayne's competitive debut. I couldn't wait, and for once the experience lived up to the expectation. The boy has absolute star quality. We haven't seen anything like that since a young Gascoigne burst on to the scene. I even thought he was the best at 'God Save the Queen'! When he took control of the game towards the end of the first half the England fans up and down the country experienced what Evertonians have been experiencing all season.
>
> We owe a debt of gratitude to David Moyes for the way he has nurtured him so intelligently and for allowing Evertonians these wonderful experiences. It was a very emotional night. If our expectations are high that's probably good for the boy and will help keep him up there. But the boy has something special that we have to cherish and look after, and that's what we have to do at Everton.

Rooney's performance once again alerted scouts from the world's biggest clubs, but Kenwright reiterated: 'Are you trying to tell me there's a bigger club than Everton? Do me a favour, he's going nowhere.'

Eriksson was delighted with the way his side adapted to a change in formation and admitted that defeat would have almost certainly handed the group to the Turks.

'We controlled the midfield and made life very difficult for them. We also defended very well – you have to against Turkey. It was a very important game for us. If Turkey had won they would have more or less won the group. I think it was a small surprise for them that we played as well as we did.'

Beckham silenced the critics. 'I think we needed to answer a few questions – and we did. We showed passion. The "no-hopers" did well in the end. We deserved the win. We worked hard, battled hard and there was definitely a lot of passion from everyone out there. The best team won in the end. It's a great night for English football and for the young players who've come into the team.

'We put in a professional performance on Saturday and a magnificent one here. The performance was for the manager most of all because he has taken a lot of stick in the past couple of weeks. He deserved the result.'

Eriksson was delighted but went to great lengths to ensure that Rooney's precocious contribution was viewed in the correct perspective. 'With Rooney we have to take it easy. One big game is not a whole career. You shouldn't expect that he will always play, but on the evidence of the match against Turkey I can see no reason to leave him out.

'He took it in his stride. He's very mature for his age. I've been very impressed with him in training. He showed no fear going into tackles with Rio Ferdinand and Sol Campbell. You could see that he was ready.'

The England coach had concluded that Rooney was ready for the international stage after watching him score against Arsenal in October 2002. 'We've watched a lot of him but you can't be sure when you're looking at a seventeen-year-old,' he said. 'Then I went to see him at Highbury. I thought that if he could play like that against one of the best club sides in Europe he could do it for the national team.'

Eriksson has often been called a lucky manager and he confessed: 'I was very lucky in that I had chosen to watch Arsenal-Everton that day. I realised then that I had found what I was looking for. We decided after the Liechtenstein game he would start against Turkey. But we wanted to keep it from the press. We didn't want a lot of pressure on him.'

Eriksson grew animated at the suggestion that Rooney's youthful exuberance had lifted England. 'I don't think any of our players needed to be lifted for that game,' Eriksson said. 'They really wanted to win, they knew the importance of taking six points from the two games. That is what we have done, and I think it is extremely professional.'

For once Eriksson could smile about a move that clearly pleased the media. 'Rooney is an exceptional talent. With Everton he has shown it and in front of millions of people with England he did it again. It's not often you see a seventeen-year-old boy with such ambition in his play.'

Sven's appreciation for individual talent has been one of his strongest traits as a coach. When manager at Fiorentina in the late eighties, a young player came along that he could not hold back. His skill and impudence was such that Sven felt he had no choice other than to give this young man a platform to parade his prowess. That young boy – Roberto Baggio – went on to become one of the greatest footballers of his generation.

'In my managerial career I have come across seventeen-year-olds like Rooney,' he pointed out. 'What about Roberto Baggio? He wasn't a bad player, was he? Baggio and Rooney aren't the same kind of striker, of course, but they could play together in the same team I'm sure.'

Eriksson gave Baggio his Serie A debut at Fiorentina and successfully nurtured youthful talents such as Rui Costa and Paulo Sousa, so why not Rooney?

'Your career can go up and down with your physical development and skill,' he conceded. 'You can never know what will happen with a seventeen-year-old boy, mentally and physically. You have to be very careful with such young footballers, I know that. The difficult times will start now. After his performance against Turkey life will not be easy. To handle it all he has to be helped by his agent, club and his manager.'

Eriksson is fully aware of the pitfalls. Some years ago Dan Corniulsson was being touted as Sweden's answer to Paul Gascoigne. 'As a club manager I had to handle this sixteen-year-old Corniulsson, who went on to play for Benfica. OK, he wasn't as famous as Baggio but he was really good. But I had to spend a lot of time with him.

'Young players can take a dive in their career and, when they do, the crash will be very difficult. You have to spend a lot of time getting it right because it's very easy for youngsters to not keep their feet on the ground.'

The England coach was buoyant having discovered another young talent to freshen up his side after the World Cup. He said: 'Rooney is strong and extremely good linking attack and midfield. He can drop down, take the ball and turn with it. He scares defenders because he just goes into them and he plays people in.'

For Eriksson, England and the fans Rooney's performance was one that would breathe new life into the country's football. To have a genuine young talent that would stun the world coming through was so exciting, especially as it was not that long ago that Michael Owen was scoring in a World Cup at the age of eighteen.

So you can just imagine what it was like for Rooney's family sat in the Stadium of Light that night. They beamed with pride at what they were seeing, seventeen-year-old Wayne running out with the England No 9 on his back. This was no friendly game against Australia, or a sub's appearance against minnows Liechtenstein. No, this was a massive grudge match against Turkey and the fact that an experienced coach like Eriksson had staked his reputation on his inclusion was incredible.

The entire Rooney clan from Croxteth was in Sunderland to see his fantastic performance against Turkey. And they still had not got over the excitement the day after when younger brothers John and Graham were allowed a day off school to recover.

Wayne senior said: 'We're so very, very proud of him. Really pleased and delighted. We're really tired this morning after all the celebrating but it's all worth it. He played a fantastic match last night. It was great to watch. The whole family went to see him and he has done us proud. We are starting to get used to it a bit now but it's still brilliant.'

And Wayne was also the toast of his old school De La Salle Roman Catholic High in Croxteth, where deputy head Pete Bradley said: 'We're so proud of Wayne, we're made up with his match last night.

'This area is a great breeding ground for talent and we're proud of all our boys. We always knew that Wayne was a brilliant talent but like everyone else we were very surprised and pleased that he is in the England team.'

Of course, one man who just had to be there was the scout who unearthed Rooney, Bob Pendleton. He sat with the Rooney family at the game and he said: 'Jeanette was crying by the end, but what really made her night was David Beckham. He came over to her after the match and said: "You must be the proudest mum in the world tonight." She thought that was a lovely touch. You just can't put a price on that.'

But of course controversy would forever continue over Rooney simply because of his tender years. Having seen what he could do in a big-match situation like the Turkey game, Eriksson needed Rooney to play in the next qualifier at home to Slovakia.

But the build-up to that game, ridiculously scheduled by UEFA for 11 June, almost four weeks after the end of the football season, would include a whistle-stop tour and PR exercise to South Africa for the full squad, which, of course, Moyes did not want Rooney to go on.

Eriksson said: 'That game against Slovakia will be very difficult. We must not take it for granted, or of course Macedonia away. Both will be just as difficult as the final game in Turkey.

'But I think we have a psychological advantage over Turkey having beaten them. Now we have a very good chance of winning the group. It's in our hands. I'm absolutely sure that we can win the group. Life is much easier if we win the group and avoid the play-offs. The players actually feel they can win the Championship. You feel it, but it's better not talking about it.'

Moyes pleaded in the aftermath of the Turkey game for Eriksson not to place too great a burden on Rooney. He asked that the national team travel for their 22 May friendly in South Africa without the young striker.

The Goodison Park boss had used Rooney only sparingly in his first full season in the first-team squad and hoped the England coach would adopt the same protective attitude. Moyes expected his young forward to be given a break by the national coach:

I would hope that England do not include Wayne in any end-of-season trips. What's the point in us trying to look after him if he's travelling away all over the world? It's not so much the extra games which are the worry but the length of time he is away. Sven has spoken to me a few times about him and I am sure he will understand the need to protect him, as we have done.

We are all thrilled for Wayne but I was not surprised by his performance because he is a great talent. But we must protect him from overexposure. He has to come back here and work hard for Everton, which I am sure he will.

He cares about this club and is just starting out on the long road. He needs to continue to work hard on his game and he will get better. What he is doing at the moment is through pure natural ability. Nobody at the club can take credit for that.

But the euphoria that greeted Rooney's full England debut against Turkey made it increasingly difficult for Moyes to hold the boy back. Former Everton centre forward Andy Gray, writing in his *Sunday Mirror* column, said:

In David Moyes he has got a good manager who will do his utmost to make sure he keeps his feet on the ground. David has already shown his protective side by asking Sven not to take him to South Africa for England's next friendly. I understand David's reasons, but I don't agree with stopping the boy playing football.

He might be only seventeen but he is fit and wants to play at the highest possible level. Let's face it, we are hardly talking about someone who is going to get physically battered. If anything the opposition players are the ones at risk of picking up a few bruises. The boy has got a taste for it and it is going to be extremely difficult to explain why he shouldn't play.

To be honest, whatever David thinks Wayne will be in the line-up for the next Euro 2004 qualifier against Slovakia in June.

. . . If I was Rooney's manager I would take him aside and say, 'Well done son, but remember why you were there. It's because you work hard for this club, because you graft in training and show commitment and dedication whenever you play. Whatever you do, behave yourself and control the way you live your life. Because let me tell you this, Wayne – it will get away from you, son, if you let it.' Moyes will probably be exercising that advice to the letter.

Eriksson urged the nation not to burden Rooney with overblown expectations that he could prove England's overnight saviour. But 'Rooney-mania' was well and truly under way.

The England coach conceded that it would now be almost impossible for him to leave Rooney out of the national side. Having drawn fulsome applause from the rest of the England squad for an exquisite chipped goal in training, Rooney went on to earn a standing ovation from the Stadium of Light crowd.

Eriksson nevertheless challenged him to continue to impress before England reconvened for friendlies against South Africa and Serbia-Montenegro ahead of their next qualifier against Slovakia in June. Eriksson would ideally have liked the teenager to feature more often for his club: equally he would be in favour of not overloading him with too many first-team starts just yet.

The players inside the England camp lined up to explain how they were simply gobsmacked by his attitude and skill just in training. Gareth Southgate, the most experienced outfield player at the age of 33, had never seen Rooney in the flesh until they met up with England. The Middlesbrough skipper said: 'What most impressed me is his football brain. We were playing on opposite sides in training on Tuesday when he strayed offside, checked back and ran across me to stop me closing down his strike partner. It is very difficult to teach a player to do something like that but Wayne just seems to do it instinctively.'

Gary Neville was another England player who was impressed by Rooney on the training ground, as he recalled his audacious goal. 'He beat a couple of players and then chipped the keeper. It was absolutely outstanding and everyone applauded. But he's been doing things like that all week. He showed fantastic touches and anyone who saw him would have thought, "this lad just has to play".'

David James is an articulate, intelligent guy who has seen how all the hype affected Joe Cole when they were colleagues at West Ham. James said: 'Rooney never ceases to amaze me. Some of the stuff he was doing in training was incredible. He wasn't trying to be fancy or flash. It's just that he makes the difficult stuff look so easy and so natural. You look into his eyes and he is seventeen. But then you watch him play and it is as if he is thirty-two.

'I was watching him on the bus heading to the match and he didn't seem to have any nerves at all. He was just having a laugh with Rio Ferdinand and if I hadn't known better I would have sworn he was just one of the experienced players.'

Kieron Dyer observed the dressing room and also spotted that self-assurance in The Kid. Dyer said:

> Before the game, he was just sitting there laughing and relaxing; he wasn't nervous. He was chewing his gum, the way he does. We began laughing at how calm he was. He couldn't wait to get out there and it showed in his performance.
>
> I think it helps there's a lot of Liverpool players in the squad, because obviously he knows them. Michael Owen, Steven Gerrard, and Danny Murphy looked after him and made him feel at home. He joined in very well.
>
> You'd think with people coming out with all these rave reviews he'd feel under pressure, but he just gets on the pitch and helps us gain a magnificent victory. He was absolutely brilliant again and I was just sorry for him that he didn't get on the score sheet. Even his manager said he's too young and that he's still learning the game, but if he performs like that he can't be ignored.

Crowd trouble on and off the pitch before and during the game demonstrated that all is far from right with English football. But England had a new hero, as Paul Wilson declared in the *Observer*:

> The seventeen-year-old did not just run with the ball against Turkey – he carried it around the world . . . Now even Michael Owen's place in the squad might not be guaranteed, if he is not the most creative or forceful forward. Sure, England will always need a goalscorer, and Rooney is not that, but Owen will have to look sharper than he did to continue his run in the team. If England are no longer playing balls over the top looking to his speed, other strikers could audition with Rooney. One does not have to look too far into the future to see a time when the Everton player might be the undroppable one.

In Wayne's World, the consequences for Heskey, especially with Alan Smith to return to the squad, could not have been clearer.

But for The Kid himself, life would never be quite the same. He strolled down a corridor at the Stadium of Light chatting quietly with a relative in an Everton shirt. Virtually everyone who is anyone was willing to talk about Wayne Rooney – except, of course, Wayne Rooney. Players stroll or, in some cases, sprint through the 'mixed zone' after matches, a roped-off area where the media must stay to one side while the players shuttle off to the awaiting coach with the option to stop and chat to the reporters, or TV interviewers.

Rooney made his way as quickly as he could without stopping. One writer chased after him with notebook at the ready – not for a quote, but for an autograph.

Rooney himself, though, is not fussed by the attention, and is more concerned about his mum. When asked, 'Does your mum get nervous when she watches you and do you think it's funny that she now gets asked for *her* autograph?' Wayne replied: 'She still gets nervous at games but I haven't seen her being asked for her autograph. I have heard about it and I think it is hilarious. I'm sure I will see it one day.'

10

What They Said

'Rooney seems to have the lot as a player and, if he continues to improve, can become an all-time great. He has great touch, excellent skill and that most dangerous virtue, lightning pace. At times, you can see a bit of Shearer in him, and at other times there are shades of Paul Gascoigne and Michael Owen.'

— Gary Lineker

'Wayne has to be allowed to grow up in peace. The press has agreed not to invade the privacy of Princes William and Harry while they are at school and college and something similar should be enforced for young sports stars. Wayne needs to be protected at least until he is eighteen.'

— George Best

Rooney's emergence on to the English football scene was not just recorded on these shores. You do not get a talent like him smashing his way into the record books without the whole world sitting up and taking notice. Rooney's performance against Turkey and his goals for Everton had sent shock waves around world football. England found out at the 2002 World Cup in Japan and South Korea how much their football is followed and the players adored. Here is just a little taste of some of the reaction from different countries to the outbreak of Rooney-mania.

JAPAN: Rooney's rise to prominence has been greeted with enthusiasm in the Japanese media over the last few months. Fuji TV, one of the nation's biggest broadcasters, requested an interview, were denied by Everton and interviewed the manager instead. Rooney has made headlines in many of the daily newspapers and has also been featured in *Soccer Weekly* magazine, Japan's oldest and most popular football periodical. It's unlikely he'll ever achieve David Beckham status here, though. The England captain is one of the most popular sportsmen in Japan, as he discovered during the World Cup, with his image appearing on a three-storey-high advertising board above Roppongi, Tokyo's premier nightclub district. The reason? Looks, wife, and non-football celebrity rating.

Michael Church, *Daily Yomiuri*, Tokyo

CHINA: People here are very excited for two reasons. First, because Rooney is so very young, and second because he is a team-mate at Everton of Li Tie, the most popular player in China. We don't think he is the new David Beckham but the new Michael Owen. If Everton come to China [they are planning a friendly] it will be very exciting, a huge event, because of Rooney and Li Tie.

Liu Junsheng, *China Soccer*

FRANCE: The French had heard of Wayne Rooney all right, even before he played for England. More Premiership games are shown here than in Britain, including all of Arsenal's matches, so everyone saw that screamer against them at Goodison Park and wondered: 'Who the hell is that?' When *France Football* did a feature on the world's emerging talents six months ago we highlighted Rooney. There is a popular radio show, similar to Radio Five Live's *606*, hosted by France's best-known pundit, ex-national-team captain Jean Michel Larqué, and Rooney was one of the players we discussed on the show.

Philippe Auclair, *France Football*

GERMANY: In the mind of the average German there is no way that the biggest talent in the world is playing in Liverpool. We have seen him on TV and he looks good but not exceptional. Sorry. Two German papers covered England but most of the reporting about Rooney related to the risk taken by Eriksson. One described it as the bravest decision he has made. The other described Rooney as 'pure energy'.

Christoph Biermann, *Suddeutsche Zeitung*

ITALY: The perception of Wayne Rooney as a world-class star in the making has been well documented in Italy, where his formidable career rise has been followed from the beginning. With great timing *Gazzetta dello Sport* ran half a page under the headline 'Wonder boy Rooney' (in English) on 19 October. In the afternoon he scored *that* goal against Arsenal, and two days later the same paper doubled with 'Rooney's masterpiece'. Since then he has become a household name to Italian football followers. There has been a TV special, a *Corriere dello Sport* rumour of a possible move to AC Milan and a constant presence in *Gazzetta dello Sport*: 'Rooney challenges king Owen' before the Liverpool derby ('More Rooney than Owen' the following day), the parallel with Leeds United's James Milner after Christmas, not only in the sports papers but also in the quality dailies, all the details about his contract in January, up until his exploits with the national team. Headlines on that subject included, for the Australia game, 'A child in the England squad', 'It's Rooney's night' and 'Rooney debuts in disaster'. After Rooney's spectacular performance against Turkey the headline writers used English again, and the *Gazzetta* gave Rooney half a page, a big picture, and the headline: 'Yes, Roonaldo'.

Filippo Maria Ricci, *Gazzetta dello Sport*

SWEDEN: I laughed when I read that Brian Clough said Rooney looks older than his own father. That's brilliant. He is such a tough player, he looks like one of those rugged players you used to see battling in the mud in the early 1970s, or the type of guy you might meet downtown in the north wearing a T-shirt when it's freezing. He is the kind of player we never breed. He comes from a tough environment. He has started getting bigger in Sweden. Here, if we produce players like that they tend to be second-generation immigrants, from Africa or Bosnia for example. But they tend to fade and are gone by the time they are twenty. Zlatan Ibrahimovic is the exception; he came through in his teens and lasted.

Jan Majlard, *Svenska Dagbladet*

HOLLAND: He's a bull. How come? Is it the food or the beer? Seriously, we've had a big discussion about him over the last few days [since the Turkey match], especially in relation to the Dutch team and its problems. But we were talking about Rooney because we have some young talent coming up. It seems to be more normal to promote youth in the English national team. The strange thing here is that although the Dutch do it at club level they don't at international level. We will watch Rooney more closely now.

Youri van den Busken, *De Telegraaf*

BRAZIL: The game wasn't shown in Brazil, and none of the main papers reported on England-Turkey. The sports paper, *Lance*, ran a report headlined 'Rooney enchants the English' but it was all taken off the wires.

Alex Bellos, Rio de Janeiro, freelance writer

RWANDA: Wayne Rooney is an extraordinary talent and, bearing in mind that he is rapidly becoming a big name at seventeen, I think he has high prospects of becoming a star. His intelligence, superb speed and strength make him the exceptional young striker in the world. The name Rooney first got into the limelight in Rwanda after his brilliant goal against Arsenal, and since then, Rwandans keep their keen eyes on him when he's playing for Everton or England. But I think he deserves to play for a bigger club, where he could face the stiff challenge that might make him reach the apex.

Emmanuel Nsekanabo, journalist

But pundits, former England legends, managers and players still could not stop talking about the super kid from Croxteth. 'Awesome' and 'fantastic' are the words Gary Lineker used to describe Wayne Rooney. Lineker, front man for the BBC's TV coverage, said: 'Rooney seems to have the lot as a player and, if he continues to improve, can become an all-time great. He has great touch, excellent skill and that most dangerous virtue, lightning pace.

'At times, you can see a bit of Shearer in him, and at other times there are shades of Paul Gascoigne and Michael Owen. But he looks distinctive, a player who deserves to be hailed for what he is rather than who he reminds us of.'

Ron Atkinson watched the England-Turkey game from a hotel in the Canary Islands. Former Manchester United manager Big Ron said:

Sven Goran Eriksson took a massive gamble by picking Wayne Rooney and I'm delighted for him that it came off. One of the biggest things in any manager's locker is decision-making and your choices can win you a cup final or lose you your job. Sometimes you just feel something's right, even for no logical reason, and you follow your instinct.

It can be worrying but you have to trust your judgement. There was logic to picking Rooney but starting him in a game of that importance was still one of the biggest risks I can remember an England manager taking.

Don't forget, Rooney hasn't played ten full games for Everton. I'm a massive fan of Rooney but I'm not sure I'd have been prepared to put him in like that. Under the circumstances most managers would have gone with the tried and trusted. Having stuck by Emile Heskey for so long, you'd give him one more throw of the dice. Sometimes the brave or unexpected decisions are the best ones.

Atkinson made comparisons with Norman Whiteside, who was sixteen when he gave him his United debut:

They're different players in that Rooney's quicker, although Norman was very quick-thinking, but they seem to have similar make-ups. The biggest similarity is in their temperament.

Some months ago I was asked if I would pick Rooney for England and I suggested he should be put into the side immediately because you could see that the step up would not affect his nerve.

Like Norman, Rooney has never looked like a boy among men and doesn't seem to be fazed by anything. It is a massive quality for a kid to have because the rest of the team instantly recognise it. Beckham, Owen, Scholes, Gerrard, they are big, big players. But you could see they were not in the least bit worried about having a teenager among them because they know he can look after himself.

Before long Whiteside . . . looked like he'd been playing international football for life, and it's the same with Rooney. That's what impresses me most about the kid. He seems to have almost a gunslinger's temperament. Even after the Turkey result, all the adulation and the standing ovation, he wasn't leaping about. I got the impression he was pretty much on the same level as before the game.

My reaction as the game progressed was that I didn't want Rooney to tire. When Sven took him off I wondered whether he had done it deliberately like they do on the continent so he could get the big ovation. I am sure, in fact, that it was really to get Kieron Dyer's energy into the dying stages, but he could have been forgiven if he had wanted the kid to get his moment of glory.

Atkinson knows that Rooney's life would now change for ever. He added: 'There will be temptations. All of a sudden he can't just go and play with his mates in the street or take his parents to Butlins. That might be the problem for him. The things he might want to do will be a problem. His life is going to take off now on a different tangent and how he deals with that will be crucial.'

The verdict from the original child prodigy, George Best, confirmed Rooney's credibility as a genuine immense talent. Best backed Rooney to fulfil his billing as the next superstar of English football.

Former Old Trafford star Best said, in April 2003, he believed Rooney has the mental strength and the ability to avoid following the line of young English prospects into oblivion: 'Every year you see a young player between seventeen and twenty coming through who looks good but for some reason does not get any better. They get to a certain level but don't go on to become what I consider to be world class.

'Just look at people like Thierry Henry and Robert Pires. They came here with people not having heard much about them but have gone on to become world-class talents. You don't see that with British players. Wayne is the exception.'

Best, now 58, struggled to cope with the fame, money and pressure that came with being a football superstar with Manchester United from 1963 to 1974. He made his debut as a seventeen-year-old but, after a career blighted by late nights and alcoholism, he walked out of top-flight football at the age of 26. The same off-field pressures await Rooney, but Best was convinced the youngster will deal with all that is thrown at him:

Wayne is going to be special as long as he has the right people to look after him. Wayne seems a sensible lad but if he thinks he's got pressure now, things are going to get ten or even twenty times worse.

The press have been going on about Wayne Rooney for months and after the England–Turkey match the coverage got even worse. Now everyone seems to be worrying about putting too much pressure on the lad. I totally agree, and the concern for the seventeen-year-old is commendable. But the real pressure for Rooney won't come from playing top-flight domestic and international football, it will come from the press themselves.

The number of stories already written about Rooney is ridiculous, but at least most of them have been about football. I know that some journalists are now sniffing around his private life, and following him and his girlfriend. That has to stop right away.

When I was Wayne's age, the only press coverage I got was about my performance on the pitch. It was three or four years later that things got crazy. Young stars today don't have the luxury of those years growing up and being able to make mistakes in private. They are so important to me, even if I didn't learn from them. Wayne has to be allowed to grow up in peace.

The press has agreed not to invade the privacy of Princes William and Harry while they are at school and college and something similar should be enforced for young sports stars. Wayne needs to be protected at least until he is eighteen.

That said, this would also mean he had to stay out of the limelight, no parties, no celebrity girlfriends, and, above all, no multi-million-pound sponsorship deals. That's a big financial sacrifice, but the minute he becomes a commercial commodity, then it's a free-for-all.

Now well past his sell-by date, Paul Gascoigne was once a legend in his own boozer who failed to live up to his immense potential. This made Gazza perfectly placed to pass on advice as Rooney faced the first major intrusion into his private life. Already the tabloid media was insatiably fascinated by everything from a tattoo on Rooney's upper shoulder of his girlfriend's name to insights into the domineering aspects of his mum. His girlfirend was snapped strolling to school, and the paparazzi was following his every move.

Gazza said: 'Learn from my mistakes and you'll be one of the greatest players in history.'

Gazza's performances and his tears at Italia 90, where England lost the World Cup semifinal on penalties, made him a global superstar. But the stardom came at a price. He has never been out of the spotlight in thirteen years since and it took its toll. Injuries also wrecked his career, but there was no let-up in the interest in every aspect of his life – on or off the field. Much of it, he admits, he brought on himself. There were times he found it all too much and turned to drink. He knows all the dangers lurking round the corner for Rooney. Gazza, who finished his Premiership days at Everton just as a fifteen-year-old Rooney was bursting through the ranks there, said:

So many people have said how much Rooney reminds them of me. Wayne probably won't realise the half of what is to come for him. Now the world knows about him his life will never be the same again. I went on benders at the wrong time and that was my fault. There was a lot of pressure from the media and it backfired on me. Whoever you are, you will have your good times and bad times and I have faced pitfalls. You never know what is round the corner.

You think the world's your oyster but you have to be careful about the things that can drag you down. You have to expect the unexpected. He can learn from my mistakes and I'd say to him enjoy your football and don't change anything for anybody. Be yourself. That's what he has to be careful of – changing just because people tell him to and not being true to his roots.

I heard he got a lot of stick because his family were going on holiday to Butlins. Why was that? If that's where they are most comfortable, then what is the point in getting on a plane to Florida?

He's going to have to learn to deal with every aspect of his life being examined. But he is at a great club which will help him all the way and in David Moyes he has an understanding manager who will make sure he keeps his feet on the ground.

Gazza was a star with his home-town team Newcastle United when he was eighteen, but he did not make his mark on the England scene until the age of 23, after he had moved to the bright lights of London. Rooney, however, was six years younger and just out of school, with an immense burden to carry. 'I would tell Wayne to stay exactly where he is and listen to the people closest to him – his manager, older team-mates and his parents,' said Gazza. 'I didn't leave Newcastle to join Tottenham until I was twenty-one. I did it because I was offered a much better contract to go to London, but when I got there I was under so much scrutiny it was unbelievable.

'Wayne, though, has everything he needs where he is. He has already got a very good contract and is at a club which is going places. He still likes to have a kick-around with his mates in the park, just as I did when I was a youngster at Newcastle. That's great.'

Except Everton might not have been so pleased if he got injured playing street football!

Gazza added: 'Like me, he enjoys playing the game so much and, believe me, that's where you get away from all your troubles. I would go and play for the first team at Newcastle and then I'd go back and play with the lads in the park. You should never lose track of your friends; good friends stick by you through thick and thin.'

So, advice from two of the most notorious world-class players. Just days after Gazza delivered his words of wisdom, he disgraced himself yet again by being so drunk he was staggering around Heathrow telling staff he was on his way to China, but boarded a flight to the States bound for a rehab clinic. He is now publicising his own autobiography after recently drying out in the US.

How all the intrusion into Rooney's private life would affect him on the field was the next big test. The player himself wanted to stress that he was a normal kid just trying to play football. And like everybody he had his own heroes and players he found toughest to play against. Wayne's role model is Alan Shearer, but he does have many players he admires, particularly among the defenders. He explained: 'No one individual, but I do admire Sol Campbell. He is a big, strong player who reads the game well, although I have scored two goals against him! He is definitely the toughest, but there are a number of great defenders playing in the Premiership who make life difficult for strikers.'

Talking about how his success had affected his personal life, Rooney said: 'Outside football, I'm just like anyone else. I go out with my mates for a game of snooker or I sit in the house watching videos and playing on the computer with my girlfriend.'

When asked if he had much trouble fitting back into normal life with friends and at home after such huge days as scoring against Arsenal and playing for England, Wayne said: 'Not really, but sometimes after the England games especially there is a lot of press around and you have to be careful of where you go. But to be honest it is normally just the same and there has been no real big change.'

Cool as you like.

But to whom did Wayne owe his success? He thought about that one and said: 'I couldn't thank just one person. Without question I have to thank my family and I also owe a lot to everyone at Everton and England. I also have to thank the people at ProActive who have helped to advise along the way, but most of all I have to thank the Everton supporters who have been absolutely brilliant to me since I have been in the team. Thanks.'

Everybody in the world seems to have an opinion on Wayne Rooney. But who better could Rooney have to offer to help him deal with the pressures of fame than brilliant Brazilian Ronaldo himself.

In the modern era the Real Madrid striker knows more than anybody what it is like to have to deal with the pressure of fame and expectation. The same could be said of David Beckham, but Becks has not played in two World Cup finals like Ronaldo.

Ronaldo took some time out from his busy football fixture list in the 2002–03 season, when Rooney first emerged, to talk about the pressures on Rooney and tip the Everton striker to enjoy a trophy-laden career. The Brazilian superstar has become the latest addition to the Rooney fan club as word spreads across the globe of the Goodison starlet's precocious talent.

Like Rooney, Ronaldo was just seventeen when he made his mark in international football as a member of his country's 1994 World Cup-winning squad. And the Real Madrid star said: 'I've been in Rooney's position so I'd like to help him. The most important advice I can give him is to tell him to stay balanced mentally because he must not allow himself to become crazy at his own success. That is why so many talents have disappeared without achieving their capabilities.'

Ronaldo himself suffered from the pressures of success at an early stage of his career, culminating in his infamous 'fit' before the 1998 World Cup final against France. The European and World Footballer of the Year exorcised his personal demons by helping his country regain the World Cup in Japan and South Korea in 2002. And he insisted: 'Wayne will have no choice but to live with the pressure that comes with being a young star. But he must do his best to forget all about that and enjoy everything about his life and his football.

'A football career can fly by very quickly so I hope he has as much fun as possible by playing wonderful football and winning great titles. There is no reason why he cannot start winning trophies now.'

He added: 'From what I've seen, the boy has a big presence and a big future, but everyone around him must do their best to take care of him when he is away from the pitch. If this happens, he won't have to lose his objective, which must be all about playing football.'

Football is just like pop music these days, with the top stars enjoying the same fame and attention as the top performers in the music industry. One fanatical football follower is Robbie Williams, a Port Vale supporter, who follows English football and the Premiership wherever he is in the world.

Williams actually labelled Wayne Rooney a god. The former Take That singer said during an unscheduled visit to Liverpool in late 2002 that he was a big fan of the Everton teenager. Robbie was due to go to Manchester, but bad weather conditions forced his helicopter to land in Liverpool instead. During an interview with Radio City, Robbie joked about his visit: 'My helicopter broke down so I decided to come and say hello – it's great here.'

When asked about the young star he said: 'Wayne Rooney is a god, he's just what the game needs. He's scoring bags of goals and he seems like a real character – I'm a big fan.'

Getting back to a little more reality, those people involved in Rooney's football upbringing had every right to urge caution over his development at this stage. They did not want to see everything blow up in the young lad's face.

Everton youth-team coach Colin Harvey was one of those concerned about his progress. He said: 'There has been an awful lot of hype about him. It is now up to the coaches and the people who deal with him to see that the talent comes to fruition. He's a level-headed lad and to play in the team he knows he has to play as a team member, which he does. It's up to him how far he goes. He's got a special talent, but he's got a long, long way to go.'

It is right to say that everybody in the game did not get carried away with the youngster's staggering achievement. But ex-Everton midfielder Barry Horne, a senior executive with the Professional Footballers' Association, was right when he said Wayne's world would never be the same again after his astonishing debut season.

The former PFA chairman said: 'You have to accept that once you are a centre forward playing for a massive football club like Everton, and then England, you are no longer an ordinary person. And, like it or not, Wayne will be treated differently. There is now a general perception that high-profile footballers are public property. He will need his friends, family and club behind him.'

Wayne's parents had originally said they would like the family to continue living in its Croxteth home, but Barry said: 'Time might change that. It's a bit different for mums and dads, brothers and so on staying where they are, but there might come a time when it's best for Wayne to find his own place not too far away.' Which is exactly what happened when Wayne's fame eventually proved too much for him to continue kicking around in the streets where he grew up.

Former Everton child prodigy Francis Jeffers knew what Rooney was going through, as he was hailed as a Goodison Park saviour when he emerged on the scene. He moved on fairly quickly to Arsenal for £10m, and although he had scored for England, which Rooney had yet to do, he has not received quite the same attention as the younger star. He was loaned back to Everton last season, but has since returned to Highbury.

Jeffers said: 'In a way there are parallels between what's happening with Wayne and the way it started for me. We are both local lads, playing in the same position, who've grown up watching the club on the terraces and then gone on to play for them. But I've never seen anything like Wayne, though. He's a complete one-off, although he does remind me of Thierry Henry in the way that he goes at players, as they both ooze confidence.

'I know him quite well and he's a really nice lad and so level-headed. It must be so difficult with all that attention and being so young, but he's taken it all in his stride.'

Rooney's team-mates had eulogised about the young Rooney all season. Before his proper breakthrough Canadian hotshot Tomasz Radzinski said: 'We have two very quick strikers in me and Chaddy [Chadwick], one big man in Dunc [Ferguson], and Kevin [Campbell] who is a combination of everything, good speed, body strength and technique.

'Then we have Rooney. I still haven't had the pleasure to watch him in action but from what I've seen at this training camp, he can do things with a ball that many people won't learn in a lifetime.' Not bad praise.

Rooney played most of his games in the 2002–03 season alongside skipper and former Arsenal star Kevin Campbell. He admitted that playing alongside Wayne Rooney is 'a joy and privilege'. Campbell played a guiding role with Rooney as the veteran and teenager spearheaded Everton's remarkable assault on the Champions League zone. The 33-year-old said it is the youngster's desire to learn from the veteran in the Everton ranks that could turn natural talent into one of the greatest players in the world:

I have given Wayne bits of advice, we all have. And the great thing about Wayne is he listens. It's one thing giving advice but it's another for a youngster to listen and take it on board. So when you see him going out there and putting that advice into practice, then you know you've really got something special. I love playing alongside anyone because that means I'm in the team! But to be honest it's a joy to play alongside Wayne.

To play alongside someone so young and so gifted is a tremendous privilege for me as the oldest member of the squad. Defenders have got years and years of him to come and I would hate to be in their shoes! He's going to get even better. He is a special talent, he's a special boy and a

nice boy. We all want to see him fulfil his potential because he can be up
there among the greats of world football.

Rooney, though, had even been causing problems for some of his
own team-mates. Midfielder Li Tie revealed he cannot understand a
word the youngster says. The Chinese star had been taking English
lessons since arriving in August 2002 for a year's loan; he is still at
the club. 'I can understand most of the players, apart from Wayne
Rooney. He is from round here and has a local accent. The accent of
the Liverpool people is difficult for me to understand.'

It should have come as no surprise that legendary boss Brian
Clough, who usually has a word of advice for everybody, rightly
warned Rooney to be wary of burning out after his impressive
England debut. The former Nottingham Forest and Derby manager
believed the seventeen-year-old could be in danger if he let fame go
to his head.

Clough said: 'He's absolutely incredible at seventeen. He's
seventeen going on forty-seven now. It is a different world to when
I was seventeen.'

Clough considered Rooney's full England debut in the 2–0 win
over Turkey showed the maturity of the player on the pitch. 'He put
in a mature performance which was incredible for his age,' Clough
said. 'He stood his ground with people who had been in the game
fifteen years, people who were in the game before he was born.'

But Clough voiced concern over the long-term effects on Rooney
of having fame and fortune at such a young age. 'I think, "What's he
going to be like when he's forty-five?" With the pressure on him, if
he doesn't handle it right he will be burnt out. He's getting things so
quickly I am concerned for him.'

Clough admitted England coach Sven Goran Eriksson had done
the right thing by resisting the calls to put Rooney in the team earlier
than he did. 'I admire the England manager for not putting Rooney
in straight away,' said Clough, who also praised David Moyes's
handling of the player. 'I admire the Everton manager for treating
him as one of the lads.'

Clough also claimed that had he been England manager today he
would have been able to help Rooney. 'If you could have worked

with anybody to keep your feet on the floor, I was the man,' he said. Well, it would not be 'old big head' if he did not make one arrogant comment.

11

Street Striker

'We have this philosophy about Wayne which will present him as the real thing. He is a product of his environment, the streets and the terraces. He is not manufactured. He is a real person and I don't want to lose that appeal. We have launched a trademark brand and called it Rooney – Street Striker.'

– Agent Paul Stretford

The Rooney phenomenon had almost become uncontrollable as everybody wanted a piece of the young striker after his exploits for England. People may have compared young Rooney to Pelé, but the brilliant Brazilian grew up and plied his trade in a completely different era, and almost a different game. The only similarity is that, at the end of the day, all that really matters is putting the ball in the back of the net.

Outside of that, though, the world of football has completely changed. Sven Goran Eriksson made the point after Wayne Rooney's heroics against Turkey that so much depended on the advice he will receive. Of course, most of that will come from his manager David Moyes and his family – but just as important in this commercial world is his agent. Rooney's agent is Paul Stretford, who heads up a Stock Exchange-listed company called ProActive, and who confidently predicts that his new client will become one of the richest and most famous sportsmen of all time. Rooney's day-to-day contact at the company is Mick Doherty, head of player recruitment. He has known Wayne for several years. An image-rights deal formed an integral part of Rooney's first professional contract with Everton, and ProActive worked on developing an image that already exists of the home-town boy made good, still in tune with his roots. Stretford said in spring 2003: 'We have this philosophy about Wayne which will present him as the real thing. He is a product of his environment, the streets and the terraces. He is not manufactured. He is a real person and I don't want to lose that appeal. We have launched a trademark brand and called it Rooney – Street Striker.' This is football at its free-market best.

Stretford added: 'The life-change he and his family have had to contend with has been cataclysmic. Most seventeen-year-old footballers come through the system gradually. His progress has been like a volcanic explosion. That has a lot of plus sides but the downside is that he is a young lad who will make mistakes. But the important thing is that he learns from them.

'Wayne seems shy when you first meet him, although those who know him best will tell you he is anything but that. It is important that people see him as that and not as ignorant or arrogant.'

As his agents exercise so much control over Rooney, it is vital that they are the right company to develop his talents on the field by protecting him off it. There are mixed feelings about his link to ProActive. Clearly they exert as much influence as his family and even his manager at Goodison.

Stretford said: 'Wayne won't become a brat because of his lovely, genuine family. Jeanette answers all his fan mail and is very switched on, the powerhouse of the family. I really hope the nation as a whole recognises that in Wayne we have a real treasure who should be cherished. We should all be proud of him.'

Hardly out of school, the biggest name of his generation of footballers has already been the centre of one of the most acrimonious and controversial rows behind the scenes between agents. Local Merseyside agents complained in late 2002 that ProActive poached Rooney with offers of a £250,000 house for his parents, £150,000 cash and promises of a new £13,000-a-week contract with Everton. The dispute still continues.

ProActive now represent Rooney on a five-year agreement; the agency is a co-director with the teenager and his mum, Jeanette, in a company called Stoneygate 48 Ltd, which was set up with the purpose of handling commercial deals as part of his image-rights contract with his club and endorsements negotiated by ProActive. The company is being handled by Leicester-based tax experts Powrie Appleby, in documents available at Companies House.

Someone had to handle the hype, though, because when somebody like Wayne Rooney comes along, the football world goes mad. The kid is unlike anything England has ever seen. But what it means, of course, is that Rooney will continually be surrounded by mayhem.

For example, take Everton fan Keith Sorrell. He is hoping a special bet at the bookies will net him £10,000 . . . sometime around the year 2010. Just before Rooney made his record-breaking England debut in February 2003, Sorrell wagered £20 at Stanley Racing at odds of 500–1 on all three Rooney brothers playing for England at senior international level in the same side. Only on Merseyside could there be such optimism.

Keith, 33, from Walton, hatched the idea after watching Wayne, the eldest Rooney, become the youngest player to play in the senior England side against the Aussies. As a result Keith then asked the bookmakers for his special bet on the seemingly impossible happening.

Never before in the history of senior international football have three brothers played in the same England team, though eight pairs of brothers have. Wayne's brothers Graham and John are both talented players and are tipped for stardom, although Graham may well make his mark for England wearing boxing gloves, as he is also a gifted fighter. But this did not seem to deter Sorrell. Everton season-ticket holder Keith said: 'Wayne's brothers are brilliant at football, too, so if they grow up to be anywhere near as good as him then I'm in with a shout. It would be great for Merseyside and make me a very happy, and rich, man.'

A spokesman for Stanley Racing said: 'We are always happy to organise special bets for customers and wish him and the Rooney brothers every possible luck.'

So there we have it, the football world had gone mad. Nobody really expected the Rooney factor to explode just as it did, but very soon shirts with the name 'Roonaldo' splashed all over them were hot property around Goodison Park.

In fact, the demand was so high that Everton were forced to hire call-centre group Avarto Services to help handle orders. The Pier Head-based group, formerly known as Bertelsmann, was first called in by the club as an emergency measure at Christmas 2002 to cope with the surge in demand for Rooney-emblazoned shirts. Shirts bearing the teenage player's name are the most popular with Everton fans.

'It was such a rush at Christmas that we were taking calls before any contract was signed,' said a spokesman for Avarto. 'They liked what we did for them then and now we are handling order fulfilment for the club for the next year. It's not just Rooney. Li Tie shirts have been going well, too,' the spokesman added.

But it did not stop there. Rooney may not be old enough to pop in for a drink, but incredibly the Everton wonder kid Wayne has had a pub named in his honour.

Rooney's Bar is just yards from Goodison Park, and was opened before the Kid could even legally call in for a pint. The Westminster Road pub, formerly known as The Sefton, was decked out in colours celebrating the Everton and England striker ahead of its grand opening. Licensee Ken Speed is a lifelong Blue and explained it was an honour to name the bar after the Croxteth-born star:

He's the most famous seventeen-year-old in Merseyside, so I don't think he is able to get served anywhere, let alone here. We hope that we will be able to get him in for his first drink, though, when he finally reaches his eighteenth birthday. We don't think we'll be inviting him for the opening, though. It would be just right that the police pop in to see if he's here and sees us sitting around having a pint.

We are having a big party to celebrate our opening so we are all geared up for the launch. At present, we have a normal opening-hours licence, but we hope to change that in the future. If anything else, there are the night games which don't finish until ten, so we don't want to throw out a load of football fans as soon as they arrive.

With royal-blue walls, an Everton clock and pictures of Rooney adorning the wall, the pub already looked the part in order to have his name above the door. But this was never going to be as simple as it sounded. Good fun it might have been naming a bar after the kid, but typically Rooney's agent was not overly impressed considering anything and everything named after the striker is worth money, and being involved with a pub was not quite the image he was trying to create.

Stretford commented: 'Neither Wayne, his family or club was asked for permission to use his name. This could be damaging. Wayne is too young to be associated with a bar. I've given the pub a week before taking the matter further.'

But Ken, who spent £100,000 creating Rooney's Bar, was not happy when he faced the threat of legal action: 'It's only a bit of fun. This will create a rift between Wayne and his fans. If Mr Stretford wants a fight, he'll get one. But if Wayne walked in and asked me to take his name down, I wouldn't hesitate.'

The next problem was a trade in fake banknotes over the Internet with Rooney's face on them. Again it did not amuse his advisors, as ProActive said: 'We are aware of the Wayne Rooney novelty banknotes. These are not officially endorsed by either Wayne or Everton, whose imagery they utilise. We would encourage people to bear this in mind before they consider purchasing any of the notes.'

Everton club spokesman Ian Ross said: 'It's become open season on Wayne Rooney commercial activities. It seems some people regard him as a bandwagon they can just jump on and exploit, and I'm sure the police will have an interest in investigating this matter.' So much for football being fun.

Of course, what people had to realise, and ProActive certainly did, was that, despite his age, Rooney was already a marketing force. The image-rights clause on his £13,000-a-week contract with Everton meant that he makes money on any sponsorship, merchandising and endorsement which uses his likeness in words or pictures.

He has already made his first million thanks to the popularity of replica kits with his name and number on, which earned him £3 for each one sold. Rooney is one of only a few in the UK who have such image rights. Normally, celebrities copyright either their name or a characteristic, such as Paul Gascoigne's 'Gazza' or Damon Hill's eyes behind his visor.

Whatever future Rooney has on the football pitch ahead of him, his name and face could soon bring him riches beyond his wildest dreams. It is understood that he is currently discussing a clothing range that would carry his name. Add this to the T-shirts, mugs, mouse mats, key rings, car stickers, videos and books that will eventually bear his face, name and examples of his considerable talent, as well as any private sponsorship deals he sets up, and his endorsement earnings will far exceed those he gets for playing football.

As Stretford added: 'I can confirm that Wayne Rooney is one of the elite band of players whose image rights are of such importance that they are able to negotiate a special contract. Wayne Rooney as a proposition is unique. That is why he is not only a footballer, but also newsworthy.'

This is the first time an Everton player has had such a contract. The club has paid Rooney a fixed sum, believed to be tens of thousands of pounds, for permission to use his image on their merchandise. Now it needs to get that money back. Andy Hosie, marketing director, said: 'We are planning an area in our megastore devoted to Wayne for a range of dedicated products. We have to make money out of this for Everton because we have paid him a sum of money for his rights. However, we don't want to do too much and overexpose him.'

Image rights are still relatively new in the UK and so far celebrities have tended only to trademark their names or certain characteristics. Dr Geoff Pearson, who lectures in football and law at the University of Liverpool, said: 'English law is lagging behind the likes of the US and Far East which have publicity rights. The courts here are reluctant to introduce them.

'Players that are involved in commercial deals will start to trademark their images and will have rights to prevent others passing them off. Those players who don't make money from their images will not be making any loss by others using them.'

But, though it undoubtedly helps in the case of Beckham and Owen, there is more to having an image than just a pretty face. The potential for fame, the player's talent and their uniqueness are all taken into account. James Dow, of financial experts Dow Schofield Watts, said: 'Rooney will appeal to a male audience. He's a very quiet lad who doesn't really do anything apart from play football.

'He's very much a blokes' bloke from the wrong end of town. It's a Cinderella-type story which will appeal to those people who will also come from the wrong end of town. Someone like Mike Tyson would have the same sort of cachet.

'They have to have that special something, but they have got to build an image. But they must make sure their endorsements are consistent with their image and that it isn't distorted by doing different things.'

There can be good and bad sides to his image. The bottom line is that Rooney is still a kid who comes from the back streets of Liverpool. As a result, when he was browsing in a London estate agents', probably dreaming what he was going to spend all his money on, he was booted out because staff who did not know him thought he was trying to 'case' £1m homes.

When in autumn 2002 Rooney and team-mate Alan Stubbs walked into posh Chelsea estate agents Kinleigh, Folkard and Hayward, wary staff suspected the two were would-be burglars and asked them to leave before they called the police. The pair had wandered down the exclusive King's Road to kill time before Everton's Worthington Cup match against Chelsea, after arriving early at the club's Stamford Bridge ground. But staff failed to recognise Rooney or Stubbs, who were wearing club tracksuits and trainers and chewing gum.

An Everton source said: 'One of the agents simply refused to give the pair any details of their properties. The agent thought they were burglars who had come to London to "case" some big houses before robbing them.'

The source added: 'Wayne and Alan just left without making a fuss but were laughing all the way to the ground. The agent had mistaken them for a couple of scallies on the rob.'

A spokesman for Everton said: 'We have heard about this story. Even the classiest estate agents in London need to learn that sometimes appearances can be deceptive.'

But, of course, Rooney has been recognised for what he has done on the pitch, and therefore as a result he was voted Young Sports Personality of the Year 2002 at December's BBC sports awards. Wayne was given the title in an award voted for by a panel of journalists and sports stars.

In keeping with Everton's determination to shield Wayne from the glare of the media, he said nothing upon collecting the award. Typically, though, being in the spotlight, Rooney was criticised by people in the media who should know better for collecting the award with his tie undone and while he was chewing gum. Maybe the poor lad was just hot and nervous.

Turning to the ugly side of Rooney's notoriety, and the jealousy that goes with it, during the 2002–03 season vandals damaged his family's new car. The Croxteth family's people carrier was attacked twice in a fortnight by vandals using nails to puncture its tyres. Wayne senior was forced to spend more than £140 on replacement tyres after discovering they had been damaged as it sat outside the family home. The navy-blue Ford Galaxy is used by Wayne's father to drive his son to and from training sessions and Goodison Park.

The family decided not to report the damage to the police or to make any comment on the attacks, but neighbours at their old house said they are shocked at the vandalism and believe the offenders have travelled to Croxteth from another area of the city.

Doreen Driscoll, who lived nearby to the Rooneys said: 'It's horrible and I can't believe anyone would do it. He is a lovely young fellow and everyone loves him round here, especially the kids. It's probably people from elsewhere doing this.'

Another neighbour said: 'There are brainless people who would do that kind of thing. Maybe it's because Liverpool are top dogs and he is an Evertonian.'

But vandals did not stop there as next they moved on to the family home. The house, which Rooney shared with his parents and younger brothers, was peppered with paint-filled pellets, which hit the wall and the family car on the driveway.

Rooney's father said in the *Liverpool Echo*: 'We don't know if people are doing it because they are jealous but we are not going to report it to the police.

'We've had tyres slashed on cars before, but what can you do? The kids were in the bedroom where the window was hit and they thought it was stones being thrown. I don't know why it happened, but there's nothing we can do.'

Next-door neighbour Tony Melia said: 'It's terrible some petty-minded yobs should do this to Wayne's house. They are just twisted and jealous of what Wayne has achieved. He's a terrific lad – always very friendly and well liked around here – so I can't imagine it was locals who did this. It must be outsiders. It's horrible to think that somebody is having a go at them for no reason, but we will all rally round and try to keep an eye on the house for them.'

Another neighbour added: 'There's no reason for this to happen except pure spite. It's disgusting. Wayne's been built up to being a superstar overnight. But he's still just a lovely young lad to us and these louts should leave him and his family alone.'

There was a media fascination about Rooney's car ever since he forced his way into the nation's attention after his performance against Turkey. Rooney was spotted one Friday night sitting and talking with girlfriend Colleen in a Y-reg Renault Clio outside the house, and later went for a meal at the Kung Fu Chinese restaurant in St Helen's five miles away to celebrate Colleen's seventeenth birthday.

It was even reported that they had vegetable spring rolls and then main courses of mixed vegetable chow mein and sweet-and-sour chicken with fried rice, washed down with Coca-Cola, and the bill came to £40 – who cares?

A worker at the Kung Fu, who no doubt tipped the paper off, commented in perfect Cantonese: 'They seemed a lovely couple.' But it was also reported that Rooney presented the birthday girl with a £2,000 designer watch. That is where the envy originates.

A few days later it made headline news that Rooney had bought his first car, even though he hadn't yet passed his test, spending £15,000 on a trendy Mini Cooper in blue and white, naturally. Rooney had failed the written part of the examination earlier in the year and was planning to retake the exam as soon as he had the time.

But the stories of really big money were at the heart of the trouble for Rooney, so it is no wonder that they moved to another house. For the Rooneys, what Wayne had achieved was like winning the lottery – things would just never be the same again for him or his family.

Quantifying what it might be worth to a seventeen-year-old making such an instant impact on his England debut was quickly seized upon with great glee by an eager media. After his brief appearance against Liechtenstein as a substitute he was linked with European giants like Real Madrid, Bayern Munich and AC Milan. But it was a year before that his club manager David Moyes foresaw that a player, completely unheard of at that time outside of Goodison, would be worth £20m – he's now rated as worth more than double this – and he wouldn't even think about selling. Moyes had just become the Everton manager, and although he is usually reluctant to heap unwanted praise on players, he couldn't disguise his excitement when discussing the sixteen-year-old sensation in the club's junior ranks.

'He's got everything,' Moyes enthused, 'movement, pace, power, an unbelievable football intelligence. He's as good as any player I've ever trained, easily the best for his age. I wouldn't sell him now for ten million pounds. I wouldn't sell him for twenty million.'

A £20m payday in endorsements was an easy figure plucked out of the air by a media indulging in a feeding frenzy on anything Rooney, with page upon page on the sports and news pages. The *Sun* stated that his performance 'rocketed him into the superstar bracket' and it was just about the same everywhere else, and not just the day after. It was a story that ran and ran.

But the *Sun* were scraping the barrel by wheeling out that most clichéd of all agents, 'Monster, Monster' Eric Hall, with the nerve to call him a 'top agent'. The ever-quotable Hall said: 'Whatever Wayne was worth before the game, he is now worth a lot more. Sponsorship deals intended for David Beckham will now be going to Rooney. Companies who want to appeal to teenagers will want to go to Rooney.'

Rooney's agent Paul Stretford had hit gold with Rooney and he knew it, because it was a tough fight to win his signature as the bandwagon began to roll. Stretford's patience was certainly stretched by the interference of Hall providing his expert opinion about his client's commercial worth. Stretford said:

There is no doubt Wayne has the potential to earn an awful lot of money and there is always a risk that could take away from his hunger for football. But I really don't see that scenario happening with him. Wayne loves his football and that is the main drive in his life. He wants to achieve and become one of this country's best players and won't be diverted from that by anything, or anyone.

People are going to put temptation in his way and there will be distractions in his life, both close and far from home. The making of him is how he handles them and that is why we are here to help him.

He is very caring and generous around his family but he is not stupid with his money. Things are being set up in such a manner that he never will be. He is very aware of the need for investment and he will not take all his money and blow it.

A major part of our work so far has been having to say 'no' as far as commercial offers are concerned. We are taking a long-term view. In the first instance there will be four or five long-term partners. They will be blue-chip brands. It is very difficult to quantify what they will be worth.

I have read the remarks of an agent, who is the antithesis of what we are trying to do. He claims Wayne has become worth so many millions overnight. But we are not looking for that quick hit. He will be carefully managed for the next twenty years.

The sky is the limit but it will be done in a controlled manner. I am not going to put a headline figure on it, but the deals we are talking about will be substantial and record-breaking both in size and length of term.

Such is Rooney's appeal that applications have been lodged with the UK and European trademark registries, to ensure he can cash in on his new-found fame and equally to make sure nobody else can. One application is to protect his name, another to cover his signature, and the third is listed as 'Rooney 18', reference to his Everton squad number. That was even before he played against Turkey.

Next it was the turn of the FA to benefit from Rooney's name. Sven Goran Eriksson and Rooney reinvented the national side and it inspired a shirt-selling bonanza. England's shirt suppliers Umbro placed orders for one million England shirts worth £40m for sale over the following six months, as supplies of the letter 'E' ran out throughout sports stores on Merseyside and even outside Liverpool in the weekend after his full England debut. JJB Sports in Chester actually ran out of 'E's' within 24 hours of England's win over Turkey. Jamie Tovey, manager of that store, said: 'We've had hundreds of people coming in to get England shirts with Rooney on the back. Every other shirt was Rooney.'

Such was Rooney's breathtaking debut in that vital European Championship qualifier, that it created a fervour of interest that even surpassed the World Cup. Head of marketing at Umbro, Martin Prothero, told us: 'The three and a half weeks of interest in the England team during the World Cup was repeated in just three or four days after the game with Turkey. We will be selling one million England shirts in the next six months.' The leap in sales would fully justify the company's £150m nine-year contract with the FA.

In turn, the FA were grateful to Eriksson and Rooney for the resurgence in belief in the England team. Umbro launched their new kit in the week preceding the Turkey game at the Stadium of Light, and the new design was destined to be a record seller. The FA embarked on a new sponsorship 'partners' programme of which Umbro are by far the longest-contracted partner. The FA could not afford to have a £150m contract in jeopardy at a time when they were so strapped for cash, because of the cost of building the new Wembley.

The really big bucks for Rooney, though, would be generated by a new boot deal. Under contract with Umbro, Rooney's deal was quickly running out and rival manufacturers were eager to sign him up, notably Nike, who wanted Rooney as their main rival to David Beckham, who was on Adidas's books.

Nike were reputedly offering £3.2m for a three-year contract to make Rooney the richest teenager ever in football and join their stable that included Thierry Henry, Ruud van Nistelrooy, Rio Ferdinand, Roberto Carlos, Luis Figo and Edgar Davids. Even Eric Cantona remains on their books. It was suggested that the American sportswear giants had already outbid Umbro and the deal would kick in for the start of the 2003–04 season. Nike are the market leaders for the mega boot deals; their strategy is now quality rather than quantity. Umbro told us that there is no way they would compete at more than £1m a year 'guarantees', as it was totally unrealistic.

Earlier in the 2002–03 season, Umbro executives spotted Rooney pictured wearing trendy Adidas footwear and tracksuit and duly dispatched a gentle reminder to his representatives, as an Umbro spokesman told us: 'It was no big deal, we are dealing with a very young lad, and if it was a Shearer or an Owen it wouldn't have happened.'

It alerted Adidas to the potential to make a bid for the boy's signature, but when they contacted Paul Stretford, his relatively new agent, it was confirmed just how much Nike were ready to pay. An Adidas spokesman said: 'As far as we're concerned, the deal with Nike's been done. They are offering the young lad a fortune and we're not prepared to match it.'

It was estimated that Rooney's earnings over the five years of his new £13,000-a-week Everton contract would be approaching £8m. The highly respected, award-winning veteran *Daily Mail* columnist Ian Wooldridge was appalled by the mercenary attitude of a sport he had long since come to detest. He wrote:

Fatted calves are being roasted across England to celebrate the arrival of the greatest footballing talent since Paul Gascoigne. Wayne Rooney, just seventeen, appears not to have a nerve in his body.

But does he have a better brain in his head? Gazza, now begging for a game alongside a paddy field in China, sends Rooney his best wishes and warns him not to plunge down a familiar precipice that yawns in front of brilliant sportsmen. It is the cash that, suddenly, cascades at their feet.

I refer not to the enormous salary Everton will have to pay to keep him, but the £3m-plus that Nike, the American sportswear conglomerate, have already thrown at him to attach his name as an endorsement for the 'Wayne Rooney football boot' which will imminently emerge in the marketplace.

This, they trust, will overtake sales of the 'David Beckham football boot' for which their deadly rivals, Adidas, pay the England captain £3m.

Where do these prodigious perks come from? Quite simply from the pockets of indulgent parents.

Wooldridge dislikes the 'murky commercial world out there', as he concluded:

Overnight Wayne Rooney has become part of that world. At this very moment, his advisors are being bombarded with commercial offers to lend his name to jewellers, car manufacturers, bespoke tailors and celebrity magazines. He is the new cash cow, the new Beckham, the new goldmine for his handlers. And who will be paying for it? You.

Former England captain Alan Shearer has become a multi-millionaire from his off-the-field commercial spin-offs as well as his lucrative playing contracts after becoming a £15m record signing for the Geordies. Shearer says: 'It is good the way Everton are looking after him. It is a tricky situation for David Moyes. But I think he is an excellent manager and it is great the way he is trying to look after Rooney. We must not forget he has only had eleven first-team starts. He shouldn't be thinking about boot deals and new contracts. All the endorsements will follow, but let's not forget what he's best at. Nothing should get in the way of that.'

Rooney was rapidly becoming a global product, albeit nowhere near the David Beckham status. The Everton press office received a request from a Hong Kong newspaper wanting to know if Rooney had ever been to the place. A Bristol PR company enquired after the player's favourite sweets and an Ontario publication asked whether Everton would be taking an option on Rooney's future possible offspring!

Even jokes have been told about the young Everton striker, and if you did not think he was the biggest thing in the game, just read this one:

Ronaldo, Luis Figo and Wayne Rooney are standing before God at the throne of Heaven. God looks at them and says, 'Before granting you a place at my side, I must first ask you what you believe in.'

Addressing Ronaldo first he asks, 'What do you believe?'

Ronaldo looks God in the eye and states passionately, 'I believe football to be the food of life. Nothing else brings such unbridled joy to so many people, from the slums of Rio to the bright lights of Barcelona. I have devoted my life to bringing such joy to people who stood on the terraces supporting their club.'

God looks up and offers Ronaldo the seat to his left. He then turns to Luis Figo. 'And you, Luis, what do you believe?'

Figo stands tall and proud, 'I believe courage, honour and passion are the fundamentals to life and I've spent my whole playing career providing a living embodiment of these traits.'

God, moved by the passion of the speech, offers Figo the seat to his right. Finally, he turns to Wayne Rooney and asks him, 'And you, Wayne, what do you believe?'

'I believe,' says Rooney, 'you're sitting in my seat.'

However, as ever with fast-found fame, nothing can be straight-forward. Many people have wondered how Rooney will keep his feet on the ground with the acclaim and riches he has enjoyed – and inevitably there comes jealousy. At the end of the 2002–03 season Rooney's agent, Paul Stretford, had the unenviable task of telling the young striker and his family about threats from extortion gangs who want a slice of the forturne that has been pouring in since the youngster became famous. The story broke across the front page of the *News of the World* on 6 July 2003. It highlighted the very real threat that lies in wait for Rooney in the future – he thought it was only knee-high tackles he would have to watch out for.

Stratford claimed in the story that he had been menaced per-sonally, and he believed the thugs making the threats were capable of killing him. He had seen gunshots fired into his next-door neighbour's house in Wilmslow, Cheshire (which is close to where Sir Alex Ferguson lives) in March 2003, and feared they were meant for him. Stretford said: 'This is a very dangerous situation and I'm now going to have to consult with a lot of people. It's dangerous for me and my family. I'm not prepared to say another word on this issue.' He himself had received a death threat, and was told if he did not do as instructed then Rooney's legs could be broken. It is unlikely any of this would ever happen, but it is nasty and unsettling, especially for someone as young as Rooney.

The newspaper reported that while Stretford had minders around the clock, Wayne and his parents had decided they did not want personal protection – yet. Even so, the security in their Sandfield Park home had already been made state-of-the-art, with CCTV and steel plates in the gates to the house. But the news was certainly worrying for Rooney. The warning came just before he played in his fifth England international against Slovakia at the end of the season, which you will read about later.

If Wayne had not previously thought his world had changed much, he did now.

12

Now for Alan Shearer

'Rooney even bullies defenders – and it's great to see a young kid do that. He knows the tricks of the trade all right. He is some player. No one gets in his way. His birth certificate might say seventeen, but he doesn't look seventeen. It is maybe too early just yet to be using the word great about Wayne Rooney. But, if he keeps his mind right – and I'm sure he will because he has the right people around him – the signs are there for him to become a fantastic footballer for years to come.'

– Alan Shearer

Wayne Rooney's next assignment after Turkey was going head to head against the last England No 9 of distinction, Alan Shearer, and his Newcastle side still aiming for the Premiership title. Rooney only returned to the Everton side at Arsenal because of an injury to Tomasz Radzinski, and it was a stunning goal in that game that forced a late change of mind from the England coach to pick him for the qualifiers against Liechtenstein and Turkey. With Radzinski still sidelined, Rooney was to start against Newcastle on Sunday, and another special performance would make it very difficult for Eriksson to rule him out of his plans, despite Everton boss David Moyes's wishes.

Moyes had the tough decision as to whether to rest the whiz kid after his heroics at the Stadium of Light. The media spotlight that Moyes had warned about was starting to kick in, as in the days after the Turkey game pictures of Rooney leaving his Croxteth home were starting to appear in national newspapers. In one he was photographed in a French national soccer top. At least it was blue.

But Moyes's team's injury problems in attack made that decision for him, and Rooney would start against Newcastle, although Gary Lineker said at the time:

> It will be interesting to see how many minutes Rooney is on the pitch against Newcastle. He started the first Premiership game against Arsenal at Highbury only because Moyes had so many other strikers on the injury list, although his goals against the champions this season will do nothing to ease the clamour for him to start for his club.
>
> Moyes would have an easier task of protecting his star asset if his team were stuck in mid-table. But, thanks to his brilliant management, they are still in the running for a Champions League spot and, after so many miserable years trying to avoid relegation, everyone at the club will do everything to try and achieve that.
>
> As a club which gave me countless happy memories, I would love to see them playing against Real Madrid and Inter Milan next season. However, that is a big ask for a club who have only once finished in the Premiership top ten and, stepping back for an objective view, I feel they are more likely to end up in the UEFA Cup. That would still be a remarkable achievement by Moyes, who has turned the club round without spending much money.

But Kieron Dyer reckoned Newcastle had the player to put the brakes on Roonaldo, £9m defender Jonathan Woodgate, who watched from the England bench at Sunderland: 'We have one of the best defenders in the country to look after Wayne – Woody is ideal for the job. It's going to be another huge match at Goodison but that's the way I like it.'

Dyer believes Shearer will always have the final edge over Rooney as he explained: 'Alan is a goal machine and, to be honest, I don't think Wayne will have his goalscoring record. When Alan came in for his debut as a seventeen-year-old he scored a hat trick against Arsenal playing against world-class centre halves.

'As you've seen with Wayne Rooney, he just shows no fear. They're both as strong as an ox and they've got many of the same strengths. But they're also very different. Wayne does a lot of his work outside the box.

'But he's an awesome player, as you saw the other day. Just think what he'll be like when he reaches his peak.'

Worried Moyes reiterated his fears that Rooney could soon suffer burnout if he is not handled properly by England. The Premiership's youngest manager had seen his carefully laid plans to control Rooney's progress and exposure to the big time largely wrecked by Eriksson's decision to plunge the boy into his full international debut. Moyes had already stated he would prefer Rooney not to play summer friendlies for England, while Eriksson planned to include him in his squad for the next European Championship qualifier against Slovakia in June, and before then there were two friendlies.

Now Moyes spelled out his concerns more fully. With Rooney on course to start Everton's home game with Newcastle because of Radzinski's groin problems, the Goodison Park chief said:

I'm concerned that Wayne started training with us when he was sixteen and just out of school on 1 June last year. This season at the moment won't probably finish for him until the middle of June.

That's over a year of constant football, so the points I am trying to make are that we have to look after him and we have attempted to do that the best we can. I think England should try and do that as much as they can as well.

What I have said is that of course Wayne should be involved in all international games, to play for England is a great honour for him and I would never stop him doing that. But I'm just saying Wayne has to have some holidays and some break and if he doesn't then we will be looking at burnout. Taking him away continuously I don't think will be right for a boy who is just seventeen.

But Moyes accepted that Wayne's world has been changed for ever. Moyes said:

I've not found he has had problems keeping his feet on the ground, but this is bigger than the Rooney performances against Arsenal and we are into a greater audience.

I'm waiting to see how it has affected him. If it does then he will soon get a slap around the ears. I'm not worried at all about what has happened to Wayne this week because we will carry on handling him just the way we have done up until now. That's the way to do it and he's getting enough exposure already without him getting any more. And that's the way he wants it as well.

Wayne handles things incredibly well, and I haven't noticed any difference in him since he's been back from international duty. He seems fine, he's come back confident and he's buzzing. For a boy of that age to be thrust into such a big game and come through it so well, it's hard not to be affected by it, especially with the reaction in the media afterwards.

But he's the sort of character who handles things well, and it is my job to ensure that we get him back down, get him calm and concentrating on Everton. We'll keep doing that, we'll keep him in line if we have to, but he's a great boy, and he's got a great attitude.

It's asking a lot for a boy of seventeen to come through such a big game and all the media attention. It's my job to ensure that he does, but it helps that he is such a strong character. There's a bit of mystique about him, especially the way he goes from being shy off the pitch to assured and confident on it.

The Everton boss accepted that he would now face ferocious interest in his young forward, but he wanted to give the teenager as normal an adolescence as possible under such difficult circumstances. He explained:

What I am asking, is that you don't build the boy up too much, don't expect too much from him, because he is still exactly that – a boy. You have to be careful not to steal his adolescence from him. I want people to know how difficult it is for boys to be thrown into this. You want the boy to enjoy himself, have as normal an adolescence as possible, because if he's not enjoying his life, then you won't get the best from him out there on the pitch. I don't want to chain him up, I want him to do the normal things boys do, go out there and enjoy himself, but with a bit of added responsibility.

What I ask is, if the country treasures him as we do at Everton, then they have got to help us take the strain off him – and that means letting him live his life. Let us deal with him the way that has seen him come this far, and we will get far more out of him. It's not about what he does at seventeen, it's what he does at 23–24 that's important.

Injuries to Radzinski and the fact that Duncan Ferguson was still not a hundred per cent match fit pointed to Rooney playing from the start against Newcastle – only the second time that season that he would have made back-to-back starts in the first team. Moyes continued:

> He did really well in the Turkey game, we are all delighted for him, but we have a really important game with Newcastle now and that's what we are all working towards and concentrating on.
>
> International football will bring him on no doubt, but to be fair I felt that he was already there anyway. I was always trying to keep him locked up a little bit because he has always had the ability.
>
> They keep telling me what the England people saw in training, but we see it every day here. He played well for England but I have to say he can play much better, there are still parts of his game he will have to work on and I want to be able to do that for him.
>
> All the things that you've seen is natural ability, nobody can take any credit for what he has got because it is just wonderful ability from a wonderfully talented footballer. But there are parts of his game that, if not worked on, will be shown up when you play at that level. And to try to be the star everybody thinks he is, we have got to make sure that we improve those parts of his game that we feel need work.

Moyes suggested that England would need to wait six years for Rooney to develop into the real thing. He insisted: 'I was pleased for him on Wednesday and it proved the right decision to play him. He looked tired when he came off but you should take into account the strain he was under. That is why we try to play down the pressure and why there will be no media work for him. He is not comfortable in front of a camera or microphone – that will probably change as he grows older.

'He was back training with us on Thursday and Friday and seems fine. If there had been any difference he could expect a slap around the ear!'

Despite the adulation over Rooney's England display Moyes said the teenager has played *better* for Everton: 'There is no extra pressure on me to play him – and that won't change. We had him watching a couple of clips from his action in the last game against Arsenal. We also wanted him to watch one or two other players' movements. We are trying to teach him things which will make him better.

'If he questions my decisions he would get a kick up the backside. He's still a young boy. What I love about him is that he comes alive on the football pitch.'

Sir Bobby Robson, who was so enthusiastic about Rooney playing from the start for England, now had to worry about any potential backlash. As he sat in the stands in the Stadium of Light, even the former England coach couldn't have envisaged such a debut from the kid. Now his team would be up against Rooney straight away. Even so, Sir Bobby believed it was imperative to encourage the lad and urged 'the young Alan Shearer' to follow the Newcastle legend's example to turn his talent into greatness.

Rooney was ready to go head to head with Shearer as the Magpies attempted to continue their Premiership title challenge at Goodison Park, giving the new England sensation the perfect chance to meet the man the nation wants him to emulate. For Rooney, it was a chance in a lifetime. He had always admired Shearer since he was a schoolboy – not that long ago, then – and he imagined that the Toon hero would be his ideal strike partner. As Rooney said: 'My ideal partner would be Alan Shearer because I used to watch him when I was a kid and I tried to model myself around him.

'But I would have to say that I would be happy to play for England alongside any player. However, I know I need to be progressing at club level to continue to be selected for my country.'

Robson was convinced Rooney can develop into the goal-scoring centre forward that Shearer once was for his country and still is for Newcastle. The 71-year-old Newcastle boss, who managed young stars including Paul Gascoigne and Ronaldo, advised Rooney to forget the temptations of fame and fortune in order to fulfil his potential. Robson enthused about Rooney's performance against Turkey:

Wasn't the young boy terrific? His is a phenomenal talent that must not be denied nor restricted.

Rooney would appear to be the young Alan Shearer. I see all the similarities. Alan is good with back to goal and at the art of holding the ball up. Rooney's the same. The lad can do that.

There is an art to leading the line and both can do that. Alan has been a great traditional striker. Movement, turning to face the goalkeeper, the art of playing on the turn. He has been the masterclass for everyone – but he has done it for ten years. Rooney looks to be equipped with those same values but we will have to take care of him. He needs careful nursing and management but I'm confident Everton will do that.

Off the field is just as important as on the field. Alan has been a superb role model to everyone with how he has conducted himself off the pitch. He has been perfect in his attitude.

Everton have got a star on their hands, that's not in doubt. David Moyes has brought him on. But I don't think he will be leaving him out on Sunday. It's the master and the apprentice with him and Alan Shearer meeting on the same pitch. It's a great story. It's not the old and the new. It's what has been and still is, because Shearer could have played on Wednesday as well.

Robson wanted to see him in a run of England matches rather than base the hype surrounding the youngster on one match: 'I have to say the boy did fine. He looked very accomplished for seventeen. It was a remarkable performance of strength and skill. But let's remember he's played one game and a very good game. You have to be writing about him when he's been playing two years.'

Robson was confident Moyes would guide him through the difficult next two years while he matures, and warned that the biggest danger to him is temptations that he will discover away from football. The United boss, who saw his greatest prodigy Gascoigne fail to deal with the pressure, said:

He needs protection and guidance. I am sure David Moyes and Everton understand that. It is important we don't go overboard and ruin a superstar. There's a danger of that. He needs careful nursing and management. David is very capable of doing that. So far he has played and he has been left out.

Off the field is just as important as on it at seventeen. Alan is the example to everybody. In that sense Alan has been superb, the best role model for any player. He's a good pro, good character, been perfect in attitude. Shearer has been marvellous in that respect – exercising control off the pitch and how he's handled himself. We have all got to look after Rooney, guide him, protect him, be strong with him. The only danger is to himself, isn't it? But on the evidence of Wednesday, I love the boy.

I have seen Rooney four times and on each occasion he's done something marvellous. Just look at his goal against Arsenal. It is a great story for the country as a whole.

Like Dyer before him, though, Robson was confident that Jonathan Woodgate would silence Rooney for Newcastle:

My only disappointment was that he was taken off with a couple of minutes of the Turkey game remaining – I was hoping there would still be time for him to pick up a bit of a knock that would keep him out against us!

A lot of nice things have been said about the kid and rightly so. It will have motivated him and that won't help us. I'm not saying whether I would prefer it if he starts against us or joins the game as a substitute.

Frankly, I hope we don't have sight nor sound of him. I have signed one of the top three defenders in the country and I have to be confident we'll come out on top. It is a tough game and these games are really significant. We know what Everton means. It could determine where we finish.

Shearer was a member of the Rooney fan club before the whiz kid's stunning full England debut. The Newcastle skipper hoped his team-mates would not be next in the youngster's firing line at Goodison Park – and his trepidation proved to be very well founded. Shearer – 63 caps to Rooney's two at the time – had almost left school when the young Scouser was born. But the former England skipper was as excited as everybody else about the teenage striker's potential. He said:

He is big, he's strong, he has a huge physical presence about him already, he is good in the air, he's not afraid, he loves getting stuck in ...

I could give you a long, long list. He excites me *that* much, he really does! Mind you, I wouldn't mind if he was kept on the bench tomorrow – although, come to think of it, Everton have Tomasz Radzinski, Kevin Campbell and Duncan Ferguson who can do plenty of damage themselves.

Rooney even bullies defenders – and it's great to see a young kid do that. He knows the tricks of the trade all right. He is some player. No one gets in his way. His birth certificate might say seventeen, but he doesn't look seventeen. It is maybe too early just yet to be using the word great about Wayne Rooney. But, if he keeps his mind right – and I'm sure he will because he has the right people around him – the signs are there for him to become a fantastic footballer for years to come.

Gazza-mania happened over an extended period and you have to remember that Paul lit up a whole World Cup finals with seven fantastic performances. I also remember Lee Sharpe leaving Torquay for Man United, but it took him a little time to make his breakthrough there. I am not knocking Wayne but he has had one terrific game at home to Turkey. We need to remember that was just one match.

But in my lifetime, Wayne has something very special for his age . . . unique in fact.

Shearer had been a huge admirer ever since Rooney's wonder strike clinched Everton's 2–1 victory over Arsenal in October 2002. There is much of his own barnstorming style in the Evertonian. Shearer added: 'He takes everything in his stride. He doesn't allow any opponents to bother him, for a seventeen-year-old he really is remarkable. Just look at the way he handled the occasion on Wednesday. He got the crowd going and gave the whole side a lift during the period leading up to half-time.'

But Shearer joked: 'I do have one criticism. After that great run to the edge of Turkey's box, I couldn't believe it when he passed to Michael Owen. I was yelling at him "shoot . . . SHOOT!"'

But Shearer knew his side had to forget about Rooney and concentrate on Newcastle's title bid. 'Every time we have been asked a question this season we have come up with the right answer, but we have nothing to fear. It will be a tough, tough game against Everton. Moyes has done a fantastic job, we'll go out and give it our best shot. But, if he plays, there is a certain young man we will have to watch very closely indeed.'

There was a particular word of advice for Rooney from one man who had coached both Shearer and Rooney, Everton coach Alan Irvine. So Rooney respected his opinion when he said the kid needed to become like the former England captain and goalscorer.

Irvine said: 'We've told Wayne he won't score thirty goals a season all from long range, so he's got to get into close scoring positions – just as Shearer does.'

Irvine firmly believes that doing this will advance Rooney's career. He said: 'We'll never stop him from shooting from twenty-five yards – but it was nice to see him scoring a goal you associate with top strikers against Newcastle. He was in the right position to get rebounds and deflections. Shearer gets those sorts of goals all the time and Wayne can learn from that. He won't get thirty goals a season from outside the box, but like Alan he can do that by being in the right place at the right time in and around the six-yard box.'

Geordie Steve Watson, now playing for Everton, knew the Rooney factor was inspiring Everton and would be of enormous benefit against his former club. Utility man Watson, once a Newcastle United star, believed having Rooney around was the incentive Everton needed to dent Newcastle's title hopes and boost their own dreams of securing fourth place in the table and Champions League football: 'It is fantastic for the club to have Wayne here and starring for England in a very important game, and at just seventeen. Let's just hope that now he's back with us we can reap the rewards of that performance – especially against Newcastle.

'We all know Wayne and I don't think there is any time since he has started with us that he has been lacking in confidence and not willing to try things. You can't help but be impressed with the way he played on Wednesday night. Everybody in the country was proud to have him as an Englishman and there was nobody prouder than everyone here at Everton.'

Watson can justifiably have empathy with Rooney, having become the youngest league player in Newcastle's history at 16 years and 223 days in November 1990, some 64 days younger than Rooney was when he debuted for Everton. Watson recalled:

Wayne plays the way I did back then, without fear. He's making waves. They're a fair bit bigger than the ones I made, mind. I was the same as Wayne, four or five months out of school and playing for the home-town club I loved. I ended up playing twenty-two games that season and it wasn't really until the summer when I sat back and thought: 'Jesus, what have I done?'

It hits you. At the time you're training every day and games are coming up every week, and it's not for a year or so that it all sinks in. It may take that long for Wayne to realise just what he's crammed in already, and he's already achieved more than I ever did. The boy's played on the biggest stage possible and he hasn't batted an eyelid. He's achieved things most can only dream of, and he's seventeen. You don't really feel pressure when you're that young, you just enjoy your football.

It's only a year since Wayne was playing for his school team [that is, he was at school and playing for the Everton youth team] and he probably approaches matches now like he did then. The standard may have changed, but he believes he can terrorise any defence anywhere in the world. There is no fear. Wayne's handling everything well but you don't feel any pressure at that age. That only comes a couple of years later when you're trying to keep your standards up.

I lacked strength when I was sixteen, but Wayne's got that in abundance. On Wednesday he was bullying established international defenders off the ball. As an England fan that was fantastic to see, but as an Everton player you worry a bit – you're naturally a bit selfish and want to save the best of Wayne for the club. At least he hasn't played that many games so burnout shouldn't be a problem.

Everything that's happened with Wayne has been justified because he really is that special, but everything that's happened to us has been justified as well. People talk about what a fantastic season Southampton have had and what a good job Gordon Strachan is doing down there.

They have and he is, but what about us? Maybe it's best we keep quiet and, in a perfect world, claim a Champions League or UEFA Cup place. Then the world will turn around and realise we've come from nowhere. We've worked hard on making it difficult to play against us – we like getting into people's faces – and we haven't got any huge egos in the squad or any players who demand special treatment.

No one took us seriously at first, but then no one took Newcastle's title challenge seriously either. They've got wonderful energy and speed in their team. If they keep the young lads there then they can carry on progressing; we can do the same.

Rooney's presence was becoming more profound by the match as he was described as a 'phenomenon', and an 'absolute freak of nature' – especially after his games for England.

Moyes has seemed dour in his endless preaching for restraint and caution but even the Everton manager got caught up in the whirl of excitement. 'I was at the Stadium of Light and I was thrilled for Wayne,' he said, attempting to dispel the long-face impression of the manager solely worried by his parochial issues, rather than the wider aspect of the global game. He said:

Although it's hard for a Scotsman to own up to, I was supporting England because I wanted Wayne to score. I nearly jumped out of my seat when Wayne went close to scoring. I was ashamed of myself. It's a fact that we are all behind him, but my job is to make sure that Everton supporters see the best of him at the right time.

He's not to be a one-cap wonder. He's not to be a one-season wonder in the Premiership. I'm trying to make sure that doesn't happen. Wayne still has to come back here and work hard at his game. He has just started out on a very long road. In time he will learn and understand more about the game. The better known he becomes the more strings to his bow he'll get and that is what makes a great player.

Once he had regained his composure, it was immediately back to the sensitive job of nurturing Rooney's development while simultaneously sheltering him from the hysteria.

'I hope he will be given space for his continued development. He has to be allowed to develop off the pitch as well as on it. We are all men now and we know the years between seventeen and twenty can be a difficult period. We all have to allow the boy to get on with his life and not chase him about and make it unmanageable and unliveable.

'I want him to do the normal things that other boys do, it's just that he has a bigger responsibility. I want to be allowed to handle him as

I have been and will continue to. I hope people looked at him after that game and can say he has been handled right.'

Robson, while absolutely focused on gaining a win he reckoned would be one of their best of the 2002–03 season at a club who, like themselves, had lost only once at home that campaign, was aware of the impact Rooney would have on proceedings – not least in terms of the 'howling' atmosphere the mere sight of him was expected to generate.

Robson could not help admiring the boy, although he was quick to add another cautious voice to the vigilance preached by Moyes and Sven Goran Eriksson:

Rooney has been given a chance because England haven't filled the void left by Alan Shearer as well as we thought we might.

He has taken it with both hands. In view of Wednesday's performance, I can't see England not having him in the side the next time they play competitively. Clearly he's a special player but he's only played one game. If we're sat here talking about him after we qualify for Euro 2004 and he has a good championships then we know we have a good player on our hands.

Will he be the same player in Turkey in October? That will be a bit of a different situation. When the country took Gazza to their hearts, they did it after he had performed for seven games in the World Cup, all the way to the semi-final. He did it at world level, not for one game at Euro 2004 qualifying level.

Avoiding injuries is important to Rooney. Gascoigne got a very serious injury at an early age, doing a mad thing in the cup final, and was never the same again.

Rooney had not had a day off since he reported for pre-season training at the beginning of last June. Tempting though it was to want to rush him into the next available opportunity to gain international experience and work on the budding understanding with his team-mates, Moyes was being sensible when he requested Rooney might be excluded from England's friendly against South Africa. Moyes said: 'His body is asking for a breather. When he has had that, he will come back feeling stronger and fresher.

For a boy that age, he could do with a bit more rest than just three weeks.'

Tony Cottee, who had been such a hero at Goodison Park, gave his advice in a 'first-person' article in the *Guardian*:

My first call-up probably wasn't as much of a shock as Wayne Rooney's was, and I was a little older. I've got to say that I don't think normal seventeen-year-olds should be anywhere near the England team, but we're not talking about a normal kid in this case.

I thought he was top class against Turkey. He maybe took twenty minutes to get into the game but from then on whenever he touched the ball he looked able to change things. But in many ways the first game is the easy one – things get harder from here.

We've just got to look after the kid. It's easy now for him to get caught up in the money and the fame, but he's got good people round him who will be making preventing that a priority.

Like many other 'insiders' preaching caution and restraint, Cottee felt it advisable to put Rooney back on the bench for the next game, as he explained:

The best thing that could happen would be if he's on the bench for Everton tomorrow [against Newcastle]. Keeping him out of the starting XI would just be good for keeping him under control.

By the time I made the England squad I was 21, I'd been playing for the first team at West Ham for a few years and scoring goals all the time, so I felt I'd earned the right to be there.

I'd also just missed out on the squad for the 1986 World Cup in Mexico, or so the media told me. There had been a lot of clamour for me to be in the squad, but with a lot of good players ahead of me it was always going to be difficult to establish myself.

In the end it never really happened, and I ended up with seven caps, six of those coming as a substitute. My England career was finished by the time I was 24 and, while there were a few occasions after that when my name was mentioned, I never got another chance.

It was like a dream come true, playing for England. There is something special about it. But when you've had success at such a young age,

Wayne (centre front), aged eleven, with his Our Lady and St Swithin's Primary School team and headmaster Tony McCaul.

De La Salle Catholic Boys' School, Wayne's secondary school in Liverpool.

The Rooneys' old family home on the Croxteth estate.

As the schoolboy's bedroom window shows, Rooney was a big Everton fan from an early age.

Wayne quickly progressed from the Youth team *(left)* to the Reserves *(below)*, aged sixteen.

The game against Arsenal that propelled Wayne to fame in October 2002 after he scored his amazing goal.

Wayne collecting the BBC Young Sports Personality of the Year award in December 2002.

With Everton manager David Moyes after Rooney's signing, January 2003.

The England v. Australia match in February 2003, when Rooney came on as a substitute at half-time to become England's youngest ever full international.

Bitter local rivals: Everton playing Liverpool in April 2003. Rooney is seen here tackling Salif Diao.

Taking on Turkish defenders in England's World Cup qualifier, April 2003. This was the first international game in which Rooney started.

Rooney scored a stunning goal when Everton played Charlton in August 2003.

Scoring the opening goal past Switzerland's goalkeeper in the European Championships in June 2004.

Rooney and Beckham celebrating his Euro 2004 goal against Switzerland.

A national hero: with his fans after scoring in England's win over Croatia.

everything just seems to come naturally. I know I felt – and I'm sure Rooney was the same – that when I was bashing in the goals aged seven or eight I was a little bit different from the other kids.

It is a bit daunting when you break into the squad, but I'd had a bit of practice. I was a mad Hammer as a kid, like Rooney is an Everton fan, so to be a supporter and then suddenly find yourself playing and training with the people who had been your heroes is a strange situation.

The England squad may be a scary prospect, but you know you deserve to be there because the manager's chosen you.

Things were a bit different when I made my debut. There wasn't the intensity in football that there is now, and of course it was a friendly in front of less than 16,000 people in Stockholm.

Even so I've got to say I didn't particularly enjoy the England experience. Obviously playing for your country is special, and those seven caps have got pride of place at home, but I was always quite a private lad. I didn't want to see my name up in lights but, once you're playing for England, that kind of attention is inevitable.

If I've got one word of advice for Rooney now, it's to forget about everything else and just think about the football. The rest will come from there.

And, of course, I never scored. I only had a couple of chances for England, and it's my one real regret in football that I didn't manage to take any of them. But to play for twenty years and end up with only one regret isn't such bad going. I'd be very surprised if Rooney has the same problem.

When the Newcastle game actually arrived it was almost hard to believe that Rooney was making only his eleventh start in the Premiership. But typically, on the back of his full England debut, he destroyed Newcastle United's championship challenge.

Everton began at a quite unreal pace. Shearer made a point of shaking Rooney's hand just prior to the kickoff, and the seventeen-year-old's response was to almost score inside the first minute. A through ball put him behind Titus Bramble. He was flagged offside, but only a fine save at his feet by Shay Given kept the ball out of the net.

That set the tone, and on eighteen minutes the seventeen-year-old gave the crowd the lead their noise demanded. It was a clever cross from Gravesen that created it, allowing David Weir to flick on, and there was Rooney, darting in front of his marker to steer home a powerful and confident reaction header. He could have scored soon after, too, with only the reactions of the Newcastle keeper Given denying him.

On forty minutes, Woodgate stepped out of defence and produced a fine ball to find Laurent Robert on the edge of the box. One touch and then a strike of outrageous power and the ball was in the roof of the net.

But Rooney's running often panicked the Newcastle defence. Eventually he picked the ball up on the left after a tackle by Gravesen – that ended up being the talking point of the match – and skipped past three challenges before slipping a delightful ball in to Campbell, who was pulled back by United's Woodgate. David Unsworth converted the penalty after a long wait.

Rooney was the match winner with his insatiable enthusiasm as Everton continued their unlikely pursuit of a Champions League place, lifting themselves into fifth, four points behind fourth-placed Chelsea.

It was fierce stuff, and Rooney, Richard Wright and Joseph Yobo came off worst from challenges by Given, Shearer and Olivier Bernard that incensed the home fans. But they were soon going wild when they got the goal they'd been praying for.

Newcastle argued that their pursuit of Arsenal and Manchester United was damaged by referee Neale Barry, who ignored a foul on Olivier Bernard by Thomas Gravesen in the build-up to the winning goal. Rooney ignored the prone Newcastle player before playing the pass that allowed Kevin Campbell a sight on goal that was stopped only by Jonathan Woodgate's illegal penalty-area challenge. He didn't stop when Bernard was lying injured, not because he was seeking to gain any unfair advantage, but because he did what he always does with the ball at his feet – run at trembling defenders.

Moyes had shouted for the ball to be put out of play but the Newcastle players were furious. In Moyes's team's defence, Bernard had clearly not taken a head injury, the usual circumstances when teams stop play when in possession, even if Gravesen's tackle did look bad. Robson said:

David Moyes apologised for his players not putting the ball out. My players might not have done that either. The ref could have blown the whistle and stopped the play. It was entirely in the ref's hands. It's tough for refs, it's not easy.

But we lost the match through it. I haven't spoken to the ref. There's not much to say. I'll lose my rag with him. He had a decent match. It's not easy the way the game is played. You can't get every one right. He was on the spot and I was surprised.

The lost points would have been vital. We have dropped points but this is a big result for Everton. They were strong, combative. They played nice spells of football. It was hard fought from first to last. It should have gone our way but for a questionable decision.

As the Newcastle boss said, the match was about Rooney. He scored – in the words of his own satisfied manager Moyes – a real centre forward's goal to give Everton the lead, and then won the match with one of those runs that are fast becoming his trademark. Robson said: 'That has killed any hope we had of hanging in there and nicking it from Arsenal and United.'

Shearer cleared Rooney of any blame in the controversial incident, even though the kid was jeered by the Toon Army when he played on after Thomas Gravesen's X-rated tackle on Olivier Bernard. Shearer said: 'I asked Wayne if he had realised how badly Gravesen had fouled Olivier and if he could have kicked the ball out of play. To be fair to the lad, he told me he did not know how bad the challenge was and didn't realise Olly was down.'

Rooney left the field to a standing ovation from the home fans, having had the same impact on the title race he had on England's Euro 2004 campaign. Another man-of-the-match award then. But what does he do with them all?

The boy striker said: 'I have a designated place where I put all my match stuff – Everton shirts, England caps and I have put the bottles of champagne I've been given in there, too. I've not been tempted to drink them – honest!'

Unsworth celebrated Everton's 2–1 win by toasting the talents of the new England hero. 'He's not bad is he? The most important thing with Wayne is that he's going to get better. He listens not just to the manager but to his older team-mates. If he carries on as he is doing, he will do really well.'

Anything was possible from England's new golden boy and it seemed fitting that he completed the most memorable week of his young life with a goal against Newcastle.

England coach Sven Goran Eriksson missed the late Toon rally, leaving Goodison Park fifteen minutes early with a broad smile after admiring Rooney's goal and the lad's sheer strength and courage. He kept going after a bone-jarring collision with keeper Shay Given in the ninth minute. It is not often Rooney stays down but he needed lengthy treatment before he could continue. He was in the wars again in the second half before completing the game.

Eriksson would have agreed with Robson's assessment: 'He was contained and curtailed for most of the match but, when he got the ball, those flashes show what a talent he is. He did some fine things and got the first goal.'

After three frustrating games without victory, Everton were boisterous again, propelled by their talismanic teenager. 'We've come a long way since we lost 6–2 at Newcastle twelve months ago,' said Moyes. He was almost apologetic when he was asked to dissect Rooney's contribution. 'If you don't mind, I think I've spoken enough about Wayne now,' he said politely. But no chance, if Moyes expected to have a Rooney-free zone.

Would he have played if Tomasz Radzinski were fit? 'Really, there's no point getting into it. It's hypothetical. Sorry.'

Kieron Dyer was more determined to make his mark on the international scene as a result of Rooney's success. Dyer said:

Wayne was superb and it's incredible to think he's only seventeen, but he got his chance in the position he is best – centre forward. That is what I want with England, one game in the central midfield role which I play for my club. In some ways it's good that managers think you can play anywhere, but in others it's bad because you lose out to those who always play in the same place. My biggest disappointment in football was being left out of Euro 2000 and Kevin Keegan explained it was because he didn't know my best position.

Rooney-mania had kept going in the national press, and the *Daily Star* still had the boy on their front page, although not this time the main item. 'Rooney whacks Tooney' was the headline, with a picture of him celebrating the goal on the front, another on the back page and a kick-by-kick 'Rooney Watch' inside.

The Times referred to Rooney's latest exploits next to their masthead on page one with a picture of his thumbs-up goal celebrations and the headline: 'The Unstoppable Wayne Rooney – Everton's young star halts Newcastle', while a huge picture of the boy adorned the front page of the *Daily Mirror* – and yes, there was still a war in Iraq going on!

The *Sun*'s chief football writer Shaun Custis wrote: 'Roo-mania is sweeping the land and, astonishingly, the life of superstar England skipper David Beckham has been reduced to a sideshow.'

Everton were flying and their next assignment in the hunt for a Champions League spot was a relatively glamourless contest where defeat would relegate West Brom. In the build-up co-striker Kevin Campbell talked of it being a privilege and a delight to play alongside Rooney.

At 33, the oldest member of the squad had formed a successful partnership in recent weeks with Rooney. Campbell had also played the elder statesman, offering advice when required, but already rated Rooney among the best in the world and the one to inspire Everton to the verge of European qualification.

Campbell talked of the 'Wayne Factor':

We have gone from strength to strength and Wayne's arrival on the scene has been a major factor. It's a tremendous joy to play alongside someone so gifted. He really can go on and be up there among the greats of world football. You know his quality and stuff but you don't realise what a big talent he is until he gets on the pitch . . .

It is a privilege for me to work with him and see the things he can do. It's frightening. I am always prepared to offer advice but not all players listen. Wayne always does, which is no surprise to me because he is such a nice lad as well as being a special talent. I don't envy any defender who will come up against him as his career develops.

At the start of the season we would have settled for mid-table but we have been up there for so long it would be a terrible disappointment if we missed out now. In previous years we have been involved in a fight for survival.

Albion boss Gary Megson confessed to being one of Rooney's biggest fans. In the first meeting with West Brom in 2002–03 he had the ball at his feet as he faced Darren Moore, stopped and put his hands on his hips! Megson said: 'I think it is marvellous the way that he has handled himself.

'He's going to be a star in his own right and for him to lift a club like Everton at his age is a great testimony to him and he's also now doing it with England. There is a lot on his shoulders but he seems to take it all in his stride. What happened with him and Darren Moore was him showing to all his mates on the streets what he can do.'

The good news for Everton was that Rooney-mania was catching on with the rest of the team, and Campbell squeezed Everton closer to the Champions League with a vital first-half winner in the 2–1 victory over Albion.

13

Enough to Make You Spit

'Before we all go mad, let us remember how old Wayne Rooney is. He is seventeen. He is not perfect and he should not be put up on a pedestal after five minutes. We all leap so quickly on to new heroes. We expect them to have views on everything and live a life without fault. So when Wayne Rooney spits on the pitch in front of Liverpool fans everyone is suddenly up in arms. Let's give the lad a break.'

– Jimmy Greaves

Everton boss David Moyes has done everything in his power to shield Rooney from excessive publicity. Apart from one press conference to announce his first professional contract, Moyes made it clear there would be no more interviews in the 2002–03 season because Rooney lacked the maturity to handle a grilling in front of the cameras.

As Everton prepared for the Mersey derby on Easter Saturday, though, Rooney's name was on everyone's lips again. The world was going mad as Rooney was being compared to the real Ronaldo who had won two World Cups, and the likes of Joe Cole – another so-called wonder kid – seemed like they were history.

Everton's own Brazilian, Rodrigo, insisted it was far too early to make comparisons between Ronaldo and Rooney. Rodrigo said: 'I have known Ronaldo for a long time. We are the same age and I have followed his career from when I was a young player in Brazil. I don't think you can compare him with Rooney because they are different players and only time will tell if Wayne will go on to become as great a player as Ronaldo. I hope he does.'

Cole, then aged 21 and still playing for West Ham, made his England debut in May 2001 against Mexico at Pride Park. He had been elevated to captain of his club but for his country he had slipped back beyond belief in public perception as the next saviour – that role is exclusively Rooney's.

Cole said: 'I'm not envious of Rooney. I'm happy with my life. I still feel I'm making progress, it hasn't been meteoric like, say, Wayne. Not as explosive as somebody like him, or as I thought it was going to be.'

The youngster would play from the start in the Mersey derby. Everton assistant boss Alan Irvine said: 'It's not too much of a gamble now to play Wayne. He has been fantastic, especially with the way things have gone in recent weeks.

'Wayne was in a tough position when he was coming off the bench because Tomasz Radzinski and Kevin Campbell were doing very well. We have tried to be fair to the players who have been in the team and playing well throughout the season. When someone has come into the team and done a good job we have left them in.

'Nothing changes now as far as Wayne is concerned and Tomasz will now probably have to compete for his place, despite the fact that he has had a fantastic season for us. He has shown he can compete at international level and Premiership.'

Of course, there were to be further comparisons between Rooney and Owen, but the people who really had to worry were Liverpool's defensive partnership, which was an unlikely combination. Djimi Traore and Igor Biscan replaced absent central defenders Sami Hyypia and Stephane Henchoz. Traore went head to head with Everton's super kid in the derby at Goodison Park.

With Liverpool lording it over Everton for so many years it seemed strange for them to meet with both sides chasing a Champions League spot. Traore said, though: 'People talk about Rooney and what impact he may have. But don't forget that we have Michael Owen and many other players who can score goals.'

Jerzy Dudek, like the rest of his Anfield team-mates, was wary of Rooney. After a spell out of the side he had returned a stronger, wiser man – and back to the sort of form that made him the most admired keeper in the Premiership the previous season. Now he could not wait for the Goodison showdown with Rooney and Everton:

I've been very impressed with Wayne Rooney, everyone has. People like him make football special, he gives something special to the Premiership and he is like Alan Shearer in that respect . . . His presence makes the league better. He has so much confidence he must feel he can do anything at the moment.

When you start your career you have nothing to lose because people don't know you. I hope that continues because clearly, the real test is still to come. As defenders keep a closer eye on him and get to know some of his ways, it is bound to get more difficult for him.

By the time the game starts, I will have watched lots of videos to get an idea of what to look out for. Looking at the goal he struck past David Seaman at Goodison, it is obvious you have to be ready for anything. He has great movement and likes to surprise opponents, keepers included. We must be on guard, especially if we are to stay on course for a Champions League place.

Moyes warned Liverpool that the balance of power on Merseyside was about to shift. 'This may be an important game but, believe me, there are going to be bigger ones than this. We have progressed this season, but this is just the start. At the start of the season, Liverpool were in a different league to us, but not now. We are really ready to compete with them now.' Unfortunately for Moyes, a year later this prediction did not come to fruition, as during his second year in charge Everton returned to their normal relegation battle.

Owen brought a sense of perspective to all the Rooney hype when he said:

Everton are by no means a one-man band and have a few good players who we're going to have to keep a very careful eye on. Obviously Wayne falls into that category because his talent is there for all to see.

But it's important to remember he's only started seven or eight games and that Everton have really improved as a team this season. Their position in the Premiership tells you that. They've done brilliantly to get where they are and, if they go on to secure a place in Europe next season, it will be an unbelievable achievement.

Everyone is still anticipating how good Wayne is going to be. While they are doing that, we'll make sure we are on our guard for wherever a

goal threat might come from. I feel we've more of a chance of winning at
their place than at Anfield, as Everton can sit back at our ground, where
a draw is a good result for them.

Owen, scorer in his previous five league games, saw the
emergence of Rooney as a challenge and he was determined to meet
it head on, particularly as his only previous derby goal was from a
penalty. And on this occasion it was wonder-goals from Michael
Owen and Danny Murphy rather than Rooney that gave the Reds
victory in a brutal Goodison derby that saw Everton finish with nine
men as Liverpool leapfrogged them into fifth place.

The Blues had made great strides under Moyes's stewardship in
the 2002–03 season, and for long spells looked capable of beating
their neighbours for the first time in seven attempts.

Everton should have taken the lead in the nineteenth minute
when Rooney showed that he's as brave as he is brilliant. He
challenged Dudek for Gravesen's cross and forced the keeper to
spill the ball. Having spent the first half relying too heavily on
the high ball to Rooney, Everton emerged after the interval, at
Moyes's instruction, more willing to pass the ball through the
team. They consequently looked more dangerous. But this was
not Rooney's day, starved of service and having to come far too
deep for possession.

When David Unsworth cancelled out Owen's first-half stunner
from the penalty spot in the 58th minute, Everton looked likely
winners. But within seven minutes their belief had been punctured
by a long-range Murphy strike good enough to win any match.

Their woe was complete when first David Weir and then Gary
Naysmith were sent off for two bookable offences. There were also
another six players booked – four from Liverpool – as referee Paul
Durkin struggled to control the game.

While Houllier took great delight in putting Moyes's Everton
revolution into perspective, it was the prospect of Champions
League qualification that was most important.

Liverpool had chalked up a victory in this 198th meeting of the
Merseyside clans, in the week that marked the fourteenth anniversary of the Hillsborough disaster. Houllier dedicated this win as a

tribute to those fans who died at that tragic FA Cup semifinal back in 1989.

As the win put Liverpool in with a real chance of securing a Champions League place, for Everton there was now only the prospect of a place in the UEFA Cup to play for.

Moyes snapped: 'I keep telling people but they won't listen. You have to let the boy grow.' But not everything was quite what it seemed in the aftermath of this fiery game. Just nineteen days after front-page headlines hailing him a national hero, Wayne Rooney was now the tabloid villain.

If anything could illustrate to someone so young the pitfalls of the game, then this surely must be it. In fact it was an example to anyone, young or old, that a week is a long time in this game.

Rooney was caught on camera spitting in the direction of mocking Liverpool fans during the Merseyside derby, although not actually hitting any spectators or, indeed, intending to do so. The official Anfield website said fans reported the incident.

Rooney faced trial by TV as the nation witnessed the act. It was announced that police were investigating, as several Liverpool fans complained that Rooney spat in front of them during the second half of the Reds' ill-tempered 2–1 victory at Goodison Park.

Rooney had reacted to taunts from Reds fans by eyeballing supporters and then spitting on the turf in front of them after failing to gain a free kick near the touchline when tangling with Liverpool defender Salif Diao.

Officers studied all the video evidence from the game, including CCTV and ITV and Sky's pictures. A spokesman for Merseyside Police said: 'We are aware of an incident involving Wayne Rooney at the derby match on Saturday. Sufficient people have come forward to report the incident and there is no further requirement for witnesses. We will be viewing all the available video evidence from the game, including the CCTV coverage, before deciding whether to speak to Everton and Wayne Rooney.'

Inspector Tom King of Merseyside Police added: 'Wayne Rooney was baited by the crowd and that incident is being investigated and we are speaking to the people who have come forward. I will be speaking to Everton Football Club later this week to see if the incident was recorded on video, and any action to follow will be determined by the outcome from those talks.'

Everton were confident that the video evidence showed Rooney did nothing wrong. Ian Ross, the club's head of public relations, said: 'We are aware of the allegations and we will be discussing them with Merseyside Police as soon as possible.' Rooney faced being charged by the FA, but they had to wait for the official match reports before commenting.

Rooney was caught up in the fallout from a particularly nasty Merseyside derby. Thugs defaced a memorial to Hillsborough victims before the match. The memorial to the 96 fans who died was daubed with blue paint just days after the fourteenth anniversary of the tragedy. In a separate incident, a statue of Everton's legendary striker Dixie Dean had a red headband painted on it. Officials of both clubs condemned the vandalism.

Friends of Rooney feared a backlash against his family. Previously vandals had slashed his dad's car tyres and their home had been splattered with paint pellets. Only a month earlier Liverpool's El-Hadji Diouf had been fined and suspended for spitting at Celtic fans in a UEFA Cup tie at Parkhead, and Liverpool's Stephane Henchoz was accused by Sheffield United boss Neil Warnock of spitting after a Worthington Cup match at Anfield.

If the pressure of success was one aspect of the job, then this was a vastly different kind of pressure as the headlines were ones neither Rooney nor his family wanted to see.

Only days before, the *Daily Star* had lauded Rooney on their front page – now the same paper's front-page headline was 'Loony Rooney', as the incident also warranted page three of the *Guardian* – 'England star Rooney, 17, in spitting inquiry' – and page five of *The Times* – 'Spitting image puts Rooney in trouble' – while the *Mirror* led its front page on the collapse of West Ham manager Glen Roeder and had this headline on the spitting incident – 'Rooney Accused in Spit Bust-Up'.

But the *Sun* columnist Jimmy Greaves and the *Daily Mail*'s Ian Wooldridge both backed Rooney. Wooldridge's argument, under the headline 'Stop this spit roasting, give Wayne a break', was pretty conclusive when he wrote: 'Why can't we allow this young Wayne

Rooney to mature in his own good time. He is supremely gifted, a fate which seems to have evaded our nation's footballing apartheid city.'

Under the headline 'Rooney's just a boy', Greaves argued:

Before we all go mad, let us remember how old Wayne Rooney is. He is seventeen. He will not in the next week be putting together a plan to rebuild Baghdad. Nor will he be revealing a cure for the SARS virus. I am not sure whether Rooney will be predicting another fall in interest rates either. He will probably be kicking a football around, hanging out with his mates and checking what woolly hat or expensive watch David Beckham gets next.

Because Wayne Rooney, you see, is just a kid who plays football. He is not perfect and he should not be put up on a pedestal after five minutes. We all leap so quickly on to new heroes.

We expect them to have views on everything and live a life without fault. So when Wayne Rooney spits on the pitch in front of Liverpool fans everyone is suddenly up in arms. Let's give the lad a break.

So far, I have been impressed with the way Rooney has carried himself. He has the right people around. Everton's David Moyes is the right manager to guide him and he has a close family.

This latest uproar reminds me of that TV programme, 'The Trouble with David Beckham'. Some C-list chef explained what is wrong with Becks – because he was red-carded at France 98.

But he is a perfectly normal lad – and Rooney is the same. He is not a nasty guy so let's not try to suggest he is nor is he about to cure the world of all its ills. Wayne Rooney is just a kid who loves playing football – so let him get on with it.

But Rooney was finding it tough just to get on with it.

The Goodison club had dozens of calls from Liverpool fans insisting Rooney did nothing wrong, and that the youngster had been subjected to a nonstop barrage of verbal abuse by a section of away supporters at the game. An Everton spokesman said: 'We have had lots of calls, from our own fans as well as Liverpool's, saying Wayne did nothing wrong and shouldn't be in trouble.'

Moyes was at first unaware of any moves by police concerning the spitting incident. He said: 'I don't know anything about that as the club came down to London on Saturday' – to play against Chelsea at Stamford Bridge just two days after the spitting incident.

A spokesman for Merseyside Police said: 'We have had the opportunity to speak with supporters who put their complaints forward and we have also had the chance to see a video recording of the incident. Wayne Rooney will be seen by a senior police officer at the earliest opportunity in the presence of the club manager and he will be given suitable advice. No further police action will be contemplated once we have done that.'

Though Rooney was a key figure in bringing Goodison alive again, Moyes was not afraid to discipline him and immediately fined the young starlet. He said: 'I spoke to Wayne about that and he now knows he has to be careful about his actions. I will clip him around the ear when I think he deserves it but generally he is a good boy to work with and a great trainer. Our job is to teach him, to enhance his play and, to be fair, he is a great listener. We understand that Wayne Rooney plays a big part in this club but no more so than all the other players.'

Everton spokesman Ian Ross said: 'The club is happy that this matter has been dealt with so swiftly. We are just delighted this matter has been resolved.'

The contest against Chelsea was a huge setback for Everton. Marcel Desailly was the man of the match, while goals from Eidur Gudjohnsen, Jimmy Floyd Hasselbaink, Jesper Gronkjaer and Gianfranco Zola lifted Claudio Ranieri's side to third in the Premiership. Everton's limitations were cruelly exposed.

Rooney produced his show of petulance, whacking the ball into Petit's midriff when referee Mike Riley failed to penalise Desailly for a challenge on him. The youngster was lucky not to go into the book.

Desailly was presented with the Ten Season award, honouring him as the best defender in the history of the Premiership, and his performance matched such an accolade. Claudio Ranieri billed Rooney as a panther, but the youngster was a pussycat up against Terry, Gallas and Desailly as he, and the rest of the Everton team, looked shot to pieces.

Everton dropped to sixth after the defeat, and a disappointed Moyes admitted: 'The Champions League is beyond us now. We've tried our best to make it a reality and I'm hurting like hell. Now we have to hang on to a UEFA Cup place. That would still be a fantastic achievement for the club this season. This squad has competed with the so-called bigger clubs and we've been in the top six virtually all season.'

Once again Rooney faced a defining moment, with all the additional pressure of the spitting incident and his manager publicly declaring it was time for a break after five full Premiership games plus his England commitments.

Moyes argued: 'In recent games Wayne has been a little bit below the standard he has set himself. But you can't expect something wonderful from him in every game. He was sixteen at the start of the season and is only seventeen now, and we are pleased with his progress . . . I'm concerned about the effects of playing him in too many games and if Tomasz Radzinski had been fit and available at Chelsea, I would have given Wayne a bit of breathing space.'

With the former Anderlecht striker still struggling with a hamstring injury, Moyes had no other option with Duncan Ferguson still a fitness doubt. Moyes had said: 'Is Duncan capable of playing ninety minutes? As for Wayne, he will be fine.'

Now it was crunch time for Everton and Rooney as Moyes stressed: 'If we had been relegated a year ago it would have been the end on several counts. This is just the beginning and I am very thankful for the season we have had.

'If we win two of our last three games we shall be back in Europe. If we don't we could finish seventh or eighth. People talk about two consecutive defeats but what about the sixteen wins in the Premiership? We are well placed to qualify for Europe and I would rather be in our position than in the chasing pack.'

Rooney was supposed to be tired but no one told him, as he popped up again for the clinching goal in a 2–1 victory over Aston Villa. To Rooney's remarkable debut season he added another first – his opening goal at the Gwladys Street end of Goodison Park – and, in the context of his club's quest for European football, it could not have come at a better time.

At a time of year more often associated with relegation contests, Everton were seeking a place in Europe for the first time in eight years. And as Everton's European dreams were slipping away, Rooney, who had glittered all afternoon, struck a peach of a winner in the third minute of injury time.

His eighth strike of a phenomenal campaign brought universal praise, starting with Robbie Earle's analysis of the game on *The Premiership*. 'Rooney has the X-factor,' said Earle, no doubt having thought of that line for some time, as he argued that 'he demands to be out there'.

After going behind in the first half through a Marcus Allback strike, Everton had battered away and forced an equaliser through Kevin Campbell's header. But the priceless winner just would not come. With Blackburn, one place behind, winning at Leeds, it looked as if Everton's hold on fifth spot and UEFA Cup qualification was in real danger.

After two damaging Easter defeats, Rooney had plenty of joy switching from flank to flank, picking the ball up deep and running at defenders. Villa's ageing back four were exposed to the wandering, scampering Rooney and the youngster clearly enjoyed himself.

Everton were still behind when Moyes opted for a third striker, sending on Duncan Ferguson for Unsworth, with Naysmith dropping to fullback. The change worked a treat. Ferguson provided extra physical threat and Villa panicked. A corner was only half-cleared on 59 minutes and pumped back into the box by Naysmith for Campbell to crash home a close-range header for his eleventh goal of the season. Villa, too, brought on a third striker, sending on Darius Vassell for Oyvind Leonhardsen. But it was Rooney who almost set up a second for Everton. First he fed Ferguson, whose shot was saved by Enckelman, and then Rooney saw his effort from the follow-up stopped by the keeper at full stretch.

Everton fought desperately from then on, searching for the winner they knew they needed if they wanted to stay in the hunt for a UEFA Cup spot.

And then, in injury time, Rooney rescued his side. He struck the winner with a sweet volley from the edge of the box after an Alan Stubbs free kick had been headed out to him. Seconds after his goal Rooney was brought off to a standing ovation.

The reception he received from the Goodison bench showed just how much his winning goal meant. He was showered with congratulatory back slapping and hugs. Rooney tried to concentrate on the final minutes, but he couldn't help smiling.

Moyes was quick to play down the hype. 'I just told him it was a decent goal he'd scored, but he should have scored a couple more. We've patted him on the back and said well done, but there have certainly not been any high fives. It has become the norm for him to score goals but we mustn't be ecstatic about each one he scores.'

Villa manager Graham Taylor refused to lavish praise on the Everton starlet, insisting that opposition managers had as much responsibility as Moyes in keeping Rooney in touch with reality. Taylor explained:

I don't want to get carried away with Rooney because I don't think that's fair on the boy himself.

All I will say is that it is foolish for people to already be looking at him as a role model. He's only seventeen and should be allowed to develop. That's why I'll say it was a good strike from him rather than a fantastic one.

What I am concerned about is that the kids we have got coming through at Villa get the same opportunity to develop. They need stability and I only have another season after this on my contract. I'm not saying I want to be like Bobby Robson and manage until I am seventy, but they do need some security.

I am very, very disappointed to have lost. Rooney's winner was an obvious sickener, but I wasn't happy about their first goal either. I wonder whether I have run over a black cat. I don't know what we have done to be so cruelly treated.

Moyes, in analysing the game, said:

We weren't at our best, but I am delighted because it was an honest performance and I felt we deserved the three points. It was a great goal from Rooney, but I will still tell anyone who will listen that he is tired. I was thinking of bringing him off, but decided against it because he's the kind of player who can come up with a bit of magic like that.

The European finish is there now. We can reach out and touch it. Blackburn are pushing us very hard but we know this season has been a marvellous achievement. We are in a great position, we still have a chance of finishing fourth or fifth.

We shouldn't be surprised it was Wayne who got the winner. It was a great goal. At times Wayne was an inspiration to us because he continually wanted the ball. That's a great trait in any player. He doesn't hide, despite the fact that we've all seen slight signs that fatigue is creeping into his play.

Wayne's tired; just because he scores in the 92nd minute it doesn't mean he is not tired. There was the thought to bring him off but on the bench we decided that Wayne was probably going to be the one who came up with something special late on. At first I thought it was from nine or ten yards, but I have seen it again and it is from eighteen yards on the volley. It goes through the boy's legs but right into the bottom corner.

To become a top centre forward you have to put the work in to get the chances. We are working with him to make him better and looking to improve his finishing. We don't want to flog him to death, but we've not got many games left. If we had Tomasz Radzinski fit we could have used them both sparingly towards the end of the season.

There have been signs in training, not just in matches, where he hasn't looked quite as sharp, his finishing hasn't been quite as clinical, he hasn't run quite as much. You see little glimpses but it has been a long hard season for him.

He's fatigued and I'm seeing it on a daily basis with him. I want to get that spark back, but he's probably played about ten months of football now this season. That's a long time for a young boy like that.

However, regarding Everton, Moyes went on: 'The fact is that he can't have a rest at the moment. We need him. If he's fit, he'll play the remaining games for us. Wayne has had to cope with an awful lot more than most lads of his age who play in an under-19 league on a Saturday morning and the odd reserve game.

'I think his body will definitely be stronger next season. When they come back from the summer break after their first year the players look more like men, more advanced physically. That's what I hope will happen with Wayne.'

After a week of gory headlines, Rooney was the hero again. 'Rooney rules again' heralded the *Observer*, while 'Destiny's Child', was the *Mirror*'s offering.

With Manchester United the final act of a season not even scriptwriters with the most vivid imaginations could have dreamed up for Rooney, Moyes admitted: 'It will go down to the last game now,' after Everton had performed the seventh comeback win of their season against Villa.

Thierry Henry and his Arsenal team-mates feared they had lost their Premiership crown after United took advantage of their slip-up at Bolton to forge five points clear with their win over Spurs. Even if the Gunners were to win their last three games, there would be nothing they could do if United beat Charlton at Old Trafford and then Everton on the last day of the season. Henry believed, and hoped, that Rooney could provide the final twist in the championship race at Goodison: 'We're hoping that Everton can do us a favour on the last day. They are playing United but Rooney has no fear about who is he playing against or where he is playing.

'He has that lovely arrogance. He doesn't worry about the opposition. When Rooney's playing against Marcel Desailly, it's like he's playing in the street. I don't think it's a lack of respect – he just wants to go out and play.'

Henry was speaking after being named the PFA Player of the Year, in which Rooney, surprisingly, came second to Jermaine Jenas for the Young Player award. Players' union leader Gordon Taylor was highly complimentary of Rooney: 'Everybody is keeping their fingers crossed that he isn't marked out of the game in more ways than one. Otherwise there is no end to what he can achieve. The future of English football is bright when you look at the players listed.'

With the last game of the season looming, and the trip to South Africa, Rooney's participation was still under discussion. In fact the whole club-versus-country issue, which had been seen so vividly in the Australia game, was up for debate.

David Moyes was among the Premiership managers who met Eriksson at London's plush Landmark Hotel to thrash out the hoary old problem, clearly wanting Rooney spared the gruelling trip to South Africa for a friendly.

After a two-hour meeting with Moyes and four other top Premiership managers, Eriksson said: 'Why should he not go to South Africa? I haven't picked the squad yet. It is too early. But if he is picked, he *will* play. Why not?'

Sir Alex Ferguson, Peter Reid, Sir Bobby Robson and Alan Curbishley were also present as part of the first stage of Eriksson's mission to convince Premiership chiefs not to stand in the way of players representing their country.

The FA stressed Rooney's name was never mentioned specifically at the get-together. Acting chief executive David Davies said: 'We didn't talk about individual players. But a whole range of issues which needed to be discussed were covered. It was an excellent meeting. I have no doubt all the managers are supportive of the England team.'

Moyes, though, refused to confirm whether he would back down over Rooney. He said: 'I don't want to go into that now. There is still a bit of time before the South Africa game comes around.'

The next day Eriksson debated these issues with Arsène Wenger, Gerard Houllier and Gordon Strachan. The FA proposed a charter be drawn up which all managers would be asked to sign. They would propose a limited number of friendlies and get-togethers throughout a season – and ask for the thumbs-up in writing. All players selected would then be expected to attend – without fail.

Eriksson refused to back down and insisted he would pick any player he wanted – and play them for however long he wanted. The compromise was that Eriksson agreed there would be no more friendly international dates during April after 2004. He commented: 'When we are talking about friendly games in March or April the club managers defend their interests and they should do – it's what they are paid to do. I understand that.

'We had meetings with the managers and that was very good and I think we're going to go on with that every year because it's very good sitting round a table and discussing the problems. I think I have good relationships with all club managers.'

Moyes was dismayed by the comments from the England manager after their meeting. Eriksson had assured the Everton manager that neither would say anything about the striker, so Moyes was naturally surprised and angered. He said: 'All I'm going to say is that Sven and I have agreed to meet in the next week or so to discuss the situation.'

The Everton boss was actually proud that his teenage star had been picked for the national side but he believed the expectation was too much for a seventeen-year-old. Amazingly, Rooney had played just the second 45 minutes against Australia and 89 minutes against Turkey to suddenly become indispensable at international level. Moyes explained: 'I am doing my best to protect Wayne. I want to bring him along at the right pace and not put him under any undue pressure.

'I think Wayne should play for England, he is good enough. But we have to be careful about the expectation that is heaped on his shoulders. If he does not live up to people's hopes when playing for England and is sent back to us crying, we are the ones who have to pick up the pieces.'

Moyes did not want Rooney to go to South Africa, but he admitted: 'If Sven picks him there is nothing I can do about it – that is the bottom line.

'People forget how young he is. He has been involved in every Premier League game this season bar the four when he was suspended. He has not had an injury and it has been a hell of a long season for a boy. People have to appreciate that.'

Moyes would not have been impressed with the meddling of Alan Shearer on the issue. Shearer argued that Rooney should go to South Africa. The former England captain said: 'It would not do him any harm to go out there and learn his trade a little bit more. Then, after the Euro 2004 game against Slovakia he can have a good rest.'

While the England debate continued, so did Everton's fight for a UEFA Cup spot. Before the Man United clash Everton had to take on Fulham. Moyes wanted four points from their two remaining games to clinch a place in the UEFA Cup. Ideally, he did not want the club's fate to depend on the clash with Manchester United.

Moyes said: 'This is a proper match. Fulham have something to play for and so have we. It will be like a cup tie.' Fulham were aiming to guarantee their Premiership survival. Their then caretaker-boss Chris Coleman said: 'Rooney's a superb player although we can't concentrate on just him. The only way to stop him will be to kidnap him in the car park.'

Regrettably, Rooney was wound up to the point of distraction by Luis Boa Morte as Everton lost 2–0. The Portuguese striker had been sent off for sparking a fifteen-man brawl in the same fixture the previous season, and Everton protested that he was guilty of a handball that resulted in Fulham's second goal. He had several verbal clashes with Rooney. Coleman said: 'As for what happened with Rooney, that is Luis. He gets involved sometimes. I'm sure Wayne Rooney's the same. He looks like he's got a lot of passion as well. It was handbags, nothing malicious.'

Fulham were safe from the drop after picking up three points courtesy of two own goals. As it turned out, Arsenal's home defeat by Leeds handed Manchester United the title before the last game at Goodison, and United were to be presented with the trophy after the game with Everton. Safety fears prompted the police and Everton officials to issue an urgent plea to ticketless United fans to stay away on the last Sunday of the season.

But Moyes did not have a problem with Alex Ferguson's champions taking centre stage after the match, especially if his side could have a party of their own to celebrate qualifying for Europe. Fergie fan Moyes said: 'I think it is right the ceremony will take place at Everton after the game. In years to come I would like to think we could be going to Old Trafford to receive the trophy as champions. When United lost at Manchester City in November, eight-tenths of the country did not expect them to come back so strongly – but I am not surprised they did. They are the best team in the Premiership and it was all down to Fergie's fantastic managerial skills. He has shown everyone who is the boss and the rest of us should look up to him.'

Moyes's men were in pole position to qualify for the UEFA Cup, providing they did not lose and Blackburn failed to win at Spurs. The manager added: 'My message to the team is we are ninety minutes away from Europe, which could be a stepping stone for this club.

He then gave a somewhat contradictory assessment of the game ahead. 'I don't think the task is made any easier because United come here as champions, but I admit it would have been tougher if they still needed something out of the game.'

The game was a 41,000 sellout, with United's allocation 3,000, and Manchester United skipper Roy Keane was concerned that Rooney should be getting the right advice. Keane commented:

I hope Rooney is looked after, but I'm sure he will be. A player like Rooney is going to have so many hangers-on. Football can be a ruthless business and you have to look after yourself. You have to be careful, especially with the money young players are earning today.

It's very rare I get as excited about a player as I have about him, but when I've sat down and watched him he has been absolutely unbelievable. He's got me out of my seat a few times this season.

When the lads came back from England they said he was fantastic in training, they said he was strong, fearless. But then, when you are that age, there is no fear.

Moyes was convinced that Rooney's love affair with Everton is so strong that he will never be tempted to move. Moyes wouldn't swap Rooney for any other young player and felt privileged to work with the most natural footballer he has ever seen. He said:

The thing that makes Wayne Rooney so unique is that he really loves Everton . . . I can't see the day coming when Wayne said he wanted to move. Even if he was coming to the end of his contract I'd be a hundred per cent certain that he'd sign another.

But the one thing our club must never do is take Wayne for granted. We have got to make sure that we eventually give him the kind of team a talent like his deserves. In the past Everton have let too many of their young players leave. The fans still remember lads like Michael Ball, Franny Jeffers, Richard Dunne and Phil Jevons, and I am sure they worry that the same will happen to Wayne.

I can understand why the players I have mentioned left because Everton failed to provide them with assurances that they could achieve their ambitions at Goodison. There was no money at the club, the team weren't doing well, so it was understandable that they saw their futures elsewhere.

That's why the one thing I demanded from the club when I took the job was that they wouldn't dismantle anything I built. We've made great strides this season and I already know I won't have a lot of money to spend regardless of what happens this weekend.

But that doesn't worry me. I believe that even a little money can be made to stretch a long way if it is spent wisely. Expectations will rise next season regardless of whether we are in Europe, but I think it's a football manager's job to raise expectations. It's my responsibility to give the fans a bit of hope and I think I've done that.

We will have a team good enough to give Wayne the platform a talent like his deserves. He is such a natural. Even at this age, he has the ability to do most things asked of him. He can virtually do everything on a football pitch. He can drop deep and run at people with the ball, he can drift off into wider areas. People at Everton tell me he spent a season at centre half, so you can see he's just a terrific footballer.

Moyes wanted Rooney to look and learn from players under Sir Alex such as Beckham and Giggs. He explained: 'David played for me [on loan] at Preston and, like Ryan, he is a good role model.'

Despite speculation to the contrary, the Everton manager planned to keep Rooney in the side against Manchester United. He said: 'Rooney will be given the chance to round off a terrific season by showing Sir Alex what all the fuss is all about. Just imagine if United need a point for the Championship, we need a point for Europe and it was a draw with just a few minutes to go. Everybody's happy, Sir Alex has a big smile on his face, we're all delighted with a UEFA Cup place, nobody's doing anything else to hurt each other . . . and then Wayne Rooney gets one!

'You couldn't tell the boy, you couldn't have a word in his ear. It would be just like him to go on a run, beat four players and blast one in from thirty yards. Tell me, what would I say to Sir Alex then?'

Moyes was just thankful that Sir Alex had wrapped up his eighth title in eleven seasons. But it did not seem to make any difference to the Champions. Wayne Rooney was handed the cruellest lesson of his young career at Goodison Park as United wrecked Everton's UEFA Cup dream.

The teenage wonder boy failed to convert three golden chances to put the Toffees back in front after David Beckham had brilliantly levelled Kevin Campbell's early opener. And the price he paid was high as Ruud van Nistelrooy blasted home his 44th and final goal of an incredible campaign, becoming the first Manchester United player in history to score in ten successive games, and ensured they collected their hard-won trophy as winners and holders of an eighteen-match unbeaten record. It was all pretty tough on Moyes, who had done so much to revive the fortunes of the ailing Merseyside outfit, but ultimately ended the season without a tangible reward.

Sport, though, has a strange way of making even the greatest look humble at times and when Naysmith fed Rooney with a perfect cross along the edge of the six-yard box, he was presented with the kind of opportunity it is easier to score than miss. Even the scoreboard flashed goal, but by then Rooney had his face buried into the ground, struggling to take in how he had failed to put his team back in front.

The chance which came next, after he had been booked for berating the linesman who deemed his shove on Silvestre had been worthy of a foul, was almost as good as Alan Stubbs lofted a long pass over the United defence. There was no flag even though Rooney looked a couple of yards offside. With Ferdinand desperately trying to make up the lost ground, the young striker took his shot early when more composure was probably due, and promptly sent the ball rasping wide of the post.

It did not take Laurent Blanc long to emphasise Rooney's potential. Introduced as an interval substitute for the final 45 minutes of his illustrious professional career, he found himself in direct opposition to the teenager almost immediately, and promptly sent him crashing to the ground – the only way he could halt his touchline run.

Still the youngster's agony was not over, although while the finger could be pointed at him for the earlier misses, little blame was due this time as he twisted on to Duncan Ferguson's downward header and smashed a shot on the turn which Carroll saved with his legs. Van Nistelrooy's late winner only increased his woes.

The impending row over Wayne Rooney's participation in the South Africa trip and the disappointment of missing out on a UEFA Cup berth would not be allowed to overshadow David Moyes's belief that Everton were the most improved side in the Premiership in 2002–03. In his usual single-minded manner, Moyes refused to feel sorry for himself or his players, admitting they had got what they deserved. However, he also passed on the credit for a vastly improved Premiership showing to his squad, rather than accept the accolades with which he has been showered since succeeding Walter Smith at the Merseyside outfit.

'There are winners and losers in this game and you end up where you deserve,' said the former Preston boss. 'You have to give credit to Blackburn, they have done well to get a great result at Tottenham. There is no silver lining in the sense that we haven't done anything other than do better than we did last season.

'You have to recognise that, though, and a lot of the credit must go to the players and the way they have turned themselves around. They are probably the most improved squad in the Premiership. We just couldn't get over the finishing line.'

14

The Moyes Effect

'The only man not doing handstands after the Turkey game was Rooney's club manager.'

– Gary Lineker

It needed a strong man for a tough job – and David Moyes was just perfect. Looking after the phenomenon that is Wayne Rooney was going to be one hell of a challenge for his manager. And that was what Moyes faced at the start of the 2002–03 season. Nobody outside Everton knew quite what a jewel Moyes had on his hands. Just ten months later and Rooney-mania had swept the world.

The Everton boss's guiding hand of iron had brought him into confrontation with England boss Sven Goran Eriksson, but Moyes could not have cared less. It was Everton and the kid he was worried about.

No wonder Rooney could not praise his manager highly enough. He said: 'David Moyes, my manager at Everton, has helped me so much over the past season. He is right there when I make a mistake and he always tells me where I have gone wrong and how to go about not making the same mistake next time.

'I think he has helped the club by achieving a team spirit that hasn't really been there in recent years. The lads have also benefited from the way he coaches the team and the results have reflected that.'

Not half. But what is the background of this gruff, fierce Scot with a twinkle in his eye?

Born in Glasgow on 25 April 1963, where he started his playing career with Celtic, Moyes the player clearly underachieved. Something went badly wrong for the promising Celtic centre-half in 1982.

Just turned twenty, with a Scottish Championship medal under his belt, he had begun to establish himself in the first team when the Bhoys crowd started to turn against him.

He had to move on, and he was offered trials by both Arsenal and Sunderland, but the proud young boy was not prepared to do auditions (unlike the manager, who makes maximum use of the loan system), and turned both opportunities down. A move to Manchester City under former Celt Billy McNeill fell through, and Moyes found himself plying his trade in the lower regions of the Football League. He says: 'It sounds daft to say that I turned down a move to Arsenal and went to Cambridge instead, but I did. It just did not work out for me.'

It was a big shock for the Scottish youth and schools international to be given a free transfer to Cambridge United in October 1983 but he buckled down and got on with it. From there he went to Bristol City two years later for £10,000. Two years on from that and he commanded a fee of £30,000 to go to Shrewsbury. In August of 1990 he returned north to Scotland and Dunfermline on a free transfer. He adds: 'I scored a winner against Celtic at Parkhead in a 2–1 win. I have to say that was enjoyable.'

From Dunfermline, after a few weeks at Hamilton Academical, he moved to Preston North End in September 1993. The Deepdale crowd took to Moyes's commitment and composure, and Moyes became team captain and later assistant manager under Gary Peters, before succeeding Peters as manager at Preston in 1998.

In his first full season at Deepdale Moyes very nearly took Preston into the Nationwide First Division, but North End were knocked out of the play-offs by Gillingham who went on to be beaten by Manchester City at Wembly in the final.

Moyes had worked his way up from player/coach to assistant boss to manager at Deepdale. There were rumours he was on the verge of a lucrative move to Old Trafford as assistant to Sir Alex Ferguson, but Moyes remained in Lancashire with the aim of taking the club into Division One.

He has the same Glasgow roots that spawned Sir Alex and Fergie recognised a kindred spirit when he watched Moyes cut his managerial teeth at Preston. He advised him against jumping at a couple of tempting job offers that came his way and included the Scot on a short list of two when he was looking for someone to replace Brian Kidd as his assistant back in 1998. Ferguson eventually opted for Steve McClaren. Now Moyes is being touted as a possible successor to Sir Alex. He said:

> Do I compare to Sir Alex? Well, we're both Scots, but that's about it to be honest. I have asked Alex on a few occasions for advice, particularly during my early days in management. I did meet with Alex when he was looking for a number two to replace Brian Kidd and I would have loved the job.
>
> I knew at the time that there was someone else in the running and Alex eventually made an excellent decision in appointing Steve McClaren. I was disappointed because, when a Sir Alex Ferguson or a Sir Bobby Robson comes knocking, you don't turn them down. Maybe Sir Alex felt I was a bit too far down the road in terms of the fact that I was number one at Preston and it would have been him making all the decisions at Old Trafford. It would have been a tough decision to make, but I think it would have been impossible to turn him down. It was the kind of opportunity I would have loved.

In May 2000, Preston were promoted as Champions of Division Two and made an impressive start to life in the First Division, establishing themselves as outside contenders for an immediate promotion to the Premiership. The season's outcome was perhaps beyond Moyes's expectations. The Lily Whites ended up in the Nationwide League First Division play-offs. They overcame Birmingham City in the semi-finals but Bolton Wanderers came out of the final at the Millennium Stadium in Cardiff with a 3–0 win that took them into the FA Barclaycard Premiership.

The season was over but the Preston boss was on the list of possible candidates for several managerial jobs that became vacant close to the end of the season. Moyes had worked wonders during his four years at Deepdale and had nearly taken the famous Lancashire club all the way to the top flight having led them up from Division Two to the First Division play-offs in two seasons. The hot-seats at Manchester City, Southampton and West Ham United were all mentioned in association with Moyes. He signed a new five-year deal with Preston and looked as though he might lead them to the play-offs once again but was allowed to talk to Everton following the dismissal of Walter Smith from Goodison. Eventually Moyes left Preston North End to become the successor to Walter Smith at Everton on 15 March 2002.

And in his press conference he won the blue side of Liverpool around in seconds with an unscripted statement that would have touched the soul of every true Everton fan. It could have come from the mouth of Bill Shankly, it was that evocative. He said without prompting: 'This is the people's club on Merseyside. The people on the streets support Everton and we hope over the next few years to give them something to be proud of.'

A young and ambitious manager, Moyes's first task at Goodison was to attempt to keep the Merseyside club in the Premiership. Horrified about the fitness levels, he immediately ordered training twice a day and instilled a work ethic that had long been absent. He certainly got off to a good start; having received a hero's welcome from the Everton fans, Moyes saw a David Unsworth goal in the first thirty seconds and a Duncan Ferguson strike earn his new club a 2–1 win over Fulham and some breathing space in the relegation battle.

Everton went on to finish the season in fifteenth place, seven points clear of the drop zone, and Moyes set about building for the future and a new era at Goddison. It was a fresh start for Everton from a man who meant business and who still had a lot to prove. With such little success as a player he has put everything into being a manager to be reckoned with, and he has proved beyond doubt that he will not be messed about. He also has the Martin O'Neill factor about him. He is inspirational and his enthusiasm and desperation to win rubs off on everybody around him.

The buzz around Goodison Park is different under Moyes. Director of Communications Ian Ross couldn't speak too highly of the man at the helm. He said:

I've never met a more thorough man in my life. He's the first in and the last out every day and on the Monday he comes in with a week's training mapped out. He's absolutely dedicated to his work and he is a pleasure to do business with. He studies the opposition in minute detail, listing their strengths and weaknesses, then tells each player what to expect and what is expected of them. He studies scouting reports and goes over and over things until they are how he wants them. His motivational skills are beyond belief and sometimes it is hard to remember that he's working with the same players that were so downhearted and dejected just a few months before. He's instilled tremendous self-belief and we're all reaping the rewards. It's a delight to watch Everton play now and be part of the Renaissance.

By transforming Everton's fortunes in less than a year, Moyes confirmed his reputation as the best young manager in the country. He might appear to be Mr Grumpy, but he is more than just the perceived overprotective Wayne Rooney baby-sitter. 'I want Wayne Rooney to turn thirty and be able to say to himself, "David Moyes was all right for me",' he said.

But Moyes has ensured a place in the little book of football quotations. When Wayne Rooney resumed his club commitments after becoming a national figure with England, the no-nonsense Everton manager said: 'If there had been any difference he could expect a slap around the ear!' However, it fails to beat George Graham's observation: 'Wayne Rooney has a man's body on a teenager's head.'

But Moyes's slaphappy comment brought widespread derision. Even Robert Kilroy-Silk got into the act in his *Sunday Express* column – before his well-publicised departure from the BBC and his return to politics with the UK Independence Party – when he labelled Moyes 'Mr Misery Guts In Chief'. Moyes would not worry too much about Kilroy-Silk accusing him of being a killjoy, as the Everton manager faced multiple challenges to the way he handled the precocious talents of Wayne Rooney.

Protecting him from the glare of the media was one of Moyes's priorities in that sensitive debut season. In fact, earlier in the season, Everton held a board meeting to formulate a 'Rooney protection policy' that largely consisted of seeking the media's co-operation not to oversell his prospect – some chance. Moyes explained why Rooney needed protection:

Wayne has been great to work with, he's more natural on the field than anyone I know. He's not so natural in company, other than his own. He's still not comfortable, he struggles in company other than people he's grown up with. But that's what you have to expect when a kid's left school at sixteen and gone straight into work, he's not going to feel comfortable. Yet because of who he is, everybody expects Wayne to be the bee's knees at everything.

In time he'll be able to handle his own media and press conferences, but at the moment we're making sure we handle him right, making sure he's not misquoted or misunderstood. At the moment, he's very good but if I told you all his failings and all the work he still has to do, then we could be here all night.

But I tell you what, his strengths are incredible. He came straight in from school, there was no breaking him in with youth-team matches, he was into first-team training from day one and in the first team pre-season. He didn't look out of place at all, and that's the greatest compliment I can pay the boy.

I understand everyone wants a piece of him, but do you understand me when I say I want to protect him? What we've got to do is get players to gel with him and I'll scrap and fight to do that.

But he has not surprised me with his progress this season. I was aware of him as a twelve-year-old because he was already building an amazing reputation, so he hasn't surprised me to that extent. I saw him play in the FA Youth Cup final last season just after I joined and he was astonishing. I told Alan Irvine, 'I've seen a boy who will be in our first team from the start of the season.'

But when you see what he does every day in training, you're no longer surprised by how good he is.

Moyes has earned great respect for the way he has handled the teenager and he explained:

I have to be very careful in the way I handle Wayne because I'm not his schoolteacher, I'm not his father, I'm not some kind of authority figure laying down the law at every turn.

I'm his manager who has to do what's right for him and the team. There is so much going on around young Wayne at the moment. Have I enjoyed all the hype and hysteria surrounding a seventeen-year-old? Yes, because I'd rather have this seventeen-year-old than any other seventeen-year old in the world.

I have enjoyed every minute working with him. He's great to work with and I hope that, when he becomes the great player that he will be, he remembers his time under me with the same affection.

Moyes was prepared to upset anybody to keep Rooney under wraps. Sky TV were annoyed at the way Moyes spoke to their reporter at West Ham. The Everton manager was angry that cameras had followed Wayne off the bus, down the tunnel and during the warm-up. He wanted and expected them to back off and he made his point clearly. Sky's Richard Keys started to refer to Rooney as 'He who can't be named'.

The media were cruel as well as kind. Kind to Rooney's exploits on the field, but cruel when he collected the BBC Young Sports Personality of the Year trophy only to be criticised for looking dishevelled, chewing gum and with his tie askew. Then again, what teenager wouldn't look totally bewildered and out of his depth in such circumstances, when he only feels at home on the football field or in the company of his friends and family. During the televised awards the cameras picked up the youngster picking his nose and the microphones homed in on him as he mumbled, far more nervous than when he made his England debut.

But Moyes adopted a more direct approach by barring the media access to his player, akin to the way Sir Alex Ferguson wrapped young players like David Beckham and Ryan Giggs in cotton wool. The strategy was simple, to keep the kid's feet on the ground, and to avoid the kind of burnout that put Michael Owen's career on hold for a time. It's this challenge that has put him on a collision course with the England management. Gary Lineker observed: 'The only man not doing handstands after the Turkey game was Rooney's club manager, David Moyes, who has already asked for his player to be left out of the summer tour of South Africa.

'Moyes has done a fantastic job in protecting Rooney but his performance against Turkey has blown the doors off the glass case that his manager was trying to keep him in. I am sure that Moyes will still try to be sensible in how he uses Rooney.

'He might be built like a man and play like a man but, at seventeen, he may not yet be ready to play every week, especially as he has now become a box-office attraction.'

But Moyes had his point of view, even though it might not suit England's cause. The Everton manager was fighting hard to prevent a prodigious talent from being crushed by expectation. 'At the beginning of the season, people were prepared to accept Wayne was just a lad growing up,' Moyes said. 'But now they think of him as a 23-year-old, a mature professional ready to play. Think of the things that you do between seventeen and 23. Wayne's not 23.'

Moyes's approach was to use Rooney sparingly – often to the frustration of the club's fans. But this did little to quieten the immense media interest, and part of the nurturing process was to keep a naturally shy boy out of the limelight.

Rooney is not articulate, and no scholar. But he is smart enough to clam up when a microphone is shoved under his nose. However, banning interviews only fuelled the media hunger.

Moyes also faced a media-management problem in that at times Rooney seemed a bigger story than the club itself. If Rooney-mania got out of control it could cause resentment among the players and overshadow the fact that Everton's success and Moyes's management method are based on the belief that football is a team game.

Moyes made an impact in his first full season as Everton manager to the extent that Fulham wanted to replace Jean Tigana with a Moyes clone – that is, a young British manager able to work with limited resources, such as Alan Pardew at Reading (now manager of West Ham), Steve Cotterill or possibly Chris Coleman (who is now their manager).

His best work is performed on the training ground. A typical morning session starts with lots of shuttles, followed by possession work and the traditional Old versus Young training match. Moyes is often the referee, which is just as well as the fixture generally has a bit of needle: the veterans, needing to continually reassert their prowess over the younger generation, are led by figures such as

Kevin Campbell, who generally want to show new kids on the block like Rooney that they can also produce a thing or two.

When Rooney misses a good chance for The Young, he is ribbed by the players. 'Nice one, Wayne.' A few minutes later Rooncy will make amends with a fine finish.

Moyes arrives at the training ground to find a gaggle of shivering autograph hunters milling around the gates. The Bellefield building is a neat and clean bit of 1950s architecture surrounded by a car park, three full-size pitches and areas of parkland. Downstairs are the changing rooms, the kit rooms and a corridor leading to a vast gym hall with its full-size Astroturf pitch. Upstairs are the offices and the canteen.

Moyes has his own office, as do Irene, his personal assistant, the guy who runs Prozone (a hi-tech match analysis facility) and the website manager. There is also a communal office for Moyes's managerial team. Bigger than the rest, it, too, looks like something from the 1950s with its cheery, bright, functional desks and chairs – but with Sky Sports News playing in the corner. This is where Moyes meets the management team every morning.

His assistant is Alan Irvine, a former Everton player whom Moyes coaxed into returning to the club. Irvine headed Bobby Robson's youth academy at Newcastle, a club doing rather better than Everton in recent years, but was persuaded to come back to Merseyside, where he was a popular player eighteen years ago. Both men share a passion for coaching and are intense students of the modern game. Chris Woods, the former England and Rangers keeper was appointed as the club's goalkeeping coach by Moyes's predecessor Walter Smith. Andy Holden (known as Taff) is the reserve-team coach. He was a no-nonsense defender for Chester, Wigan and Oldham. Jimmy Lumsden, Moyes's No 3, completes the triumvirate. Moyes brought Lumsden, who is slighter and older than the rest, with him from his previous job at Preston, but the two have known each other longer that that – Lumsden was youth-team coach at Celtic when Moyes came up through the system.

Nothing has been left to chance, especially the way he deals with Wayne Rooney.

An Everton legend, Alex Young, has no doubt that Rooney will emerge as the talent everybody expects because of the supervision by Moyes. Young says: 'David Moyes has got something extra out of the players. He can take the club forward and he's also fortunate he has Rooney.'

Moyes was acknowledged by his peers at the League Managers' Association as Manager of the Season for 2002–03. Moyes was the one of the youngest managers in the English top flight but, despite his lack of experience, he guided the Toffeemen from fifteenth to seventh in the first full season of his management, making Everton the most improved club in the Premiership. They only missed out on a UEFA Cup place on the last day of the season, and all achieved on a shoestring budget. That was a major difference from the constant relegation battles of previous regimes. The club have only finished higher on two occasions since the beginning of the Premiership in 1992, but Moyes was still not expecting to receive the accolade.

'I'm delighted and surprised to win the award,' he said at an awards dinner in London. 'The disappointment we have suffered [at not making the UEFA Cup] is immeasurable. Football is about taking opportunities when they come and we had a great opportunity this season. But when things die down, then hopefully we will realise what a good season it has been.'

More importantly, perhaps, is that with the way he brought Everton back to life, particularly by playing Rooney, Moyes had believed Everton had regained the trust of their fans and that much of the frustration and anger from the fans over past failings had now gone.

Moyes said: 'I thought it was a good season with the progress the players have made. There's a difference between a great and a good season and had we qualified for Europe that would have been the difference. But we didn't win anything, apart from winning the supporters' trust back. They filled the ground and could see that we were trying to do the best for Everton. In the future they will see us continuing to do just that.'

Moyes admitted that he was overwhelmed by the depth of support and appreciation from Everton's success-starved fans:

I have attended functions recently when the Everton fans' response to the season has been fantastic, and I have left wondering what on earth they would be like if we actually won something. I'm hoping to see it. The fans are coming back, they can see a team that maybe is not full of top players but certainly a team top in commitment, attitude and the desire to play for the jersey.

None of those things labelled against the players when I first took over, like lack of commitment and not having a good attitude, now apply. That can't be said after this season. I was pleased with what they achieved.

Everton's fans may love Rooney, but in the 2002–03 season Moyes proved to be as big a star.

15

Stormy South Africa

'He has been an explosion this season. He's doing very well at his club and has been fantastic for us. When you are playing for England at seventeen years old of course it's a sensation all over the world.'

– Sven Goran Eriksson

'Wayne rates with Paul Gascoigne. His ability is tremendous and he has the capability to go on and make a better career and make a better player than Paul Gascoigne. And it is a lot for me to say that about Wayne.'

– Walter Smith

The war of words had already begun, but this was an escalation beyond all belief over the control of Wayne Rooney. The FA and Sven Goran Eriksson had become annoyed with Everton boss David Moyes over him insisting that Rooney would not go to South Africa. They felt it was not his place to make that judgement, let alone express it to the footballing world. Eriksson made no bones about letting the Everton boss know who was in charge.

The FA and Eriksson were desperate to get Rooney on the money-spinning PR trip to Durban alongside the likes of David Beckham and Michael Owen. They were all due to meet legendary statesman Nelson Mandela on a trip England were being paid £1m to make by the South African FA. But then came the telephone call from Everton that knocked both the FA and Eriksson sideways.

According to the Merseyside club, Wayne Rooney was ruled out of England's trip after compounding a bad day in front of goal by picking up a medial knee-ligament injury in Everton's 2–1 defeat to new Premiership champions Manchester United.

'Wayne picked up an injury in the first half, then aggravated it when he was tackled by Laurent Blanc in the second,' said Moyes. 'He will have a scan in the morning but he definitely won't travel to South Africa and he is a doubt for the later matches as well.'

The news was greeted with suspicion by the FA, who had been embroiled in a row with Moyes over Sven Goran Eriksson's insistence in the days building up to the conclusion of the Premiership season that the player should travel to South Africa. The matter threatened to escalate into a full-scale row, as neither side trusted the other.

Eriksson spoke with Moyes to discover the extent of the injury to Rooney's right knee, as it looked suspiciously like revenge by Moyes, who had argued fiercely that Rooney should be spared the 6,000-mile trip.

Rooney wore a huge ice pack on the knee when he helped form Everton's guard of honour for Man United as they were presented with the Premiership trophy. FA spokesman Adrian Bevington said that England team doctor Leif Svaird would contact Everton after Rooney underwent his scan. Until the FA knew the outcome of the test, Rooney was not ruled out of the South Africa trip by Eriksson, hinting that he possibly doubted the veracity of the bulletin from Everton.

Seeing that Rooney had played a full ninety minutes and done a lap of honour at the end of the match in which he was injured, it was perhaps natural that the FA were a little suspicious of the extent of his injury. But to ask Rooney to come down to London for the FA medical staff to look at the scan taken by Everton highlighted the atmosphere of distrust that surrounded the situation. Eriksson said:

Wayne Rooney had a scan on his knee today and we will see afterwards. But, anyhow, he will come to our hotel on Sunday and we will make a decision then as to whether he comes with us to South Africa. If our doctor can talk to his counterpart then I hope we will come to a solution.

Wayne will have rest for six days and I hope he can travel. It will be very good for him because he will come into the family more and more. It is very important that David Moyes and myself have a good relationship, but it is even more important that we have a good relationship with Wayne.

Asked about the Goodison teenager, Eriksson said: 'Rooney is the best seventeen-year-old I've had. I had Roberto Baggio when he was young, and he was brilliant, but Wayne Rooney is exceptional. David Moyes has a diamond in his hands. He is only trying to protect him and there's nothing unusual about that.'

Eriksson thought he had won his power battle in the bitter club-versus-country row after meeting with eleven top-flight managers, including Arsène Wenger, Sir Alex Ferguson and Moyes, to try to reach a compromise over future call-ups and friendly fixtures.

In his interview on *Football Focus* before the final games of the season, Eriksson refused to be drawn on whether he would pick Rooney for South Africa, although he was keen to stress that he would not be overworked even if he does make the trip. 'Before I pick the squad I will talk to David Moyes once again,' he said. 'Anyhow, going to South Africa or not, Wayne Rooney will have six or seven days rest as will all the players. He will have a rest even if he comes.'

Eriksson reiterated how much he was impressed by Rooney's first international start, against Turkey: 'I thought he should be nervous. I told him three hours before the game he was playing and he just said OK. During the game he was not afraid of taking on people and it's very unusual you will see a seventeen-year-old boy playing like that.'

Moyes was still far from convinced and still very much concerned about burnout, as he said prior to the final game of the season against Manchester United: 'I think parts of his game have been very good recently, but there have also been signs that it has been a long, hard season for him. Wayne has had to start our last seven games as well as internationals. It's lucky that we didn't overplay him at the start of the season.'

The Swede went into greater detail in his media interviews about how he wanted the Everton starlet to terrorise Slovakia just as he had torn into the Turks, and that therefore it was important to be part of the build-up. Eriksson said: 'The important thing is that we beat Slovakia. That's the real one and that's why we have arranged friendly games beforehand. And that's the end I'm working to with Wayne Rooney. I'm sure he is ready for the big games. He showed that against Turkey. We all saw the impact he made and I think he is ready to play or at least be on the bench to come on against Slovakia. So Rooney *will* be picked.'

Eriksson added:

To pick him for South Africa or not at the end it must be my decision and only mine. He will be picked maybe against South Africa, maybe not. We will see. But leaving him out against South Africa, that would give him more than ten days off and I think that's too much for him to be fit for the other games, against Serbia and Montenegro and then Slovakia.

I spoke to his manager last week and by phone again this week. We maybe don't have the same opinion, but we will talk again on Monday. He thinks Rooney might need more rest and he might be right, I don't know. The important thing, though, is not David Moyes or Sven Goran Eriksson, the important thing is Wayne Rooney.

That said, the Swede confessed: 'I haven't spoken to him about this but, from what I saw when we were together, he seems very happy with us. I think he won a lot of friends among the players.'

Eriksson said Rooney's amazing display against Turkey had won the youngster admirers all over Europe. The England boss explained:

People in football, friends in Sweden, Portugal and Italy, they loved him very much. I can't think of another youngster anywhere in the world who is making such an impact. But I have to say it didn't surprise me how he did against Turkey, certainly not in the way he played.

But his attitude to the game, that *did* surprise me. He was not nervous, he was very confident. He was missing some balls but next time he was there taking chances again. That's not normal for a seventeen-year-old boy, absolutely not. I hope it goes on and everything continues as is planned for Everton and England. Then he will be a really big one and I'm happy about that.

But Eriksson complained: 'It is good we have that long together but it is crazy we have a game a month after the league has finished. It is not easy to keep the players fit and happy when everyone else is on holiday.'

Eriksson named Rooney in his 25-man squad for the friendly in Durban, saying that, while England and Everton doctors would discuss Rooney's injury, no decision would be made on whether or not he would travel to South Africa until the players were due to meet up the day after the FA Cup final between Arsenal and Southampton.

Moyes denied there was any doubt over the severity of Rooney's injury, even though he played on after taking the knock on his knee. Moyes had Rooney sent to a private Merseyside clinic for a full knee examination, and Everton claimed the scan showed he had a 'grade-one medial-ligament injury', which normally means two to three weeks out of action. Moyes declared:

> I'm sure there are a lot of people thinking I'm pulling Wayne out because I don't want him to go to South Africa. But this is a genuine injury and the scan is there to prove it. Wayne has got a tear on his knee ligament. It's not severe and won't keep him out too long, but I expect it will keep him out for a couple of weeks. I thought [by missing the South Africa game] he would have then been ready to play against Serbia and Montenegro and Slovakia and I also thought it would have given him the break he needs.
>
> It's been a real long year for the boy and at seventeen there is a lot of expectation and pressure on him. I think, at the right times, he has to be been given a break. We have to remember his age and not expect too much of him.

Eriksson hit back: 'I don't think this is a competition. It is common sense to let the doctors decide. If we do it like that there can't be any discussions about who's doing right and who's doing wrong. Rooney will have a rest this week, treatment as well, and we will see.'

Moyes expected Rooney to be fit enough to join up with the England squad and go to La Manga, the training complex in Spain that England were to visit after the South African tour.

It was clear why Eriksson made so much of an issue in selecting Rooney. On the FA's own website the England coach waxed lyrical about the boy, and Eriksson insisted that Rooney's 'explosion' into English football made him the young player of the year in his eyes:

'That's Rooney,' he said without a moment's hesitation. 'He has been an explosion this season. He's doing very well at his club and has been fantastic for us. When you are playing for England at seventeen years old, of course, it's a sensation all over the world.'

Although Jermaine Jenas was the PFA's Young Player of the Year and there's certainly no question that Sven rates the Newcastle man very highly too, it is Rooney's ability to excite that seems to have entranced the England coach as well as the rest of the country.

'He's one of those players that, whenever he gets the ball, something seems to happen,' explained Eriksson, his eyes lighting up as he described the young Everton prodigy. 'Whether it's finding a good pass or taking on a player, it's exciting and that's what makes him such an interesting player both now and for the future. He's young but I don't think he's nervous at all. He's very confident and knows what he can and can't do. He has no fear and not too much respect for the opponents.'

For Sven, one of Rooney's most appealing assets is the breadth of his qualities, which means that he can be played in differing positions up front. 'I don't know him as well as David Moyes does but I can see the qualities in him that allow him to drop deeper,' the England coach confirms. 'He can turn on the ball and then drive forward. It's very dangerous because he can beat people and play his team-mates in as well. Also, although he is not tall, he is strong, so you have the option of playing him right up front. Because of his broad talents he could play with almost any kind of partner – that makes him very useful.'

Although Moyes's specific aim was to deflect the spotlight from Rooney, the row over his inclusion for the trip to South Africa had the opposite effect – it made front-page headlines in the *Telegraph* and filled the back pages of every tabloid. Even though Moyes had signed up to the Premiership pact in which club managers agreed the Swede could pick whoever he wanted, no matter what the circumstances, the club-versus-country controversy now escalated to all-out confrontation between Moyes and Eriksson.

Eriksson called up the injured Rooney at 1.30 p.m. on Monday 12 May for the three end-of-season internationals and he said: 'There will be no compromise with Rooney.' Moyes insisted thirty minutes later that Rooney would not be fit for the 22 May friendly in South Africa.

The Swede commented: 'What I heard about the scan is that Rooney has a problem. The Everton doctor talked to our doctor and we will see the scan as well. How long it will take they didn't say. They didn't know exactly. So the FA and I decided he would be picked for the squad for the three games. He will meet up on Sunday and from there we will take the decision what to do for the first game and then the others.'

As Shaun Custis wrote in the *Sun*: 'Rooney is getting almost as much attention as Becks already and this trip is seen as a valuable part of his education.'

Eriksson argued that Rooney's case was vastly different to other missing England players. The England coach explained: 'It's different when you have Rooney, who played the ninety minutes. The others have not been playing – or were injured during the game.'

Diplomatic as ever, he added: 'I've no doubt there is a problem. I don't know the details but the two doctors agreed the best solution is he comes on Sunday. If he's fit I will be taking him to South Africa. It's good for him.

'We will not overwork him and every time he can be together with the rest of the squad he comes more and more into the family. He should be very happy to be there. David Moyes and I always talked straight and his opinion was it might be better if Rooney didn't go to South Africa. But he's always said it's up to me to decide. The only worry is we might talk too much about Wayne Rooney.'

The 25-man England squad for friendlies with South Africa and Serbia-Montenegro plus the Euro 2004 qualifier against Slovakia was:

Goalkeepers: David James (West Ham), Paul Robinson (Leeds), Ian Walker (Leicester)

Defenders: Ashley Cole* (Arsenal), Wayne Bridge* (Southampton), Danny Mills (Leeds), Phil Neville (Man Utd), Rio Ferdinand (Man Utd), Gareth Southgate (Middlesbrough), John Terry (Chelsea), Matthew Upson (Birmingham)

Midfielders: David Beckham (Man Utd), Paul Scholes (Man Utd), Kieron Dyer (Newcastle), Jermaine Jenas (Newcastle), Owen Hargreaves*

(Bayern Munich), Danny Murphy (Liverpool), Frank Lampard (Chelsea), Steven Gerrard (Liverpool), Trevor Sinclair (West Ham)

Forwards: Michael Owen (Liverpool), Emile Heskey (Liverpool), Wayne Rooney (Everton), Darius Vassell (Aston Villa), James Beattie* (Southampton)

* Joining squad after friendly in South Africa.

To illustrate how Rooney had emerged almost on a par with the England captain in terms of identifying with the country's football fans, when the FA launched the pricing for the new Wembley executive boxes and premium seating at Soho Square in spring 2003 (involving a specially built full-size box and a section of seating), there were visuals of two England players – Beckham and Rooney.

Moyes, meanwhile, on 13 May 2003 collected his Manager of the Year award at the League Managers' Association annual dinner from . . . well, it could only have been Sven, couldn't it?

Then Moyes and striker Rooney were in Belfast while the youngster conducted the draw for the Milk Youth Cup tournament. The Everton manager said: 'We all know Wayne is a smashing player. But I want him to be a great 27-year-old and not just remembered as a great seventeen-year-old . . . If he starts getting too big for his boots he will soon be brought back down to earth with a slap around the ear and he could be back in Belfast playing in the Milk Cup.'

Everton owner Bill Kenwright dismissed talk of a rift between Moyes and Eriksson:

The lad has a genuine injury and it is only natural David Moyes is concerned about that. But there is no conflict between the club and Sven Goran Eriksson. David Moyes is as thrilled as anyone when an Everton player gains international recognition.

One of the reasons he bought Richard Wright was because he felt it would improve the goalkeeper's chance of rejoining the England squad. And if young Tony Hibbert continues to make progress and also gets a chance, I can assure you the manager will be the first to congratulate him. Why would he want to bolt the door on any player's international career?

In the case of Rooney, he is merely protecting the interests of one of his players who happens to have an injury. Surely every club manager would respond the same. His first duty is to his club but I want to stress we don't have a problem with England. Our position is clear. We want the best for Wayne, Everton and England.

While all this was going on, a mild diversion for Rooney watchers came when the youngster was compared not to Shearer or Gazza, for once, but Albert Einstein. That just about sums up the hysteria heaped upon the broad young shoulders of Wayne Rooney.

With Einstein's head on the Everton shirt of Rooney on the front page of *T2*, *The Times* supplement suggested: 'The New Einstein. What Wayne Rooney's Genius Tells Us About Innate Intelligence.' Inside it read: 'It takes all sports to make a genius. Footballers are derided for having their brains in their feet. But scientists now believe that sportsmen such as teenage prodigy Wayne Rooney have an intelligence that matches the traditional academic kind.'

The son of an unemployed labourer and a school dinner lady, who left school at the first opportunity, has a mind likened to that of a great chess player, computer-like in its ability to visualise in an instant the possible outcomes of a pass, and act on them? Madness.

Nick Torpey, an English teacher at Wayne's old school, De La Salle in Croxteth, said: 'Wayne has shown that somewhere in his make-up is an iron will to succeed. He sees world-class internationals as his equals, which is amazing in itself, but what sets him apart is that he actually sees many of them as his inferiors.'

Dr Steve Blinkhorn, a psychologist and chairman of Psychometric Research & Development, said he has no problem in seeing great footballers such as Rooney, Michael Owen and David Beckham as super-intelligent:

There is a temptation to think that intelligence is the sum of taught skills and that you can beef up a person's intellect by teaching them numeracy and cognitive skills.

Charles Spearman a hundred years ago said that intellect was about seeing patterns and making effective use of them. Watching Michael Owen when he gets the ball is a joy. There is a plan there. Players like him

can see the possible range of consequences. They have a plan that goes
beyond the mere next contact with the ball. Really intelligent
performance is not purely down to cognitive capacity. If that was the
case the country would be ruled by Mensa.

Ian Ross, Everton spokesman, commented: 'Intelligence is no
longer a purely cerebral affair. Intelligence in the physical sense, in
the sporting sense, is now not only accepted, but coveted. Better
to be an acclaimed footballer with sporting intellect and a healthy
bank balance than a forgotten academic with no friends and
mounting debts.'

It took seven years of ridicule before David Beckham, who failed
his GCSEs and bailed out of Chingford High at sixteen, was declared
the Albert Einstein of football. Engineers in Japan, England and
Belgium conducted a study of his free kicks and concluded that he
had a staggering mastery of physics.

Dr Keith Hanna, of the software company Fluent Benelux, which
undertook the study, said that Beckham has figured out how to
balance the kick angle, kick speed, spin imparted and kick direction
to get the optimal turbulent-laminar transition trajectory that is
impossible for goalkeepers to save. 'Beckham can carry out a multi-
variable physics calculation in his head to compute the exact kick
trajectory required, and then execute it perfectly,' he said.

The Beckham brain – still much derided by TV impersonators –
must be computing some very detailed trajectory calculations in a
few seconds, purely from instinct and practice. Our computers take
a few hours to do the same thing.

Rooney is a different type of player, but computes action in a
similar way. His agent, Paul Stretford, said:

I wouldn't presume to know as much as a football coach, but I imagine
that if we had the technology to look into his head we'd see that he sees
everything at a slowed-down pace. While everyone else sees the
football being played at a hundred miles an hour, it's all slow motion in
his mind.

Wayne has something that you find in very, very few people. He has
such an absolute inner confidence and belief in his ability that situations

don't faze him, no matter how great the pressure. Great footballers are equally as intelligent as the most intelligent professor in their given subject.

But all anybody really cared about was Rooney's knee, and who won – Eriksson or Moyes.

16

Back in the Fold

'You must be patient even though it is difficult because he looks like a great player.'

— Pelé

Pelé collected the first of three World Cup winner's medals as a seventeen-year-old in 1958. So if there is anybody in the world who understands what it is like to be a teenager with the burden of the nation's expectations on your shoulders it is the great man. Yet Pelé warned that it is unwise for England to rely so much on Wayne Rooney. He said before Euro 2004:

Some players are exceptional when they are very young, then they fade and do not make it as far as you think. It is too soon to start talking too much about Wayne Rooney. It is much better to wait a little bit. You must be patient, even though it is difficult because he looks like a great player. He does look to have great ability.

I have only watched highlights of him and the football is excellent, but I do not know him and what his personality is like. And personality is very important. You can have plenty of ability but you need to be strong and have a strong personality to succeed.

I came to England six years ago to see a Brazilian player called Juninho. That week I saw two games and watched a young player called Michael Owen. I thought straight away that he was very special. He moved very quickly and had excellent vision. I said then and there that this player would go on to become one of the best in the world. Two years later he was in the England team.

Pelé worried that too many games may rob a youngster of vital protection as he perfects his game: 'They are expected to be men straightaway. And it becomes more difficult as you become more and more well known.

'Markers in the matches will come down on you even harder, which is why young players should be protected by their managers. It is difficult, but all those situations must be evaluated by the managers. It is not just about letting the boys play football. Be patient.'

David Moyes most definitely wanted to protect Rooney, and he eventually won his battle with the England coach to keep Wayne Rooney out of South Africa, as the young striker stayed at home to receive treatment on his medial knee injury. Moyes took the unprecedented action of accompanying Rooney to the medical examination at a Heathrow hotel after Sven Goran Eriksson demanded that Rooney report for duty despite the injury the teenager sustained against Manchester United a week earlier. The England coach's insistence on sending a copy of the scans of the injury to his head doctor Leif Sward implied that Eriksson did not trust Moyes's assertions that Rooney was genuinely injured. Moyes took club physio Mick Rathbone with him to Heathrow for the examination, while Rooney's agent Paul Stretford was also present along with Eriksson and the FA's medical team.

'I had never had that before,' observed the England coach. Moyes clearly felt vindicated when it was decided that the Everton striker would not fly out for the friendly in Durban. That undermined Eriksson's decision to take Moyes on over the youngster, in what he clearly saw as a matter of principle. In a statement the FA announced:

Wayne Rooney has had to withdraw from the England squad for the game in South Africa. The England medical staff, together with Everton's physio, assessed Wayne's knee injury and agreed that he should return to his club for treatment.

It was also agreed that Wayne will remain with Everton for the remainder of the week with a view to joining the England squad for the trip to La Manga. Sven Goran Eriksson and David Moyes were also present at the examination.

'Sven Loses Wayne-Nil' was the catchy *Daily Mirror* headline.

Until the headline-hitting issue with Rooney, David Moyes had been one of the Premiership's less influential figures. Yet Moyes refused to back down, irritating both Eriksson and the FA hierarchy with a daily series of telephone calls in which he insisted that Rooney must not link up with the squad. An FA insider even suggested that Moyes had been rude to Eriksson on the phone. However, even the FA conceded that they could appreciate Everton's concerns about their most valuable asset embarking on such a lengthy plane journey with no intention of playing.

The fact that Moyes was in the room with Eriksson as Rooney underwent his medical examination was even more proof of his unwillingness to back down.

The row refused to subside, with Eriksson confident that Rooney would recover in time to play in the crucial European Championship qualifier against Slovakia, while Moyes was far from sure about that. Rooney spent the next five days recuperating on Merseyside while the rest of the England squad had the opportunity to meet Nelson Mandela in Johannesburg on Wednesday, before playing the friendly international in Durban the following day.

Eriksson still hoped that Rooney would be fit enough to join the rest of the squad on the Friday for a six-day training camp in La Manga. Everton physio Mick Rathbone cast doubts on this when he said: 'Normally these things take three weeks to heal, but he's training comfortably with me. He's able to run in a straight line and we're happy with his progress. He remains doubtful for the game with Serbia and Montenegro on the third of June but he has a better chance for the game on the eleventh with Slovakia.'

Part of Moyes's case was one of potential double standards; he was angry that the FA had ordered a medical on Rooney, but did not make the same demand to Manchester United over midfielder Nicky Butt's ankle injury. Butt's injury was taken at face value and the United star was ordered to rest for the summer.

Out in South Africa, Eriksson remained optimistic Rooney would be fit for the qualifier and dismissed talk of a club-versus-country row, saying: 'It's been too much talking about it, but last Sunday we met together and our doctor said he will be fitter sooner if he practises every day.'

Michael Owen reassured Rooney that there was still all the time in the world to make his mark on international football, even though he had missed the friendly in South Africa that represented a chance to develop his budding strike partnership with Owen, which had shown early signs of promise against Turkey. He gave Rooney ample encouragement: 'There will be plenty of time for Wayne Rooney. He's probably got tons and tons of England caps to come. So I don't think we should be under any rush to risk him with his injury or whatever. There will be plenty of times to come, maybe even in this next month. We don't know whether he will be missing for all three games yet.'

As it turned out, Rooney did join up with the rest of the England squad for their La Manga training camp, though Moyes warned he might still be injured for the friendly with Serbia and Montenegro and the Euro clash with Slovakia eight days later: 'Wayne's injury might yet keep him out of the Serbia game. He's been running in a straight line but not kicking a ball, checking or turning. Hopefully he is fit but obviously England won't want to take a risk with him.'

Moyes attempted again to defuse any lingering suspicions of conflict with the England coach:

We were not trying to kid anybody on, which I would never do. I felt a little bit that people were disbelieving, but that is not how I work. I can only say that Wayne had an injury and I felt that Everton's integrity was being called into question.

It was a fact he was injured in the last game of the season and we did everything by the rules. We got Wayne checked out, then we attended the England medical last Sunday. We want him playing for England. Against everything people might think, it's a great honour for Wayne and for Everton.

I will do what is right with the player. That has always been my attitude, and people need now to trust me. I see Wayne every day in training and I think I know what's best for him. When I say he could do with a breather that's because I know it, and they need to trust me on it. I'm doing it for the right reasons.

There is no question of me trying to undermine England – far from it, I want to help England. In fact, nothing would please me more than to have five or six of my players in the England squad in the next few years. What manager wouldn't be proud to have the England number nine in their side? That's what I want, but I want it for years to come. I want what's best for Rooney.

The Everton manager wanted the England set-up to realise just how much of a talent they have, and work towards protecting him for the future:

We told the FA on the Sunday, straight after Wayne was injured against Manchester United, that he was struggling, and on the Monday we sent the scans to their specialist. They knew then that he couldn't possibly play, and yet somehow it seemed to get overlooked that he was injured, and they appeared to be even suggesting he could go to South Africa. The results of the scans were clear, and they knew exactly the extent of the injury.

And yet I felt that our integrity was being brought into question. I felt that they did not believe what we were saying, even though we gave them the clear evidence. Maybe it was because I said he shouldn't go to South Africa and a lot of people were probably thinking 'here's a manager pulling a fast one' – which wasn't the case.

I get on with Sven fine. But my position has not changed on the South Africa issue. A lot has been said in English football in recent years about the dangers of overplaying young players. We are supposed to be far more careful about how much we play them, and here was a young player going halfway around the world when he's tired after a long season.

We need help to protect Rooney. Suddenly, he's found out that everyone wants a piece of him. Everywhere he goes they want something from him.

Moyes also wondered how much help Eriksson would be asking for the following season in the preparation for the European Championship:

This time next year, I hope that England have qualified for Euro 2004. If they have, then are people going to be asking me to rest Wayne during the season so he'll be ready for them? You look at his performances last season, and he definitely felt it towards the end. We have to be careful with him. We are protecting him, and we hope everyone does. If they don't, well, we will carry on doing what is best for the lad, and that means over the course of his career, not just in the short term.

We don't need to push him now because, as he gets older, there will be loads more caps for him. We want him playing for England, but for a long time.

Moyes expected that Rooney's presence in La Manga would silence the critics who believed that his injury was a con. He also expected Eriksson would be sensible with his first-season professional, and ensure that he played only if he was 100 per cent fit. 'He is still injured, and he will have more treatment. But I would hope that if there's any doubt at all about him, he won't be risked. We really wouldn't want him to come back to Everton injured.'

Goodison physio Mick Rathbone kept in contact with his England counterpart Gary Lewin while Rooney was in Spain. Rathbone commented: 'Wayne is doing OK and we are in full agreement with the England people as regards the nature of the situation. He has been with us this week to do some light training and he is running comfortably.'

Oddly enough, the boy didn't look too badly injured when he was swinging a golf club at La Manga, shrugging off the row over his knee injury to show off his golf skills. He was the first to tee off after lunch in the England team hotel. Although he jumped in a new jet-ski style buggy to get between holes, he looked happy enough to test his damaged ligaments on the golf greens.

He was joined on the course by team-mates including Leeds keeper Paul Robinson and coach Ray Clemence. He was in good humour, laughing and joking as if he didn't have a care in the world. You wouldn't have thought he had just been caught in the middle of an almighty row between his manager and the FA. Ian Ross said: 'We feel confident that the England medical team would not allow Wayne Rooney to do anything that would jeopardise the recovery from his knee injury.'

The FA, naturally, issued their own statement. Adrian Bevington said: 'Any player who went to play golf, and that includes Wayne Rooney, only did so after getting permission from the physio.'

Rooney had earlier watched from the sidelines as his England team-mates took part in a gruelling training session in temperatures up in the high eighties. He worked out with physio Gary Lewin along with John Terry, while Rio Ferdinand and Paul Scholes did some light gym work. Steven Gerrard sat out training as part of his normal recovery period.

Next day by the pool at the Hyatt Regency, the centrepiece of the complex, the players and their girlfriends relaxed, Colleen stunning in a red bikini. Pictures of Wayne's already sun-tanned girlfriend inevitably made the front pages of the tabloids. In fact the pictures lasted for days: first Wayne had his kit on by the pool, then removed his shirt and lounged next to fellow Scouser Steven Gerrard and his girlfriend Alex Curran by the small and secluded La Cala beach. Naturally one shot of Wayne kissing Colleen provoked the front-page headline: 'Wayne Roodie'.

Day Two in La Manga and Rooney was off the golf course and back on the training pitch, taking part in his first major session since picking up his injury. Though he practised away from the main group, Rooney went through a rigorous hour-long work-out, whacking in shots with his left and right feet, and practising headers, twists and turns. He even went in goal. He certainly gave no hint that he was carrying an injury. FA spokesman Adrian Bevington said to the press who had travelled to Spain on England watch: 'Wayne is progressing well and the medics are delighted with the way things are going.'

Halfway through he jokingly collapsed to the ground in front of 250 holidaymakers as the FA invited fans into their training ground to watch the players go through their paces. In the sweltering sun many of the spectators chose to watch Rooney practising some 300 yards away with Chelsea's John Terry, even though the rest were training in front of them. One joker said: 'It's amazing how well Rooney can run now he's got Moyes off his back.'

Moyes was still urging that Rooney be handled with care, although he admitted the hotshot would play a larger role at Goodison next season. The Scot said: 'In most games he came on for thirty minutes – and was magnificent in a lot of them. Hopefully next season he will be magnificent for an hour.'

Moyes added: 'I always thought he was capable of that performance against Turkey . . . Those performances will become more regular as he gets stronger and fitter. But we have to be careful. He has lots and lots of games to come for Everton and lots more caps to come for England. If we think about that, he doesn't have to be pushed now.'

Back in La Manga, Rooney was involved in his first full training match and was on course to play a part in the final friendly with Serbia-Montenegro. Rooney was delighted to get involved in a ten-a-side game. He played the first half alongside James Beattie and replaced Emile Heskey on the opposing team in the second half to play as Michael Owen's partner. He did not score but looked as hungry as ever in the sixty-minute session.

Moyes gave his blessing for Rooney to resume his international career, saying, 'I want Wayne to play for England. I've no problems with him playing as long as he is fit and will be very pleased if he does get selected against Serbia and Montenegro. We have had another look at him and there is no problem with the injury. He is fit and I would love to see him start.'

The green light for Rooney also had the backing of former Liverpool goalscoring legend Ian Rush. Rush believed that if Rooney proved a success in England's next two games against Serbia and Slovakia he would become an even greater folk hero:

Wayne Rooney is still growing and still learning. But playing for England can only do him good and he will still get a month's rest after that. He will have plenty of time to get over these matches and this should not be a big problem in his development. Wayne has had a lot of pressures on him at just seventeen and sometimes you do want the lad to have a break.

Yet if Eriksson wants to pick him for experience, fair enough. Only time will tell if this will affect him in the future. Ryan Giggs was nurtured like that and Sir Alex Ferguson made sure he looked after him.

Rush insisted too much rest can have a demoralising effect on such a proven goalscorer: 'Any youngster gets itchy feet after a couple of weeks' rest. They just want to play football again. If you are fit, you want to play. I remember when I took my summer holidays in the sun, I was itching to play again after a week or so and was playing football with my kids. I don't think this will harm him because he will be getting experience and training with the world-class players in the squad.'

Rooney and Gerrard were inseparable during the six-day break in La Manga where they joked around on the golf course, relaxed with their respective partners on the beach and dined together in the evenings. Gerrard said: 'He's a nice kid. We get on like a house on fire and we speak at least two or three times a week on the phone.'

A far cry from their first meeting in December 2002, when the two almost came to blows as the Merseyside derby erupted after Gerrard took out Everton's Gary Naysmith with a late tackle, which almost sparked a mass brawl and saw Rooney run virtually the length of the pitch to confront the Liverpool man. The two players came close to blows before team-mates intervened and separated them.

Club rivalry was put to one side, however when they crossed paths again after Rooney was called up against Turkey. Gerrard said:

When we first met there was a bit of aggro during the Merseyside derby and he got involved. But Rooney is a Scouser like me. We have been brought up in similar backgrounds and I'm not into holding grudges. So I got very close to him when we met up with the England squad prior to the Turkey game. I wouldn't say I went out of my way, it was more a natural thing because he's a local boy. If I ignored him – and that's not really me – who was going to break the ice?

I wanted to make sure he didn't feel alone, lost and in his room on his own. I wanted to make sure he felt comfortable and got out. So I just went up to his room, gave his door a knock and swapped a few DVDs and CDs with him. I sat and had a few meals with him, played computer games and watched some films. I guess I just got to know him, really. I have always felt that the better you get on with people off the pitch, the better you get on with them on it.

I know what it's like coming into the England camp when you're young – it's really difficult. You don't really know anybody and you walk around with a vacant expression on your face. You're in awe of some of the players. They are the best, and the nearest you've come to them in the past is briefly in a game.

You don't talk to them. Most of them are older and well established and you're some young scallywag who has just been called up. It can be frightening and intimidating. You come in, you're shy and you don't have a clue what to say. The thing is you're away from your family and in a room on your own. You maybe train for two hours and then you have to keep yourself occupied for the rest of the day.

It's even worse when you're away for a period of time. You're maybe stuck in a hotel room for five or six days and it can be extremely boring. It's important you make friends. I was lucky because there were four other Liverpool players in the squad when I came in and Michael Owen took me under his wing – as I have with Wayne, I guess. I also became close to Gareth Barry and once I got through a couple of tough get-togethers I felt far more at ease.

People assumed that because I play for Liverpool and he plays for Everton there would be friction between us. They maybe thought there would be a few snarls, a few things said. It was bit like this crap about Liverpool players clashing with the Manchester United lads. I never saw it – it was rubbish.

Of course you tend to knock about with players from your own club because you know them so well, but that doesn't mean you hate the others and take that rivalry into the camp.

Of course, when I go out on to the pitch I want to stuff Everton with or without Wayne Rooney in the side, and that's natural. Prior to the recent get-together me, Richard Wright, Danny Murphy and Wayne went out to the pictures together. Where is the rivalry when two Everton and two Liverpool players go out together? People should put all that rivalry stuff to bed. I watch films with Manchester United lads. Everyone mixes, it's good for team morale.

Gerrard was stunned by Rooney's talent:

He's special, the best around. He's got it all at such a young age. There is ability and then there is Rooney. His talent is frightening. He's not as good as people think – he's better. Everton are extremely lucky to have him and they should do everything in their power to make sure they keep hold of him.

I'd seen bits and pieces on him, read this and that and heard other people talk about him. But I tend to judge as I find. In the week leading up to the Turkey game I thought, 'England have got a jewel here.' When you think he's only seventeen and Michael Owen is twenty-two, it bodes well for England's future.

He's a really quiet kid, extremely confident with a ball at his feet, but shy without it. He's not just a quiet lad with the media, he's quiet around me and other players. He's coming out of his shell a bit but he's not very talkative. But the better you get to know him the more relaxed he feels.

Brian Clough, however, voiced his concerns and could not help having his say again from his retirement:

Wayne is the talk of the town and he was terrific against the Turks, but there is a long way to go from the age of seventeen to twenty-five when he should be close to the finished product. He should stop eating all those sausages, eggs and chips meals for a start. It is good, working-class food as I know from personal experience, but no good when you are as solidly built as this lad. He'll have to work hard to stay in shape. That's much more than remembering to spit out your chewing gum and do up your tie when picking up your latest award.

The odds against Rooney making it to the top and staying there are high, so he needs to know about all those potential teenage greats who became unknowns. It's not the boy's fault he's overexposed, but he'll find that growing up painfully in the public eye is the price to be paid. He appears to be tough and he'll need to be. Everybody who cares about the lad has to protect him and nurture him. Our game needs heroes like him.

The next day Rooney strolled around the La Manga complex with a £13 Chucka-Chucka giant lolly. Could that have been his boyish way of laughing at Clough's remarks?

The England party returned from their 'family' get-together, and reconvened for the more serious preparation business without wives or girlfriends and kids in tow at their Leicestershire HQ. Rooney was not handed a first-team bib, indicating that Emile Heskey would start alongside his club-mate Owen, captain in the absence of Beckham. According to Eriksson: 'If they [Owen and Rooney] are a couple for the future, it would be good to play them together, but Heskey has done very well.'

But there were no special words of encouragement for the youngest member of the squad from the stand-in skipper. Michael Owen was stepping in for David Beckham, and everybody expected him to have had a special word with Rooney. But the Liverpool man was reluctant to try and force his own experience on Rooney. When asked if he had offered Rooney any advice, Owen said: 'No, I am not going to say to him this or that happened to me, but if he asked me then no problem. I'd tell anyone what I thought, but I'd hate to try and impose my experiences on people.'

As for teaming up with Rooney, he added: 'I haven't played properly with him yet. We started against Turkey, but I was knackered after ten minutes with my back. I'll tell you after I've played with him properly.'

This would have to wait for at least one more match, as Rooney came off the bench to replace Owen for the second half against Serbia and Montenegro, playing at Leicester. But for a fingertip save he might have collected his first England goal.

Eriksson used 21 players at the Walkers Stadium, and had four different captains as he exercised all his options. It was a frustrating night for England as Gerrard gave them the lead, only for Serbia and Montenegro to equalize through a scrambled effort from Nenad Jestrovic on the stroke of half-time.

Eriksson made five half-time changes, arguing that he needed to take off Ashley Cole, Gerrard, Scholes, Southgate and Owen to protect them from injury. 'They will provide the base of the team against Slovakia and I couldn't afford to have any of them injured,' he explained.

The introduction of Wayne Bridge, Owen Hargreaves, John Terry, Jermaine Jenas and Rooney gave more of an edge to England's game. Eriksson's answer to those questioning the validity of another night of serial substitutions was justified, but only just, by the second-half contributions from Cole and Rooney.

The bullish, muscular presence of young Rooney clearly unsettled the Serbian defence. He had two good shots but was easily provoked by shirt-tugging defenders. But though he was given a hard time by the aggressive Vidic, and came close to losing his temper, it did not prevent him demonstrating his potential. The young player gave Eriksson a scare when he needed treatment on his right ankle after a heavy challenge, but he was able to carry on.

Joe Cole finally came to England's rescue with his first goal for his country, a stunning 25-yard free kick in the 83rd minute. David Beckham would have been proud of it.

Four straight wins suggested the right preparation to beat Slovakia, and Eriksson accepted that he faced growing public clamour for Rooney to start, as he had already reached 'hero' status among many fans desperate for some urgency and creativity in the side: 'I know that he's becoming a big hero among the fans and that's very fair. We'll see whether he starts. I don't want to tell the formation for next week yet.'

Eriksson remained an admirer of the more experienced Liverpool forward Emile Heskey, who lost his place against Turkey, but admitted: 'The quality that Rooney has is incredible. The first time I picked him, I was asked why. I said that when he gets the ball, he makes things happen. Not every time but many times when he gets the ball, he can beat people, sees the pass or makes a shot.'

Eriksson accepted that the teenager inevitably still had much to learn, including how to control his temper, as he responded to one foul on him by quickly exacting a measure of revenge with a similarly late tackle. 'Of course, he still has a lot to learn as he's only seventeen years old. You can't expect one seventeen-year-old boy to be a perfect young man in every sense. I think he's shy and of course if you're seventeen and the manager of a country wants to talk to you, it can't be easy so I never force him to do something like that.'

Cole stands as a warning to Rooney that genuine natural talent is not necessarily enough to avoid a dip in form after making an impressive start to a young career. The former West Ham midfielder, who moved to Chelsea in summer 2003, made his own England debut in May 2001, but he has struggled to establish himself and has failed to become a regular for both club and country.

Cole had started just one senior game, against Cameroon before the World Cup, but Eriksson believed he represented the future of the team – as long as he learned to restrict his tricks to the final third of the pitch. 'It's very individual. You never know what's happening physically and mentally. Coping with being famous is not the easiest thing in the world when you are young,' he observed. 'But Wayne Rooney seems very confident and keeps his feet on the ground so far.'

Indeed, Rooney's only real handicap was a lack of experience alongside Owen, although Eriksson was not overly worried by that. Answering criticism that the pair had not played together, Eriksson explained: 'We could have done that, but we still have four practices left. John Terry and Wayne Rooney are coming back from injury and haven't had a lot of football work lately so we started with Emile Heskey and Matthew Upson.'

It seemed highly unlikely, though, that Rooney would be starting from the bench against Slovakia.

17

Long Way to Go

'It is dangerous for me, the crowd and the critics to expect him to be the best player on the pitch every time he plays for England. He is only seventeen and one of the biggest talents I have worked with and he will go on getting better and better and will stay in the England side, for sure. I am so happy he is English.'

— Sven Goran Eriksson

The 2002–03 season was building towards a crescendo for Rooney, almost eleven months after it began for him. In May 2002 Rooney had been involved in the build-up to the FA Youth Cup. Spin twelve months further forward and it was another build-up, but to a crucial Euro 2004 qualifier against Slovakia. It was the perfect illustration of how life had changed for the teenager.

But as with life, everything is not always rosy for footballers and, perhaps just in the nick of time, Rooney was given a harsh lesson in what the reality of playing among the best is about.

His rise had been meteoric, but maturity needed to go with it, and after his cameo second-half role against Serbia and Montenegro, where he slightly lost his head, Sven Goran Eriksson was concerned about young Rooney's temperament. Rooney had been sent off once and booked eight times in his debut season.

As the England manager said: 'I normally talk about discipline before every game, especially a qualifying match because it is very important we have eleven players on the pitch for ninety minutes. When we don't have that you have a big, big handicap. And I will probably talk to Wayne about this. I know we all have different characters and it's the same with football players.

'You can never say there are two exactly the same. Some are short-fused, others never get angry, but Wayne is one of those with a short fuse. I don't know why, you have to accept the character of the man, the character of the boy.'

As Rooney prepared for his fifth England cap, Manchester United legend Norman Whiteside – the youngest player to grace the World Cup finals when he appeared for Northern Ireland at Spain in 1982, aged just 17 years and 41 days – gave his advice. He had also gained a quick-won reputation as being a hard man, but insisted that aggression will keep Rooney at the top. Whiteside said: 'It helps if you've got that devilment. Roy Keane has also got a lot of devilment about him – you need that to be at the top level. Rooney is the type of player who's going to find himself in trouble with referees at times because he's got that nasty streak, which top players need. He's got that little bit of edge. I remember when I was seventeen, I was soon protecting myself.'

On the flip side, former England skipper Terry Butcher said Rooney must cut out his 'macho man' approach. Butcher, 45, won fame as a blood-stained hero during his playing days. But he reckons Rooney is in danger of becoming too bogged down by the physical aspects of the game. As the former Ipswich central defender pointed out before the Slovakia game: 'Wayne is trying to stamp his mark on senior football and sometimes you can be too impetuous. But Wayne's aggression is not necessarily a bad fault and if he is aware of it he will stop it. You can try to be a bit *too* keen, *too* macho.'

Butcher claims Rooney could have no better role model than his England strike partner: 'Rooney can look at Michael Owen. He doesn't stick his foot in here or his shoulder in there. He's done it with his pace and his intelligence – and Rooney can do the same. He needn't leave his foot in or fight the physical battles against the big guys when there is no need to do it.

'But that's just youthful naivety and exuberance. Sometimes you can just get carried away. That said, I *do* think Rooney should play against Slovakia rather than Emile Heskey. Rooney would excite me more because of his movement and pace.'

The measure of how far Rooney had come, though, was that there seemed no doubt that he would start the game, however well Emile Heskey had been doing.

Eriksson wanted his team to get the ball to Rooney and Paul Scholes at every opportunity, as he knew they would be the danger men.

'Scholes is one of the most important players we have, a fantastic player,' said the Swedish coach. 'He links the team play and we like Paul to have the ball because we know when he has it things will happen. Rooney is the same – give him the ball and I know things will happen for us.'

Eriksson was not perturbed that Rooney had not played much alongside Michael Owen. It was a major criticism after the match against Serbia and Montenegro that, if Rooney and Owen were his number one strike force, then perhaps they should be played together instead of in different halves. Eriksson, who does sometimes have some strange explanations, said: 'We talked and thought about playing him with Owen in the recent friendly, but it was more important to avoid injuries than have players playing together. We have four practice matches before the Slovakia game and if they are going to play together they can play together during the practice sessions.'

He added:

When I think back to Fiorentina and the players I had at seventeen who went into the first team, [I had] Roberto Baggio . . . Rui Costa plus others and they all went on to have very big careers. I can't see any reason why Wayne Rooney shouldn't have the same sort of career, certainly of someone like Baggio – and that would not be too bad at all.

When you are seventeen and are looking ahead, over the next five years you should be better in everything, even if you don't have to improve that much.

The one thing you can't teach a player is experience, of the Premier League and of international football. You must get that for yourself. Everyone needs to make their own mistakes. It's when you get hurt or bang your head against a wall that you learn it hurts.

Eriksson had every confidence in Rooney, which must have been a huge boost for the lad. 'In training or in a match the way he plays is very mature. He's a great talent, very clever, he can see things and he's a good finisher . . . He always has a nice smile and he gets on with the other players. He doesn't have any fear about playing football. If it's a local or national game it doesn't matter. He's very strong in that way. I like him very much. He can play up front on his own but he's good when he drops and turns people.'

Rooney, as predicted, replaced Emile Heskey in the only change from the side that started the win over Serbia and Montenegro. Eriksson seemed to feel that Rooney was the natural link man he had been searching for since he took over England:

> Heskey and Michael Owen have dropped off from the front for us, and when Teddy Sheringham played he did it very well. You can't say Heskey and Wayne Rooney are the same type of player. Rooney plays more than Heskey does. Heskey is stronger up there, fighting for the ball with the central defenders.
>
> But Rooney is maybe more natural in that role. He can do it and it's very important to have that type of player, especially when the distance between attackers and midfielders becomes too big.
>
> If we have to defend a lot in a game, with the defenders and midfielders all back, I don't like to see us having two men up front and getting isolated. You want to keep one up there to keep two of their defenders occupied. But the other one should try to look for space so when we win the ball, we can play it in to him as soon as possible.

This seemed to be a Merseyside partnership that Eriksson found just as mouthwatering as any England supporter. Owen, at 23, was due to become the youngest Englishman to win fifty caps against Slovakia. Eriksson said: 'I can understand the excitement about them. They are two young golden boys. It is a great story to tell. They can play together and I understand why people want to see it. I'm as excited as anyone about Owen and Rooney playing together.

'The country should be very happy you have them. They are fantastic strikers. I can't say whether Rooney will be as good as Owen, but he is another of the great talents. They can have a fantastic partnership and the great thing is they are very young.'

Owen took over as the country's youngest goalscorer in 1998 when he netted against Morocco at the age of 18 years and 164 days. Rooney was only 17 years and 230 days old before the

Slovakia game so he had every chance of breaking that mark at The Riverside.

Eriksson added: 'It's difficult to compare them. One is twenty-three with fifty caps, the other is seventeen with only four. I've no idea if Wayne will be better than Michael, it might be like that. Rooney is one of those great talents and Michael can maybe play for another ten years.'

Owen, though, had no doubt what would happen to all of his records: 'I would be delighted if he scores to break my record. But he's probably going to beat more than one record of mine, more than just the youngest goalscorer record. I'll become the youngest player to get fifty caps, but he started even younger than me, so he could take that off me.'

The win over Turkey had been arguably England's most cohesive performance under Eriksson. Whereas in the famous victories against Germany and Argentina they won on the counterattack, at Sunderland England had forced the pace against a quality team. Liverpool midfielder Steven Gerrard revealed: 'Wayne and Michael worked together in training and they looked terrific. We know it will take time because they're both young and haven't really played together, but I think they will develop into a top-class partnership.

'I think we've discovered the best way of playing now. It's definitely working at the moment. We maybe can't play the diamond every game. It might not work against Argentina or Germany, but that's something we have to look at in the first ten or fifteen minutes of a game.'

Eriksson had already earmarked Rooney and Owen to spearhead the challenge for the European Championship finals and the 2006 World Cup. Owen said:

There is massive potential for us as a partnership. You can never look too far ahead but there is a possibility we could stay together for England for a long time, maybe the next ten years. There are a lot of other England strikers who will come into the reckoning, and deservedly so, and the current and future England managers might have their own ideas about who should play up front.

I have only seen Wayne play a few times but there was one incident against Turkey which told me a lot about him. He picked up the ball on the left and went on a run which took him past a couple of defenders. Everyone was expecting him to shoot but he played a pass through to me, which unfortunately the keeper got to first. However, the move said a lot about his vision and awareness.

We are different as players but that is a good thing because we can complement each other. I have become more of a penalty-box player, pushing right up on the last defender and getting on the end of moves. Wayne is more of an all-rounder. He can score goals but does a lot more work outside the box. He can go past people as well as being able to shoot from long range. He has also got strength and explosive pace, which reminds me of Alan Shearer. He has also got some of Alan's determination and is difficult to shake off the ball.

Wayne is a quiet lad and is still finding his way around the international scene ... Wayne has only played around thirty-five times for Everton and many of those were as a substitute and he still has a lot to prove. But you have to trust the evidence of your own eyes and from what I have seen Wayne is the real thing.

He is one of a new wave of youngsters who are coming through the ranks like Joe Cole, Jermaine Jenas, John Terry, Jermain Defoe and James Beattie and I am sure there will be others. The future looks very bright for England.

Despite Rooney himself not being put up for interview by the FA, everybody was still talking about him. Gareth Southgate was concerned about the unforgiving glare in which Rooney was having to develop. Southgate said: 'I was fortunate to grow up without the intrusive spotlight on my private life and asking a seventeen-year-old to deal with all that must be incredibly difficult.'

Southgate believed Rooney could carve himself a role as England's new Teddy Sheringham by forming a similarly explosive partnership with Owen, as Sheringham did with Shearer during the days of Euro 96. Rooney filled the role for a significant part of the training session a few days before playing Slovakia. The Middlesbrough defender observed: 'Wayne came into the game against Turkey and played particularly well. He offers a different style of play to Darius or Emile because of how he plays. He drops in deep and looks more of a Teddy Sheringham type of player, going deeper into midfield areas and linking the play very well.

'Darius and Emile are possibly more comfortable further forward and don't have the attributes which Wayne has. It's a case of which style the manager feels is spot-on for which game.'

The game against Slovakia on 11 June was one that England were expected to win, yet never had they fielded a weaker side in a competitive game under Eriksson. A midfield including Phil Neville and Frank Lampard and a central defence of Gareth Southgate and Matthew Upson was a long way from the manager's preferred options.

As it turned out, the senior member of the young strike force grabbed a double to rescue a poor England performance. After a free kick by Vladimir Janocko from distance sailed over the defence and beat James by his left-hand post in the 31st minute, Owen won a controversial 62nd-minute penalty, which he tucked away coolly before bagging the winner seventeen minutes from time as he nipped in to head home a glorious chipped pass from Gerrard.

Rooney, who was substituted in the 57th minute, discovered that life with England is not so easy. When he lost the ball because of poor control, he took his frustrations out on Vladimir Labant as Labant was trying to break forward. It was another example of his suspect temperament.

As Eriksson headed off on his summer holidays – having secured a fifth straight win that had put England back on track for the decisive Euro 2004 qualifying clash in Turkey in October – he jumped to Rooney's defence: 'I am happy with what he did. It is dangerous for me, the crowd and the critics to expect him to be the best player on the pitch every time he plays for England. That is absolutely not fair . . . He is one of the biggest talents I have worked with and he will go on getting better and better and will stay in the England side, for sure. I am so happy he is English.'

Owen was also quick to stick up for his young strike partner who looked tired from his long season:

I thought he did well. There's a lot of pressure on young players nowadays. Some can handle it and some can't, and he looks as if he's

handling it really well. He played well tonight. It was a big game, and he
and Darius Vassell did well. We expect a lot of anyone. It wasn't long ago
that Joe Cole burst on the scene and people were saying he was the next
Gazza.

I'm sure he will go on to be a great player. I'm not going to say that
Wayne is being built up too much because I think he is a fantastic player.

I said 'Well done' to him. I think everyone was pleased with the way he
performed. He held the ball up well, had a lot of movement and kept the
ball. I thought he had a good game. Do we need to have patience? I know
that and the manager knows that. It's the outside that doesn't seem to
show that patience. If everyone realises that patience is important, we
could have a fantastic player. But it's not easy.

Typically, just as Rooney was perhaps disappointing for England
after his brilliant performance against Turkey, Sky were running
the first documentary on the wonder kid. The producers had
promised to handle the film with 'kid gloves' sensitivity to appease
the volatile Moyes.

Wayne's World did not intrude into areas that Moyes would make
a huge fuss about. A Sky spokesman said: 'The producers have been
careful not to intrude into Wayne's life and have made the show with
sensitivity towards the protections given to the player. The producers
have not approached the player for an interview.' Well, it would
hardly have been worth the price of a telephone call, considering
Moyes's ban on Rooney talking to the media.

ZigZag Productions are experienced in football documentaries,
having previously made *Football Years* and *Teddy Sheringham . . .
Close Up*. The Sky One documentary, *Rooney: Wayne's World*,
went out an hour after the Slovakia game finished. The documentary
examined 'the rise to fame of the most talked about teenager in a
generation'. The programme was a positive look at the 'incredible
last four months of Rooney's career' since his goal-scoring
substitute appearance against Arsenal at Goodison Park in a 2–1 win.

Everton legend Neville Southall, interviewed on the programme,
talked of his fears that the Toffees could lose Rooney when England
team-mates try to lure the youngster away to bigger clubs. The
former Wales keeper felt pressure from international pals could see

the lad tempted away from the club he loves: 'When he goes away with England, another player will tap him up. That's what goes on. Whether it be another player saying, "Do you want to come to play for us? You get this and you get that and you get this and we're in this and we're in that." You know, people talk.'

Rooney's performance was a disappointing conclusion to the season for the teenager, watched in the stands by his manager and his family, who had driven across from Merseyside and turned up two hours before the game. But at the end of what had been an incredible season for a lad who only turned seventeen during the campaign, his club manager, who knows him best, was proved right. This was one game too far for Rooney, who may have benefited from being around the international scene, but had also looked tired and just slightly out of his depth.

There seemed no doubt Rooney would be an international star, whose future will probably rival that of David Beckham. But there is also a need for restraint, and he is lucky that he has a manager like David Moyes. As a result of Rooney's elongated season, the compassionate Everton boss decided to give his young prodigy an extra week off before returning to pre-season training for the 2003–04 season.

Moyes admitted it had been an arduous introduction into the ranks of professional football for the young player: 'Wednesday's game against Slovakia was another big step for Wayne in his career. It has been a really long season for him and we now need to look after him and make sure he gets the opportunity to have a proper rest and recharge his batteries. We won't ask him to report for training for a full month. That gives him a week longer than the other lads who were not involved in international matches after the end of the season.'

Rooney picked up another slight knock during the Slovakia game, but Moyes confirmed it was not connected in any way with the knee injury that prevented the youngster from going to South Africa with the England squad in May. He added: 'We had a fax from England straight after the game which told us everything was fine.'

Rooney-mania was bound to continue and just get bigger and better though. The young kid could only improve from the fantastic player he already was. And if anybody needed any sign of how the Rooney saga will run and run, a day after the Slovakia game Everton suspended the sale of season tickets, as the club broke through the 27,000 mark.

A cap was placed on season-ticket sales for the first time in Everton's 125-year history as the club wished to have 10,000 tickets freely available on a match-by-match basis for supporters who, for whatever reason, were unable to purchase a season ticket.

The 2003–04 campaign was going to be a record breaker in terms of season-ticket sales, surpassing the club's previous best achieved in 1996–97. Rooney-mania goes on and on, as the new golden boy of English football was on course to write a fresh chapter to his sensational story with every game he plays. But nobody could imagine what was to follow in the next season.

Rooney had the last word on an incredible season as he explained in very simplistic terms how his life would never be the same again:

> I'd like to just wander round unrecognised with all my mates and just do my own thing. I just can't do some of the things they do. I had to stop. I've had to make sacrifices but it's definitely worth it. I wouldn't change a thing.
>
> I still see my old mates and we hang around together in the same way we always have done. I sometimes get asked for autographs, but when we stay local it's not too bad. I can be standing around and a car will stop and someone asks for my autograph. My mates get used to it now and don't give me too much stick.

There we go. Wayne Rooney at seventeen – England, Everton and Croxteth hero.

But little did he know he was about to make an even bigger impact on Europe than he could ever imagine.

18

Record Breaker

Wayne Rooney was always going to become the youngest ever goalscorer for England once he was given his debut. But nobody would ever have believed how grateful England would be for the goal.

Wayne Rooney may have been the darling of England, but when it came to going back to Everton last summer it was a different story. His first blistering season was always going to be a tough act to follow for a player who had still not yet got over his growing pains. With the burden of expectation for club and country slapped firmly on his shoulders, he had a lot to live up to.

David Moyes was at first uncertain how to handle his young prodigy. Having seen him taken to South Africa with England against his wishes, he did not want to throw him in the deep end immediately at the start of the 2003–04 season. Right through the year there remained questions about his fitness, which is why he arrived at Euro 2004 carrying a bit of weight. But Moyes did not exactly inspire confidence in the youngster by not starting him in Everton's first game of the season against Fulham.

His first-choice partnership was Kevin Campbell and Tomasz Radzinski, and of course there was Duncan Ferguson also to contend with. The fact Everton won 3–1 meant Moyes was vindicated, and Rooney had to be content with a place on the bench.

It would not be far wrong to say that this was probably the high point of Everton's season, as nothing really went right after that. Moyes seemed unsure during the campaign as to how to get the talented teenager into the side. He wanted to use his experienced strikers, but also give Rooney a run. As a result, though, Rooney was never really given an extended run in his most natural position as he was shunted all round the team. At times, in a bid to get Radzinski and Ferguson in the starting line-up, Rooney was used on the right side of midfield, which was obviously a waste of his god-given talent. Then, in other games, Rooney would be played just behind the two strikers because of the youngster's versatility.

What it meant was that the eighteen-year-old struggled to score goals because he could never find any real consistency. That and the fact Everton started the season so poorly that it was soon clear that they would have to face up to another relegation battle. It had looked like those days were behind Everton, as Moyes's arrival had galvanised the side into a seventh-place finish at the end of 2003. Those heights were never to be repeated last season as it was a constant battle for points.

Just like Rooney, Moyes himself had a lot left to prove and did not find it easy considering his hands were tied – the fact was he had no real money to spend. He had tried to buy Fulham's Sean Davis at the start of the season, hoping the talented midfielder would provide more of a constant supply line for Rooney. But the £5m deal fell through at the last minute because of the player's injury picked up in pre-season, and apart from taking former Evertonian Francis Jeffers on loan from Arsenal, Everton were unable to strengthen the side.

Although Rooney managed to pick up more bookings than he did goals in the Premiership, nine goals against ten yellow cards, many Everton fans felt that without Rooney's vital strikes, Everton would have been facing up to life in the newly named Coca Cola League Championship. His fiery temperament and suspensions will always remain a problem for Rooney, but the Kid only knows one way to play football.

His first goal of the season came in front of a watching Sven Goran Eriksson at The Valley. Rooney had only started the game because Kevin Campbell had a hamstring injury and Duncan Ferguson was suspended. As it was he scored a spectacular equaliser that showed the summer off had not dulled his talent. The game ended 2–2, but all the news reports were about Rooney's goal.

Moyes though, was still not happy with how best to deploy his marked man, and the feeling at Everton was that Rooney was becoming frustrated with the shackles being put on him. As a result, it was no surprise that he found his freedom playing for England.

Rooney was always destined to become the youngest ever goalscorer for England once he was given his debut at such an early age. But nobody would ever have believed how grateful England would be for the goal.

Though Rooney had been left out of the friendly at the start of the 2003–04 season against Croatia due to injury, his stunning goal at Charlton in August 2003 meant Eriksson could not avoid picking him for the double-header European Championship qualifying games against Macedonia and Liechtenstein. The game in Skopje on 6 September was always going to be a hostile one, and before the match many people felt it would be a step too far for Rooney and that Emile Heskey would be the better option. But Eriksson desperately needed a victory and he has incredible faith in the youngster. Just before the game he had a brief word with Rooney, to make sure the kid was OK, but Rooney was not fazed by the intimidating atmosphere or the fact the Macedonian fans burned a flag of St George.

But, as the players left the pitch at half-time, the Swede must have been cursing himself. England were a goal down in a game they had to win, and Rooney had had his worst 45 minutes in an England shirt. Eriksson thought quickly, and knowing he needed goals he asked Rooney if he had ever played in the hole behind two strikers. Rooney answered, 'No, but I'll have a go.' That was good enough for Sven.

Heskey replaced Frank Lampard, and with almost his first touch he headed the ball down for Rooney to drift in and score. It was what dreams are made of as the teenager peeled away to the small bank of England fans in the stadium. He was 17 years and 317 days old, and the youngest ever player to score for England. Victory was won with a David Beckham penalty, and Rooney left the pitch a hero.

When Rooney walked through the area where the journalists were waiting, he had his head down and was clutching his Burberry washbag, seeming almost embarrassed by what he had done. The first thing he did on the coach was phone his great Everton mate, Francis Jeffers, to find out what he thought. Rooney was more concerned with how he had played in the first half than with the goal he had scored, but like any youngster he was looking for reassurance. A statement he released said: 'It was great to get a goal and break the record, and I hope it will be the first of many in an England shirt. But it was important to get the win.'

It was left to his skipper to sum up what Rooney's first strike would mean; David Beckham said in the aftermath of the game:

> Everyone knows what a great player Wayne is. People talk about his age, but when you can perform like that, play like that and you're scoring goals like that, he deserves to be in the team. He's a strong character, he's a strong player, and has a strong club behind him. It's good for him to break records, especially so early in his career. I think he enjoyed his goal; we all did, because it got us back in the game. Wayne's got that weight off his mind, and confidence is the biggest thing it's going to give him now. It is important to get the first goal out of the way, especially as a striker . . . But his performances help the team, and he doesn't have to score every week. He works hard, puts himself about, and when you've got a player like that in your team, playing up front with Emile Heskey or Michael Owen, you're going to go places.

. . . Hopefully to Euro 2004.

Having seen what a great job Rooney had done in Skopje, Eriksson could not help but pick him to play against Liechtenstein at Old Trafford a few days later, on 10 September. He played Rooney in the hole again, and the wonder kid was an absolute star. He looked like he had been playing there all his life. The fans and press could not quite believe what they were seeing, and just as Beckham had predicted, he scored again. This time it was England's second of the night as Michael Owen had grabbed the opener. But the 67,000-strong crowd went wild over Rooney. He was given a standing ovation as he left the pitch, and he won the Man of the Match award.

Words are not enough to explain the impact of Rooney. But his team-mates cannot stop eulogising about him. There is no doubt that it is the players themselves who have been stunned more than anyone by what the kid can do. As Manchester United and England star Gary Neville said:

It's difficult talking about Rooney. People try to shield seventeen- and eighteen-year-olds, but sometimes you can't when they perform like that. His performance against Turkey in his first start was nothing short of exceptional to be honest with you, and I don't think we can talk about his age any more. This is an international football player, who will only get better. His strength, his understanding of the game, and his awareness, are fantastic.

Some players you can give the ball to when it's tight and they're the best ones; you just want to give it them and they'll turn, they'll jink out of a hole. He's got the ability to beat players. He's got that raw enthusiasm where every time he gets [the ball], he wants to do something special. He won't have that when he's 28, so we'll use it now when he's seventeen, because he's fantastic.

Wayne's not an emotional lad. He was happy on Saturday after his goal, but that was it.

As one of Rooney's best friends on the England scene, Steven Gerrard is at the moment someone who knows him best. The Liverpool midfielder's comments just about sum up the super-kid: 'He has got everything. He can go past people. He can pass. He can score goals and make them for others. He can cause havoc.'

Then came the real test of a seventeen-year-old's nerve. England faced the prospect of going to Istanbul needing a draw to qualify for Euro 2004.

Everybody knows what an intimidating place Turkey can be for visiting teams. But this was even worse because of the security fears. The Football Association were so terrified of there being violent clashes at the game – which could have risked their participation in Euro 2004 – that they refused their ticket allocation for the match. It was not a universally popular decision, but one which people understood. But it just heaped more pressure on the players because it meant they were entering a hostile environment without any of their own supporters.

It's hard to imagine how Rooney must have felt. At only seventeen he was being placed in a vicious, scary atmosphere that would be enough to intimidate the best players in the world.

Not Rooney. It is part of his character that he is not fazed by what goes on around him. He has proved time and again that playing for England for him is like playing for a Sunday league team – not because he does not care, it is just that he loves football and he trys to keep it simple.

England certainly kept it simple in October 2003. The greatest drama surrounded David Beckham's missed penalty. He lost his footing and skied the ball over the crossbar with the scores at 0–0 – not unlike his later miss against Portugal. Then came a tunnel bust-up at half-time after Turkish and Aston Villa defender Alpay had a row with Becks. As ever with these situations, pictures and footage are hard to come by. But the suggestion was that Rooney waded in to help support his skipper. It is the response you would expect from a kid who has grown up on the tough streets of Liverpool, and the scuffle was over quickly.

But Rooney was superb up front, and the whole team managed to get through the game with the draw that they desperately needed. As part of the protective shield being put around Rooney by the FA, the press was not allowed to speak to him after the game, as he was whisked away from the stadium with the rest of the squad under armed guard. The performance was up there with those against Germany in Munich when they won 5–1, and against Argentina in the World Cup when David Beckham's penalty had earned a 1–0 victory.

With life starting to become a struggle at Everton for Rooney, joining up with England was a pleasure because it meant he could get away from the pressure of a relegation battle. The next opportunity came in November when England played against Denmark at Old Trafford. It was a chance for the England fans to congratulate their side for the fantastic performance in Turkey, and it was also an occasion for them to hail their new hero Rooney. His impact had been so immense that his profile was starting to overtake that of even Beckham, famous all around the world.

Off the pitch life had been changing for Rooney. He could no longer stroll the streets as he had done only months before. He had to be protected from the paparazzi and the obvious interest in his private life.

On the pitch though, things did not change. Rooney responded to the fans' support by scoring the first goal against Denmark. It was a fantastic shot from the edge of the area, and smashed past goalkeeper Thomas Sorensen. Unfortunately for England, though, they lost the game 3–2, but it just did not seem to matter.

Back at Everton it was life on the bench. In fact, out of 38 possible league games, he only appeared in 26, 8 of which were as substitute, which just shows how sparingly he was used. His response at Christmas was to fight tooth and nail to try and make sure that he forced his way back into the team. And the way he did that was by scoring three goals in four games.

But it was not all manager David Moyes's fault. The impact of what had happened to Rooney in the past twelve months had to bite at some point, and this was it. His form had not been scintillating, and as a result Moyes was refusing to start him, in a bid to prove that he was bigger as Everton boss than Rooney-mania and the clamour for his automatic inclusion.

Against Portsmouth at Fratton Park on 13 December 2003, Rooney came on in right midfield for the injured Steve Watson. Jason Roberts had given Pompey the lead, only for Lee Carsley to equalise. But then Rooney intervened. Pavel Srnicek flapped at a Gary Naysmith cross and Rooney was on hand to drive the ball home. It proved to be the winner, and secured Everton's first win away from home since April 2003.

What was even stranger was that during the game Rooney thought he had been sent off. Referee Uriah Rennie pulled him up in the 72nd minute for pushing Steve Stone. Rooney had started to walk to the tunnel expecting a red, but then Kevin Campbell pulled him back because he only received a yellow. It was typical of the drama that surrounds Rooney, but he did not seem that bothered, although Moyes was angry with him for getting involved in the first place.

He was on a good run, though, and a week later he came off the bench to score against Leicester as he helped his side to a 3–2 win over the Foxes, with Tomasz Radzinski grabbing the vital goal.

He was at it again a week later as Moyes still declined to give him his head. This time against Birmingham he came on at half-time, which was an admission from the manager that he got his team selection wrong. There was nothing more Rooney could do than find the net, and with the type of determination he has, that is exactly what he did. It came in the 69th minute when he lashed home from a corner to score the winner. Considering Everton's precarious position, these were important points Rooney was securing for his club.

The last goals in his brief run were against Southampton, when he hit a brace. On this occasion Rooney actually started the game as Moyes could no longer keep him at bay, and a deflected shot in the seventh minute was enough to grab the opener. Duncan Ferguson doubled that lead, before Everton were pegged back by Kevin Phillips. Rooney then hit a second and looked as if he had won the match for his side, but Michael Svensson and Fabrice Fernandes scored late to earn a draw.

It was quite obvious that Rooney could not carry the club single-handed, but with no money to spend in the transfer window there was little Moyes could do about the team's shortcomings. With Euro 2004 looming, it seemed strange that while the majority of the England team that played for Arsenal, Chelsea and Manchester United were thinking about the Champions League, and the Liverpool boys were trying to qualify for it, Rooney was faced with a relegation battle.

Nobody wanted to see Everton lose Rooney, but people were starting to ask how long they could keep hold of him. He had two more England games on the horizon, and the fact that he had not been a regular for Everton meant there was no concern about him burning out, but there was a worry about his fitness.

England visited Portugal in February, where a Ledley King goal was enough to earn the side a 1–1 draw. But at the time the England set-up was surrounded by the type of speculation Rooney himself was going to have to get used to in the future. Chelsea were trying to lure Sven Goran Eriksson away from the England job, and it was this kind of drab draw that could drive him into the arms of Roman Abramovich. But eventually, despite meeting with Chelsea and discussing the job, Eriksson decided to commit his future to England, which was good news for Rooney. The Swede had given Rooney his debut and helped turn him into a star, so to lose his support and familiarity would have been a problem. Continuity for such a young player is important, so to have lost Eriksson would have been a blow.

As it was the next game against Sweden could go ahead without any further speculation. But the result was not what Eriksson would have wanted. Zlatan Ibrahimovic scored the winner in a slim 1–0 victory. But in this game there was no real sign of the type of impact Rooney was set to have at Euro 2004.

Maybe he was suffering from the demise of Everton's season. They had lost to Middlesbrough in the Carling Cup on penalties, and then went out of the FA Cup in the fourth round in a replay. Rooney did not look happy in either game against Fulham and was struggling to find his form. In fact after December, he only scored three more goals for Everton in the rest of the season. The important thing for Everton, though, was that they all secured points for his club.

He grabbed a vital winner in the return match against relegation-threatened Portsmouth. It came in the 77th minute and he danced a jig in front of the Pompey fans who had been giving him stick for being overweight. It meant that Everton moved eight points clear of the drop zone, which was a vital boost.

Against Leicester in March he scored his side's only goal in a 1–1 draw, and then he did the same against Leeds, with both opponents ending up relegated. It was a good finishing flourish for Rooney, who had endured a tough season.

After turning eighteen, he was now suddenly fair game, no longer a vulnerable boy who the country had to be in awe of. The country loved him, as they should, but life was much harder as people focused on his weight, and in particular his fiery temper, which had cost him suspensions during the season.

The biggest thing, though, was his relationship with manager David Moyes. The club were desperate to get the the most highly rated teenager in Europe to sign a new contract. But so far he was not prepared to do it. There was a whisper among informed people at the club that he no longer wanted to play for the Scot. He hated being moved about so much and felt he did not need as much protection as he was receiving.

At the end of the day all Wayne Rooney wanted to do was play football, it did not matter where, when or how much. He loves the game and the game loves him, and just as he was to prove in June, he was a big-game player with nerves of steel, and the days of being a protected youngster were long gone.

19

Roomania

'He looks unstoppable at the moment. He's the key to England's offensive game.'

— Arsène Wenger

Wayne Rooney was supposed to be England's surprise weapon at Euro 2004, the extra ingredient to add to the mix based on David Beckham's right foot and Michael Owen's predatory instincts. Role reversal began immediately with the opening match on 13 June 2004 in Coimbra, Portugal, against France, with a blistering Rooney run that brought a penalty. With England already a goal ahead Rooney's powerful surge forward had the nation on the edge of its seat, but his dynamic burst was halted only by Mikael Silvestre's blatant foul inside the box. Had the England captain scored from the spot an unassailable lead against the favourites would have produced a startling start to the tournament.

Instead Fabien Bartez guessed right and saved Beckham's penalty, and Zinedine Zidane inspired an injury-time comeback. England lost their opening game 2–1, depression set in, and the country feared the worst.

But Rooney was just beginning. He was catapulted from the back pages to the front, centre and just about every news bulletin with his one-man show against the Swiss four days later, a match in which Switzerland's West Brom defender Bernt Haas was sent off for two bookable offences.

Four minutes before Rooney opened the scoring, he chased a long through ball and slid in recklessly as keeper Joerg Stiel advanced to gather the ball, picking up a yellow card from Russian referee Valentin Ivanov. Stiel said: 'I will tell you what, Rooney was lucky, very lucky. He was the youngest one playing and that is why I did not go into him hard. Normally, in that kind of situation, I would go in feet-first and not worry. But, because it was him, and he is only a young boy, I held off.' Then he noted wryly, 'Now I know better.'

Just as Gary Lineker looked to the bench when Gazza cried in the 1990 World Cup semifinal, Gary Neville put his arm around Rooney after his opening goal. Rooney had already been booked and no one wanted to see it all ruined by a red card. Rooney admitted:

Becks and a few of the lads told me to calm down a bit after that booking, but I was giving 110 per cent and I don't want to change that. I like to play with a little bit of a temper. I think it makes my game better and I am not going to stop just because it's a major tournament like this. I'm going to carry on doing what I do best. I thought my booking for the clash with their goalkeeper was a bit harsh. I wasn't fazed by the booking because the ball was there to be won and I went in for a fifty-fifty challenge with the keeper. I was a bit late but that's the way it goes. I know there is going to be a lot more attention on me now after all this. But that is part of it, isn't it? What do people want me to do? They must know I am never going to give 90 per cent and not go in for certain challenges. I will always give it everything I've got.

You go out there, you play well and score a few goals and it feeds it all. Obviously, there is going to be pressure to keep on doing it in every game, but I just want to keep playing and keep scoring.

Rooney's all-or-nothing approach has put fear into defenders more accustomed to dishing it out than taking it. He admitted: 'The players are a lot more clever at international level and I've got to try to be just as clever. People say that nothing fazes me but I'm only a young lad and I promise you I get nervous before a game like anybody else.'

Steven Gerrard atoned for his moment of madness against France – his back pass caused James to concede the decisive penalty – with England's third goal against the Swiss. England, it seemed, were back on track. On the down side, Owen had looked listless long before he was replaced by Darius Vassell. Fortunately, Rooney showed the way.

Gerrard was in at the start of his opener on 23 minutes, rampaging 40 yards with the ball, only to be stopped by a crude foul by Fabio Celestini. The Russian referee waved play on as England had the advantage with the ball breaking to Beckham. Owen was precisely picked out by the skipper and he clipped in for Rooney, who powered home with his head from close range. Owen had at least made a vital contribution with an inch-perfect chip pass to Rooney.

England were grateful for Haas's stupidity – a foul on Gerrard followed by a bad tackle on Cole just eleven minutes later ending his match early in the second half. With the Swiss down to ten men and even more exposed, inevitably Rooney got the second, two minutes after Vassell had entered from the bench. When fellow sub Owen Hargreaves, on for Scholes, hooked a long hopeful ball forward, Vassell forced errors from Mueller and Murat Yakin before feeding Rooney in space on the left.

If there was luck as his fierce strike cannoned against the post, on to Stiel's head and over the line, he deserved it. Having celebrated his first goal with an extravagant somersault and the booting over of a TV microphone, prompting a national debate about whether he might harm himself – one national newspaper captured fans doing 'the Rooney somersault' – curiously he showed no trace of emotion when he collected his second.

UEFA confirmed that Rooney was to be credited with scoring the second despite the ball going into the net off the back of the goalkeeper's head. Eriksson had said earlier he hoped UEFA did not decide to take the goal away from Rooney. In the match between France and Croatia, UEFA originally credited the opening goal to Silvestre, before deciding it was an Igor Tudor own goal. The crucial guideline affecting Rooney states: 'Shots which are on target (i.e. goalbound) but are then deflected, or balls rebounding off the goal frame and hitting a defender or goalkeeper, will not be considered as own goals.'

Rooney's emphatic emergence as the game's new superstar was under way when, at 18 years and 237 days, he became the youngest ever goalscorer at the European Championship as he struck a stunning double, beating Yugoslav Dragan Stoichkovic's twenty-year record by nearly nine months. Whatever he had achieved before this, whatever records he had already broken, this was the one that changed his life more than anything that had gone before.

Rooney's second goal ensured a win over probably the worst team in the competition to give England high hopes of qualifying from their group stage. Forget that the Swiss went down to ten men before England managed two more goals, forget their lowly ranking, this was the perfect antidote to the French defeat. Rooney now had an impressive seven international goals to his name in fifteen appearances.

Rooney was given a standing ovation by his team-mates in the dressing room after he got England's campaign back on track in the 3–0 win over the Swiss. The youngster was thrilled:

I'm made up because when I went back into the dressing room there was a simultaneous round of applause from all of the players. It's always great to break a record and it's nice to score. I'm just enjoying myself, going out and doing well for the team. It is always nice to break records but the result was the most important thing and, luckily enough, we've won the game. After losing our opening game to France, there was a bit of pressure on the whole team going into the match against Switzerland. We knew we had to win or we could have been out of the tournament. It wasn't our best performance but we won 3–0 and that was always the main target.

David Beckham was genuinely delighted for him:

He's the youngest ever scorer at the championships and he deserves it because he worked hard and played well. He showed a lot of maturity because there was a spell in the first half when he was getting kicked from behind and a few players said to him after he got booked that he should show his frustration by scoring goals. He's eighteen years old and sometimes you can either fade out of the game or fight back as he did tonight and he was superb for us. It was hot out there so we had to pace ourselves and we were a bit nervous and anxious. But once we got the ball down and spread the play we got through them. We've got a young team and even the experienced players get nervous, but a lot of young players showed maturity and this win will settle us down because we've got points on the board and we've got a win behind us.

Normally, an FA official marches Rooney straight past the interview area where the media wait in their hundreds for the more experienced players. This time the FA decided he was ready to face the full glare of the media. A mass of tape recorders were thrust in his face and the clamour and crush that surrounded him signalled his new-found eminence. Rooney said: 'The performance wasn't great but we got the win and that's what mattered. We probably started a bit nervous but we settled down after we scored and once we scored the second, I think we knew we were going to win the game. Of course there will be more pressure now, but it's not a one-man team. It's not all on me. I'm just a young lad and I'm here to enjoy myself.'

Surprisingly he handled his first international interview well enough, even if some Swiss journalists were left desperately asking for a translation for this insightful description of his first goal: 'Eeer, not much to say really. Michael just put the ball on me 'ead.'

Rooney himself is gradually becoming more used to facing the microphones. He has told the FA's website about how his heroes Shearer and Gascoigne have helped him: 'I've seen Alan Shearer give me some advice on TV and I spoke to Gazza a few weeks ago when he came to Bellefield when we trained and did a session with us. He was telling me to keep going and playing football the way I'm doing. He's been through a lot and obviously his advice can only be good for me.'

Eriksson had nothing but praise for Rooney:

He is a fantastic player and a fantastic talent. He played very well against France and he scored two today, one more beautiful than the other. He is incredible. I hope he goes on like that for the rest of the tournament.

I can't say I know him very well because he doesn't talk all that much. But he doesn't need to – he just goes out and does it. Against France and Switzerland he was like a boy out on the school pitch. He was saying, 'Give me the ball and let me enjoy myself.' He was the man of the day in

England and all over Europe as well . . . Rooney is special . . . Rooney needs no protection. He has no nerves and already acts like a senior player. It is fantastic. Everyone loves the way Wayne Rooney is.

One problem for Eriksson, however, remained the poor form of Owen. 'It's not a classic partnership, with one tall and one short, but they still play well together. Owen played well against France and he will be better. We will see goals from Michael Owen in this tournament.'

Rooney, though, was having none of the argument that he is unsuited to play alongside Owen (in fact, former England captain Tony Adams had even advocated axing Rooney). He said:

I don't feel any sympathy for Michael because I know it won't be long before he's banging in the goals again. He's a great player and I'm sure he'll be back on target for England very soon. It's a team game and it isn't all about one player. He set up my first goal against Switzerland and I'm sure he's happy that we won the game even if he didn't score. On this occasion I've gone out there, we've done well and we've got the result. Now people are talking about the responsibility on me to deliver in the next game. But I've had to deal with those expectations from the moment I came into the Everton team. Everything I've done in my career has made the newspapers but my only concern is enjoying myself and getting a good experience from this tournament. Once the game starts you get a bit more relaxed and you just want to go out and do your best.

Rooney was shepherded from microphone to microphone, while Tord Grip was being asked whether in all his years in the game he had ever before seen a player who was so good so young. 'Yes,' replied England's assistant manager after a brief pause for thought. 'Michael Owen.' Yet Owen was being ferreted away by FA minders so that nobody could ask any wounding questions. That cameo depicted the pitfalls that could await Rooney. Grip noted how Rooney had improved in all facets of his game, 'not only in goalscoring but working very hard, helping out in midfield and defence and tackling back'.

The game in Coimbra attracted seventeen million viewers at its peak. ITV said: 'The figures are astonishing for a match kicking off at 5 p.m.' Rush hour had begun two hours early as fans left work to watch the game, though many were forced to listen to the start on the radio as they got caught in traffic jams. After the win, millions of delirious supporters chanted his name back home as they danced in pubs and clubs across the country before carrying the party out on to the streets.

Rooney picked up the Man of the Match trophy and made the day for Kathy Feeley, who manages The Stonebridge Inn in Croxteth. She said: 'Rooney was brilliant, he should have been left on because he would have scored a hat trick. There were so many people trying to get in and cheer Wayne on that we had to turn them away in the end. Everyone round here is delighted with Wayne. He is the best thing to ever come out of Croxteth – a real superstar. There was a real sense of pride written on everyone's faces after the end and the whole pub was chanting Wayne's name.'

In Newcastle the Tyne Bridge was packed by 4 p.m. as fans set off to watch the game. Crowds then gathered in the city's Eldon Square to watch the game on a giant screen. A spokesman for Woolworths said: 'Watching the national team in major tournaments is a special event for all football fans and extremely important to morale. Woolworths is happy for its managers to be flexible with staff hours to ensure that everyone who wants to watch their country play in Euro 2004 can do so.' Cross-channel Hoverspeed bosses received pleas from fans returning from French breaks not to show the game because they would miss the start and the finish. They wanted to watch the full highlights on TV when they got home.

While the nation's birth rate has a habit of increasing at times like these, Rooney was smothered in kisses by his fiancée Colleen McLoughlin on his return to the England team hotel in Lisbon – the couple got engaged in October 2003. He met up with his father Wayne Snr and two younger brothers. Despite the fact he has been cocooned in England's Lisbon HQ, Rooney has managed to stay in touch with his family and fiancée – which has helped him cope with any pressure. 'My family and girlfriend are out here, so I'm not too homesick at the moment,' he said in a video interview on The FA.com. 'And when we come back to the hotel there are lots of things to do. There's table-tennis and pool, which I'm probably equally good at, and now there's the matches, too – which we all watch together. You can't get bored.'

The squad partied until 1 a.m. They enjoyed a sumptuous open-air buffet as chill-out tunes were played over hotel speakers, followed by a string of Simply Red tracks. Wives, girlfriends and families joined in the celebration before players paired up with their partners and headed for bed. Wayne and Colleen were among the last to emerge for breakfast. Eriksson gave the squad the day off and many lay by the pool of the four-star Solplay Hotel. Rooney, who was wearing an England shirt and white shorts, sat listening to music on an iPod.

The adulation and reaction to Rooney's two-goal performance in Coimbra was mind-blowing. Unstoppable, according to Arsène Wenger:

> He looks unstoppable at the moment. He's the key to England's offensive game. I thought a lot of his team-mates played without much confidence, but he looked to me like a youngster without nerves. He just played his natural game. He didn't seem to have any fears. Perhaps he's simply too young to have worries like some of his team-mates. Michael Owen seems to be slowly getting his game together, but at the moment Rooney is the force at the front in the England team.

Wenger believed England faced a tough test against Croatia. 'Croatia will be a very difficult game for England,' he said. 'France were lucky to draw against Croatia and I was surprised by their technical and physical ability. It will be a lot harder for England than most people think.' France's surprise 2–2 draw with Croatia meant that England needed a point from their one remaining Group B tie.

Rooney's team-mates believed he was on course to become the star of Euro 2004.

Sol Campbell, who was also outstanding against the Swiss, said: 'Wayne plays with no fear. The opposition will no doubt be more aware of him, but he has enough about him to cope with that. He's young, he just wants to play and he's intelligent with it. If they target him I am sure he will raise his game.' John Terry said:

> Wayne is unbelievable, there is no other word for it. He does things in training which amaze you and nothing seems to affect him. He's risen to the challenge in every game so far. He's a quiet lad around the place. He loves playing his computer games and he seems completely unaffected by all the fuss. He just loves playing football. Teams will now look to mark him more closely but I think he can deal with it. A couple of times Chelsea have played Everton and our manager has told us to keep an eye on him. He's dealt with it, though. I think the bigger the game, the better he likes it. For a defender he's difficult to mark. He's always pulling off the front line and he also has the pace to go in behind and get a goal that way. He causes problems for defenders because they're not sure whether to go with him or not.

Gerrard has been Rooney's 'minder'. Gerrard admitted:

> I could go on all day about Wayne because he's a big, big talent. He's come to Euro 2004 and is running defences ragged. I'm just glad he's English. Wayne's already proved in this tournament that he's going to be a massively important player in the future. Wayne's only eighteen and if he looks after himself off the pitch the world is his oyster.

The key to Rooney's success has been the laid-back attitude off the pitch which allows him to turn into a snarling beast on it, as Gerrard observed:

> He goes out there as if he is going for a knock-about with his mates down the park. He's very relaxed in his approach to big games and plays as if he's got nothing to lose. There's a lot of experienced players around to do all his worrying for him. He's produced two massive performances and we need another from him against Croatia on Monday. Wayne's doing great and, like every Englishman, I hope he keeps firing in the goals throughout the tournament.

Frank Lampard also watched in wonder. Stunned French reporters had screamed 'Pitbull, pitbull' when the snarling teenager squared up to Claude Makelele, Lilian Thuram *and* William Gallas in England's opening match. Lampard said:

You can't take that aggression from Wayne, that's what he's all about. The minute you take it away you lose a big part of him. His aggression is a big strength and I'm sure he'll learn to control it as he gets older. He's a unique character. He's not scared of anyone on the international stage, which is amazing for an eighteen-year-old. It will need eleven players to take England all the way but if Wayne carries on playing like this he's going to be a big weapon for us.

Newcastle midfielder Kieron Dyer is another in awe of Rooney's raw talent:

It's a privilege to be out here with Wayne. Sometimes I look at him and can't believe he's only eighteen. At the moment he's carrying England on his shoulders. I just hope the booking he picked up against Switzerland doesn't hurt us. It would be a disaster if he got suspended. If you're talking about England's great No. 9s then Alan Shearer is up there. But Wayne has all the qualities to become one of the best ever. He creates as many chances as he takes and though he's a predator, he can also drop deeper and lay the ball off.

Gary Lineker, the BBC's anchorman out in Portugal, said: 'When you're pinning your hopes on an eighteen-year-old, it sounds a bit desperate. But the way Wayne has played in the first two games has been awesome. He has wonderful natural talent and is fearless, but he must watch his temperament.'

Paul Gascoigne, now 37, says: 'Wayne Rooney is phenomenal, there is no doubt about it. But he has got to keep his feet on the ground. He is going to come home to some reception, I know that as well as anyone.' Gascoigne, who saw Rooney's rise through the ranks during his own spell at Everton, added:

If Rooney takes a look at my life, there is stuff there and lessons to be learned that can help him. I have been in the spotlight, eighteen years of madness and hell. Every ten years, you have a new big star coming though. You had George Best, then Gary Lineker, a great pro, then you have Gazza, and now you have Beckham. The next one in the spotlight is Wayne Rooney . . . I don't fear for Rooney. I know he has a good head on his shoulders. I told him to just enjoy himself and said that he has fifteen years of football ahead of him. I have no regrets about my career. But I want Wayne to be able to say the same when he finishes.

Gascoigne was asked whether Rooney was the new Gazza. 'There's only one Paul Gascoigne,' he laughed. But he added, 'Wayne can go on to achieve unbelievable things – he's got so much talent. There were some things I knew I could get away with. Unfortunately, it all creeps up on you if you're not too careful.'

Gary Neville said:

The one thing I would say to Wayne is . . . rest. He will be on such a high. I remember Euro 96 when me and my brother Phillip were probably the youngest in the squad and we beat Holland. You are on such a high, you go and play golf, you go and shop, you go and do everything. What you should do is just get in your bed and rest, because you need every little ounce of energy you can get to go into the next game. These matches take so much out of you, mentally and physically. Wayne is a livewire and infectious to everybody. You wouldn't want to take that youthful enthusiasm away from him – but I think we might have to chain him to his bed!

Neville has been praising him ever since he encountered Rooney, then sixteen, in a reserve game. But even he is struggling to come to terms with the impact Rooney has made on these championships:

He has been phenomenal. Against France, I saw him do things against top defenders who I know and have played against, that I haven't seen other players do. He knocked them about, nudged them off the ball. I've not seen anybody doing what he is doing. I think of Ryan Giggs for Manchester United twelve years ago and Michael Owen for England and Liverpool. They are probably the only comparisons I can think of. He has come on to the world stage – against the likes of Turkey and France – and is putting in performances that are turning people's heads. These are the best players in the world and he is more than holding his own.

The only negative was his yellow card. But it angered Neville when people questioned the youngster's temperament. 'I don't care about the booking. Why are we sat here talking about little negatives about the lad? We should be praising him to high heaven every time he walks out on to that football pitch – even if, at times, he misses a chance or does something wrong. He's a human being.'

Eriksson confirmed that Rooney was to play against Croatia despite knowing that another yellow card would rule him out of the quarterfinal, assuming England achieved the draw or win they needed. 'We can't worry about that. Everybody loves him the way he is,' Eriksson said.

Thierry Henry, yet to find the net for France, joined the gallery of admirers. 'Before the tournament started, I warned people to look out for this kid. I think a lot of people were a bit dismissive of what I said because he plays for Everton, but I knew he would have an impact. He's a very special talent and could take the tournament by storm.'

Henry was particularly impressed with the way Rooney had made the most of the lack of space available during games. 'People say that I have struggled because the standard of defending in the Premiership is poor, but Rooney is scoring and he plays in England. He has had just as little room to manoeuvre as me or any others. He's just made better use of the small gaps that have appeared. All the strikers are having to feed off crumbs.'

Croatia coach Otto Baric ordered his players to target Rooney during a special team meeting. Reserve keeper Joey Didulica said:

If we provoke Rooney in the right way, he will definitely lash out. He's a fanatic and when you're playing off emotion like that, a red card is inevitable. You can see Rooney is fired up and the manager told us to prey on this weakness. All is fair in love and war and football. You've got to try and use every tactic. The defenders can just slide in and try and take him a few times – and you will get the reaction you want. He's young and aggressive and, hopefully for us, something could pop in his head. After his booking against Switzerland he had ten minutes when he was running around even more fired up and could have been booked again.

However, former England star David Platt, one of Eriksson's scouting staff, believed the Croats were not as bad as they had been painted. He said: 'They are not a dirty team. What they do, though, is put the opposition under pressure by harrying and chasing.' England took the threat seriously and were delighted that the man in charge was the sophisticated Italian Pierluigi Collina. England's assistant coach Steve McClaren made no attempt to disguise his pleasure that 'Collina will be there'. He added:

One thing Sven addressed before both the French and Swiss games was the need to keep cool heads and discipline – and he's going to make that point again. You can't take away what Rooney is but I do think it helps that we have some good senior players like Gary Neville and Beckham who in some controversial incidents in the Swiss game were going over to him and calming him down, diffusing the situation, affecting the referee. I think other players can help Wayne and that's part of the strength we have got in our camp. I think everybody looks out for everybody else within any team structure, especially with Wayne, one so young and who, as it is being said, could well be targeted.

Eriksson said: 'I am not worried about Wayne. It seems he was unlucky to be booked against Switzerland but of course he must be disciplined. We need him, though, because we have to get to the quarterfinals.' Rooney's granddad was adamant he would not rise to the bait; William Morrey, 73, said: 'He is a cool, quiet lad and he will keep his head. I'm sure he will stay calm.'

Rio Ferdinand, missing the tournament through suspension after infamously forgetting to attend a drugs test at Manchester United's training ground earlier in the season, was part of the 1998 World Cup squad in which Owen made a sensational impact. Owen began that tournament as a substitute, while Rooney has been leading the line from the start at Euro 2004. Ferdinand said:

Wayne is a bit more streetwise than Michael was six years ago. He is putting in performances of a mature, seasoned professional at eighteen. I've heard it said he plays better for England than Everton but he is a regular for England now and is not always a starter for his club. When you are in the team all the time, you have that bit more confidence. But I'm sure his manager David Moyes knows what he is doing with him. It's understandable he wants to nurse him along.

Rooney was made to do extra training before the tournament after tests showed his fitness was behind the other players. Eriksson puts great store behind preparation for the big tournaments. The extra work paid off. England fitness coach, Italian Ivan Carminati, worked especially hard on Rooney's prior to travelling to Portugal. Eriksson said, 'Wayne's fitness levels were not as they should have been prior to the tournament because he had not been playing all the games for his club. In the beginning though, in Sardinia, he did more than the others, extra work and it has paid off because he is very fit now.'

Eriksson, who as a coach in Italian club football often had to devise tactics to subdue Napoli's Maradona, was at first reluctant to compare Rooney to the young Argentine prodigy, but reflected:

Yes, I think there are similarities. Wayne runs with the ball and hurts defences in the way that Maradona did. It's difficult to take the ball off him because he's so strong and has such good balance, like Maradona. I think that Wayne is more of a centre forward but I think that Maradona was probably quicker. Time will tell. You have to remember that Maradona was one of the best players in the history of the game.

In the run-up to the Croatia game, Rooney carried the hopes of a nation. 'I'll do me best,' he said shyly.

An army of up to 22 million viewers were expected to be glued to their TV sets, with eight million more watching in the pubs. Landlords anticipated bumper takings with possibly twelve million extra pints being sunk. Supermarket beer and pizza sales hit record levels as armchair fans stocked up. Motoring groups even predicted another early rush hour as workers hurried to see the 7.45 p.m.

kick-off. Bookies expected £25m to be bet on the match, much of it on Rooney to score first.

Eriksson, whose team would play either Portugal or Greece in the quarterfinals should they get there, also backed Owen to score against Croatia, but all eyes were on Rooney.

20

The Race for Rooney

'My personal view is that there will be thousands of people who will shed tears if he ever leaves Everton. He is part of our Everton family and every Evertonian has special feelings for Wayne because of the lad he is and what he does on the pitch. I can't say what will happen to Wayne from now on but I can say that he is in good hands.'

— Ray Hall, the head of Everton's Youth Academy

Rooney had arrived in Portugal on the back of rumours linking him with a summer move to Manchester United. Arsène Wenger ruled out an Arsenal bid for Rooney but admitted London rivals Chelsea could lure the teenager to Stamford Bridge, and Everton boss David Moyes felt Chelsea were the only club in the world who could afford to sign him, particularly as his value rocketed even higher on the back of his performances in Euro 2004. Moyes said, 'Everyone seems to be talking about Wayne and I'm concerned about an element of it becoming a witch-hunt. But my point of view is Wayne should remain an Everton player.' Everton are over £30m in debt, and would have to sell if an attractive offer were to come in, but despite praising Rooney's talent, Wenger insisted:

Wayne has been a revelation at Euro 2004 for people who don't work in English football. I said a long time ago he would be one of the best and he's confirming that now. We'll have to wait and see how far he goes. If a team really want him then he could go for £30m. Chelsea could do it but that's a very high price to pay for any club in the world. But when I see a player I don't see a number, it's not how many millions he's worth. At Arsenal we have the strikers we need and are not in the market for him.

I don't know if Everton will keep him – if you are a big club then you want to keep your best players.

John Terry added his thoughts: 'I know from personal experience that he's an absolute nightmare to mark. All of Europe is now aware of him and I'd love to get him to Chelsea next season. I've not got the money to buy him but I think there are others connected with Chelsea who may be able to raise the cash!'

Pini Zahavi scooped £7m-worth of commissions for Roman Abramovich's spending spree at Chelsea but, for the moment, Rooney is not a prime target for the Russian Revolution. From his Tel Aviv base, Zahavi explains:

If he carries on like this, then yes, he can become the best, and even break the world record for a transfer. But don't forget that everybody was getting excited about Michael Owen when he scored his wonder goal against Argentina in the World Cup. They talked about a £40m player then, and look at Owen now, there are not too many clubs trying to buy him and he has only one year left on his contract at Liverpool. I told you some time ago that Owen has to continue to prove himself before he will get a big-money move, and really the same applies to Rooney. The best judges do not make assumptions on one tournament, they make an assessment over a long period. People have asked many questions about Rooney, about his attitude, about his mentality. If he proves himself on all of these points then yes, he can become the top, top player, but it is too early, of course, to make such a judgment.

On the commercial front, Rooney's value continues to soar. Already Rooney was the face of Nike, Coca-Cola, Pringles and EA Sports, and Ford provide him with a top-of-the-range Ka. Now his face was all over the television. Sports shops reported a massive surge in demand for replica England shirts bearing his name and No. 9, while St George flags printed with his moniker were also selling fast. His overnight rise in popularity also saw him made the new 3–1 favourite to win the coveted Sports Personality of the Year title – to add to the Young Personality Award he won in 2002. A spokesman at the Everton megastore said: 'We've sold tons of

Rooney stuff. I've never seen a frenzy like it.' Nike possess one of the biggest and certainly longest commercial commitments, a ten-year contract. Simon Charlesworth, a Nike UK spokesman, told me: 'In the eyes of a number of commercial partners Wayne Rooney is more valuable now than when the tournament started and he has always been tremendously valued.' If, as Zahavi advises, he carries on in this vein, then he could even outearn Beckham, who is now touching the veteran stage in his thirtieth year.

Everton don't want to sell, but my contacts tell me they have placed a 'reserved' price of £35m on his young head. Everton are among a profusion of Premiership clubs strapped for cash and carrying enormous debt, and they could not say no to a new British record fee.

The England coach inadvertently entered the realms of controversy when he said: 'If I was in club management, the first thing I'd have done this morning is find out the telephone number of his agent. He is one of the biggest talents in the game, he is not just a goal-scorer but a real all-round footballer. I'm sure the queue for his services is getting longer by the minute.' Moyes issued a terse statement in reply:

> We've not had any bids for Wayne Rooney and we would not encourage any. We want to sit down with Wayne and discuss a new contract . . . If Sven was Everton manager I don't think he would want to be hearing an international manager saying that about one of his players. First of all I would expect the England manager to know the rules. It would be illegal to approach his agent because the player is under contract. Secondly that is the last thing we want. I don't want to sell my best players. And we have no intention of selling unless my board tells me we must – or Wayne tells me he does not want to play for Everton any more.

One of Rooney's uncles added to doubts over his future at Everton. John Morrey said: 'It is like Steven Gerrard at Liverpool – he needs top players alongside him. And unless Everton can get the players that are necessary, then he would just be wasting his time in the end. He would not be developing without the support of his team-mates.'

Beckham marvelled at the way the kid was 'walking round like nothing's happened'. England's captain had some encouragement for Everton fans worried that Abramovich will sign him for £50m. They were fanciful prices, as Beckham said:

It's sensible to stay where he's happiest. If that's at Everton, so be it. He's only eighteen and as long as he's at a club that's going to look after him that's what's most important to him. I wasn't playing for England at that age. Wayne's a special talent and deserves everything that's been said about him. He's worked hard at his game. At eighteen years old, to be performing at this level, the way he is, is very special. We're all thankful he's in our team. As long as he's looked after . . . he's got a strong family behind him, he'll be around for a long, long time.

Eriksson said: 'I am not surprised about the impact he is having at home. He is man of the day, the man of England and the man of Europe. He is eighteen years old and he will be even better in the future.'

The media became obsessed. The FA had taken the precaution of banning newspapers in the team hotel, but the players rang home regularly and would know of the adulation being heaped on such young shoulders. He is popular within the England camp, but in a totally different way from someone like Gazza. Not someone who needs to stand out with practical jokes and comedy walks, but simply good at blending in.

The man who helped nurture him at Everton, Ray Hall, insists the striker is repaying everyone who has coached and guided him at Everton. Hall said: 'People are talking about Rooney-mania and because of all the media, fan and business interest, I suppose we have created a monster. But what we have got to do now is create another one. We have to keep working to make sure another lad comes through just like Wayne.' Hall expects the records to keep tumbling:

Every challenge he has been faced with he has met and raised the bar. Nothing fazes him and he seems quite at ease with the England players, even though he is the youngest. He has always played over his own age. When he was under sixteen he was in the under-19 side and then at sixteen he was in the first team. He is no different from the kid at school who is a gifted mathematician and is moved up classes to be with the older kids. Rooney-mania is everywhere and everyone wants a little piece of him.

Everton manager David Moyes dismissed constant speculation in the media that Rooney was on his way out of Everton, adding that the club had not received any offers for him. 'It seems that everyone wants to talk about it. It's as though there is nothing else to talk about apart from Wayne Rooney.' Moyes is anxious to secure the whiz kid's long-term future at Goodison:

Wayne's natural talent has got him where he is and nobody can take credit for that except the boy himself and his family. He is a particularly natural football player. Wayne doing so well for England and scoring goals doesn't create a problem for me at all. It just goes to prove to everybody what a good player he is. Wayne won't be affected by the pressure and the hype about what he is potentially worth. We know what Wayne's value is, but he is an Everton football player and we have no reason to believe that will change.

Keeping Wayne Rooney at Everton is vital for us, but we have no reason to believe there is a problem. We understand that if Everton are not successful in the future then Wayne Rooney might want to seek pastures new, but I hope we would be given the opportunity to try and succeed. I have said all along, I am not here to sell my best players. I am here to build a team. That hasn't changed from day one. Wayne certainly hasn't outgrown Everton Football Club. Of course Everton are big enough for Wayne Rooney. Everton are one of the biggest clubs in this land. We are, obviously, very pleased for him and to have him as part of the team here. To work with him is a great privilege and I have enjoyed that. Long may that continue.

But Moyes finally conceded that he would consider letting Wayne Rooney leave – for £50m. He told the club's official website:

I think if someone came in with £50m, everybody in the country would be saying that we'd be right to take it because that's a big offer. One of the things I said when I came to this club is that I don't want to sell my best players ... but I'd be lying if I said that there wasn't a price on everybody's head. There is. I can only say that I have got no intentions of selling Wayne just now unless I get told by the board that we have to or unless Wayne tells me that he doesn't want to play for Everton any more.

Bill Kenwright had always insisted that Rooney would not be sold, even though the massive transfer fee would go a long way towards easing Everton's financial ills. The Toffees' deputy chairman said:

Nothing has changed with regard to my feelings about Wayne Rooney. As for a £50m bid for him, well, there's only one person who'll ever make that kind of decision. Not Bill Kenwright, not the Everton board, but the Everton manager. And I know very well how the manager feels. David Moyes is anxious to conclude negotiations with Paul Stretford [Rooney's agent] to secure a five-year contract. It's up to the manager. I talk to David Moyes every day and we talk about Wayne Rooney in an England shirt but we also take about Wayne Rooney in an Everton shirt. It's very disappointing, though, to hear that Wayne is being hawked around clubs.

David Moyes and I agreed Wayne has to be a £50m player now. We do smile about what Wayne is worth but, then again, we also talk about who's going to be alongside him with us next season. I would turn down any bid for him and say: 'Thank you very much, what else do you want to talk about?' We know what Wayne's value is and our price is that he is an Everton player and we have no reason to believe that will change. I am not here to sell my best players and Wayne wants to stay.

Kenwright insisted that he trusts Stretford to stand by his word that the teenager will still be at Everton for the 2004–05 season:

I trust Paul. We've had many conversations. Wayne will continue at Everton. I know Wayne is mixing with England lads who have won medals and that it's hard for us – after finishing fourth from bottom in the Premiership last season – to set our sights too high. But we have to believe that we progress together. There have been no bids for Wayne, absolutely not. No approach from Chelsea, nor Manchester United. I've heard talk of Manchester United having a done deal. But I've had no contact whatsoever with United and you'd think they would ring, wouldn't you?

Rooney's emergence as a major star at Euro 2004 delighted Kenwright: 'I'm hugely proud. I spoke to Wayne the other day and told him how proud I was. He's a smashing lad . . . He's shy, humble and he's got a genius about him. He's handling the media attention really well. He's the nation's favourite son – but he's also Everton's favourite son.'

Even though Moyes is a passionate Scot, he is desperate for Rooney and England to do well.

It may seem strange for a Scot to be cheering England, but I am growing to England because Wayne is doing so well. I work in England so I want them to do well and from our point of view we have England's No. 9 there so we want them to do well and Wayne to continue scoring. I haven't spoken to him during the championships – he is being well managed with England just now – but I sent him a telegram prior to the tournament. I have let him get on with it, the same as I have the other players. I was delighted for him the other night. I watched the game at home with my family and was cheering him and England on all the way.

Ruud Van Nistelrooy advised his club to sign Rooney:

He's a phenomenal talent and the prospect of him pulling on a United shirt is frightening. I don't know many clubs that wouldn't want him in their side. He's an incredible player. And if he does become available Manchester United should do everything in their power to sign him. It certainly excites me to think he could be playing at United next season. He's making a name for himself but it's not come as a big surprise. Anyone who has seen him play knows what a talent he is. Nothing seems to worry him. He is strong, aggressive and quick, the type of player who will always score goals and gives defenders nightmares.

Rooney is reluctant to uproot from the Northwest and has told friends he favours United. Sir Alex Ferguson has monitored his meteoric rise and after watching Rooney terrorise his team at Goodison last season, he decided then that United should pay what it takes to bring him to Old Trafford.

Barcelona president Joan Laporta claims the superpowers of Spain, Italy and Germany have also targeted the boy wonder, whose transfer value has rocketed to £50m. Laporta said: 'There is no other player in football today with the quality of Rooney. You can see he is different to every other forward – and that makes him interesting. I know from talking with other clubs, their coaches, general managers and presidents that Rooney has impressed everybody. Everywhere around Europe, they are talking about him all the time.'

It was Laporta who opened the way for Beckham to leave United when he declared his intention to lure the England skipper to the Nou Camp. And though Barcelona eventually lost out to bitter rivals Real Madrid in the battle for Becks, they did beat United to the signing of Brazilian ace Ronaldinho.

Laporta added: 'I like Rooney because he is so explosive. When I first saw him, I thought of Paul Gascoigne playing as a forward because of his strength, his physique and his pride in his play. The fact he is only eighteen and already the leader of the English national team is impressive. He has a splendid future.'

Yet Laporta admitted that Barcelona are unlikely to get involved in a bidding war for Rooney and would like to see the player prove himself on a consistent basis before making the sort of bid that would tempt Everton to part with their prize asset.

He looks mature for an eighteen-year-old but he is still young and he has to demonstrate his great quality for one or two more years in the Premier League. I will talk to our coach Frank Rijkaard about him but it is probably too early to try to sign him. Everton are an important team but I know there are a lot of other clubs that want Rooney. Maybe he already has some agreement with another club. We would like to know if he does. I am sure there are some clubs who would be ready to make a bid for him this summer but the market is changing every day and we don't need to take risks by talking about how much we believe him to be worth.

Laporta, speaking in Lisbon at the launch of Barcelona's new Nike kit, also admitted the arrival of Abramovich had made life tougher for every other team in Europe.

Chelsea are rapidly becoming one of the best clubs in the world with the financial and economic capacity to incorporate many great players. They have already signed many high-quality stars for next season and we have great respect for what they could achieve in the Champions League. But Barcelona belongs to the elite. We can compete with Chelsea, United, Madrid, Milan, everyone. Every day I can feel this because every day a lot of players offer their services to us.

Just when you thought Rooney could do no more to increase his transfer value, he turned in another match-winning performance for England . . .

21

Rooney Does It Again

'Absolutely fantastic. He is not only a good goalscorer he is a complete football player and I am very happy to have him in my team. I just hope he keeps this up all the way to the beginning of July. What can I say about him that has not been said? He was absolutely fantastic.'

– Sven Goran Eriksson

Hopes were high as many people left work early to get home in good time, or else piled into pubs and clubs in their millions to watch England's final Group B match against Croatia on 21 June. Wayne Rooney duly sent the nation delirious by scoring two goals and setting up another in England's 4–2 win over Croatia on 21 June to set up an enthralling quarterfinal clash with hosts Portugal.

He said modestly: 'I just went out and played my normal game. The team played well tonight and I'm lucky enough to get two goals. We just go out there and try to do our job the best we can.' Asked about his strike partnership with Michael Owen, Rooney added: 'We play well together. Michael isn't scoring now but he set a few goals up for me and I think it's working well.'

He made himself a national hero all over again as he completed England's stirring fightback after Croatia had given them a major fright in the Estadio Da Luz.

England fans pouring into bars before the match were seeing double, thanks to Graham Rooney, a dead ringer for his star brother. He happily posed for photos after jetting to Portugal with the family. Thousands of Three Lions supporters crammed into the centre of Lisbon's main Rossio Square to watch on a big screen.

Prince William celebrated his 22nd birthday cheering for Rooney in a village pub. Wills chanted 'Rooney, Rooney' as the superkid scored his goals. The excited Prince, wearing a St George sweater, watched the game with polo-playing pals at the Tunnel House pub in Coates, near Highgrove.

Chelsea owner Roman Abramovich watched from the stands, alongside the club's chief executive Peter Kenyon and newly appointed coach Jose Mourinho – if he had any doubts about the wisdom of offering Everton a fortune for Rooney, they would have evaporated after this performance.

At the singing of the national anthem, England players were again arms-locked around each others' shoulders, singing as the Croat fans tried to drown out the music with boos and howls. Rooney, Neville and Scholes did not join in the anthem, but they all felt like signing by the end as Rooney made it four goals in two games, while Scholes ended his three-year goal drought and Lampard added a clinching fourth.

Rooney was the star turn for the third successive game as world football began to debate just how good he will be when he reaches his full potential.

Croatia took an early lead in the match. Beckham conceded a free kick on the right, and when the ball was drilled across, Ashley Cole's inadvertent touch, after being shoved in the back by Boris Zivkovic, forced a brilliant parry by David James. But the ball rebounded off the slow-reacting Terry for Kovac to slide in from close range.

England kept their nerve, though, and Rooney was everywhere, the lifeforce of the side. He set up the equaliser when Lampard flicked through to Owen and while Butina met his charge to send the ball into the air, Rooney headed powerfully goalwards for Scholes to nod home. Alan Hansen described Rooney's headed pass across goal for Scholes's equaliser as 'one of the best I've ever seen'. Five minutes later the boy wonder scored a wonder goal, as Owen fed Scholes, and from 25 yards Rooney rifled into the bottom corner with half-time approaching. For the record, Rooney's piledriver against Croatia hit the net at 58.8mph, but it was still only the sixth fastest since Sky TV started recording speeds last season (Alex Rae was No. 1 with his 73.9mph thunderbolt for Wolves against Bolton).

Owen and Rooney then exchanged passes to send the teenager away 22 minutes from time, and the finish could not have been bettered by Owen himself. Nerveless as ever, he streaked away on to Owen's return pass and stroked the ball into the corner.

Briefly, when Igor Tudor headed home to make it 3–2, there were worries, ended with Lampard's second of the tournament, rifled in left-footed eleven minutes from time.

Eriksson, mindful of Rooney's yellow card in the match against Switzerland, had already substituted him by this stage to ensure he would be eligible to play in the quarterfinals. He left the field to a tumultuous reception.

Roon-ey . . . Roon-ey . . . it had become the chant of the tournament.

As 40,000 English fans celebrated at the Stadium of Light in Lisbon, and at least 25 million TV viewers at home went wild, Rooney's parents and brothers jumped for joy in the arena when the final whistle went. Wayne Snr hardly stopped clapping all game. And fiancée Colleen broke into a huge smile as she heard the England fans chant her sweetheart's name.

Afterwards Wayne's dad said, 'Wayne was fantastic – he played his heart out. I wasn't even disappointed when he was substituted. It didn't matter as long as England won.'

Rooney's four goals in three matches made him the top marksman in the tournament and prompted Eriksson to mention him in the same breath as Pelé. 'I don't remember anyone making such an impact on a tournament since Pelé in the 1958 World Cup in Sweden,' he said.

Eriksson also stressed Rooney's work rate as an invaluable contribution:

Two goals from Rooney again, fantastic goals. He's also doing hard work for the team, is always available and he helps us defend as well. Absolutely fantastic. He is not only a good goalscorer he is a complete football player and I am very happy to have him in my team. I just hope he keeps this up all the way to the beginning of July. What can I say about him that has not been said? He was absolutely fantastic. He scored two goals and both were fantastic. He was always working, always available. I was always confident that, sooner or later, we would score goals tonight. Wayne deserves all the attention and front and back pages for what he is doing here. Sometimes I feel you should not say too much about a young player but he is absolutely incredible. Let us see if Portugal can stop him. Tactically I can tell him things but I could not tell him how to score those goals, it is better for me to say nothing. He just has an instinct. He is absolutely fantastic not only in his scoring but the way he plays football. He is good to play the ball up to, to hold it and turn with it. If you're having problems he drops into midfield to receive the ball. And then, of course, he scores goals. It is going to be a hard game against Portugal, but it will be hard for them too. I am proud of what we have done so far.

When it was pointed out that Rooney had again been denied the opportunity of claiming three goals by his substitution in favour of Darius Vassell, Eriksson joked, 'Did he say, "I want a hat-trick"? No, he didn't say it. Maybe he thought it.'

Croatian coach Otto Baric admitted: 'Wayne Rooney is a very good player, he just escaped from us.'

David Beckham hailed Rooney's stunning performance:

When you see him perform, nothing fazes him. It was a big game and he has produced for us again. He has had a great game tonight. He has produced again; he deserves all the praise he will get. We're so lucky to have a talent like that in England. It's been another awesome performance from Wayne. He's done it against France, Switzerland, Croatia and – hopefully – he can carry on doing it. A lot of people back home will be very proud of him.

Gerrard commented that nothing surprised him about his fellow Scouser:

There is no better player in Europe at the moment. On current form, Wayne is the best in this competition – it's as simple as that. If he keeps on putting in performances like that then one day he can also become the best player in the world. When you look at his form over the last three games, he can definitely help England to win this tournament. His goals have already helped us to the last eight and I'm sure he will help us progress ever further. The whole squad is buzzing and confident we can go all the way. Wayne keeps getting a round of applause in the dressing room after every game. He scores goals and his all-round play is superb. He's just spot-on at the moment and, hopefully, he can carry it on right to the end of the tournament.

It was a very mature performance from Wayne because certain teams are going to try to wind him up. He's just got to get over that and prove himself to be one of the best players in the world. The whole team is playing well and no one will want to face us now.

Portugal will be a tough game because they're the host nation, with a lot of talented individuals. It will be a great night but we'll definitely be up for it and I don't think we'll be underdogs. Portugal will be fearing us after this performance. It's going to be all about us, not Portugal . . . the whole team is doing well and, if we keep playing like we did tonight, not many sides will want to meet us.

Beckham concluded, 'We're all delighted that Scholesy has scored, as well. He does it in big games and Paul Scholes playing at his best is as awesome a weapon as Wayne Rooney. Maybe, it's a good thing – to go a goal down but still come back and win. There's a good balance in the team now and we're all working well together.'

Ironically, just as he quickly lost his Premiership goalscoring record to James Milner of Leeds United, Rooney lost his four-day-old record as the youngest scorer in European Championships. Swiss striker Johann Vonlanthen took the record, but his delight was tempered by his team's first-round exit. The eighteen-year-old, starting an international for the first time, scored the Swiss goal in the 3–1 defeat by champions France. Vonlanthen struck after 26 minutes, breaking Rooney's record. Vonlanthen was eighteen years and four months, three months younger than Rooney when he scored in the same goal at the same stadium *against* the Swiss. The PSV Eindhoven player was called into the team for this third international at the last minute following the withdrawal of Alexander Frei over his alleged spitting at Gerrard.

The astonishing goalscoring form of Rooney had helped disguise some of the flaws in England's game, while single-handedly establishing Eriksson's men as serious contenders for the title.

Rooney is not a natural strike partner for Owen, so Eriksson prefers to play him in a deep position where he acts as a link player. His control and vision is good enough to influence the build-up play and his strength and pace is such that he can run with the ball too. 'He not only scores goals but does many other things too,' said Eriksson.

Eriksson had to keep young Wayne's feet firmly on the ground. Family visits to the squad's luxury headquarters helped. Loved ones arrived after the match. 'We've been together as a squad for a month and I think it's good for the players to have a taste of normal life,' said Eriksson. 'It's good for them to talk about something other than football.'

Gary Neville, the 66-cap defender who passed his own milestone of playing more European Championship games than any other England international, knew that his club colleague Cristiano Ronaldo was vying with Rooney as the outstanding young talent in the tournament. The quarterfinal was billed as the clash of the Boy Stars. Neville delivered a timely reminder that Rooney's wasn't the only show in town, while Gerrard's assessment that his young pal is Europe's best might be premature, considering that Zinedine Zidane and Pavel Nedved were also illuminating Euro 2004.

Listen to a wise old-timer like Croatia's coach, Otto Baric. 'Rooney is a very good player, but a phenomenon? I wouldn't say that.'

His four goals had come against mediocre Swiss and Croat sides, and although Owen had yet to get off the mark his goal record remains impressive, notably for scoring against the world's elite as well as the minnows.

Yet as Neville pointed out: 'It was the game against France which was the eye-opener for me. The things he was doing to a world-class defence were fantastic. He is the real thing.'

Beating Figo, Ronaldo and Deco etc. in their own back yard would need England to defend more convincingly, rather than relying totally on Sol Campbell at the back and Rooney at the front. England's 1966 World Cup-winning star Geoff Hurst congratulated the team on beating Croatia, but warned the game against the Portuguese would be much tougher, before adding, 'We should have nothing to fear out here if we play to our full potential.'

With Rooney in such unstoppable mood there was a growing feeling that England could win this tournament. With every game, the cohesion was increasing, and England seemed to be evolving as tournament-winning teams often do. Bookies Coral cut the odds on England winning from 6–1 to 11–2, while England were 9–2 second favourites to win the tournament with William Hill.

The FA opted to protect the eighteen-year-old from the euphoria before the intensity of the clash with the hosts. Although he made a brief television appearance, he was not exposed again to the rest of the media.

But nothing could stop Rooney-mania gripping the nation.

22

Praise from the Greats

'Rooney has been outstanding. He is precious. It is a joy for him to play as much as it is for people to watch him play.'

– Pelé

Although his team-mates have been falling over themselves to praise Rooney, they are far from alone in their admiration. England's Rugby Union coach Sir Clive Woodward was one of the more unusual sporting figures to recognise his achievements. He said, 'I think he'd make a great fly-half. We should get him involved in rugby. There'd be no stopping him.'

George Best was also enthralled:

It's not often that I see a player, English or otherwise, who makes my heart beat that bit faster, who excites me and promises to deliver something out of the ordinary. Wayne Rooney does. For a lad of eighteen, he is just incredible. I'm not known for flattering modern-day footballers, David Beckham has never impressed me, but Rooney's got everything. That performance against Croatia was not only exhilarating to watch, it was, in its own way, frightening. Just how good can he get? If his career runs along the right course, he'll be among the absolute greats.

After Eriksson's earlier comments, it was only natural for the Brazilian legend to respond, and having met Pelé on many occasions and been privileged to have penned his biography with his approval, he provided me with these thoughts on Rooney: 'I was fortunate to see Michael Owen play when he was eighteen, the same age as Wayne Rooney. I pointed to Owen as a great player and in fact he became a great player before his injury. I haven't had the chance to see much of Rooney before now, but it looks to me – from what I have seen so far during Euro 2004 – he has the potential to follow in the footsteps of great players like Sir Bobby Charlton, George Best and David Beckham.'

In addition there were some comments attributed to Pelé in the national press, when he was reported to have remarked:

Wayne Rooney has already emerged as one of the best players at the European Championships. He's a very exciting talent, who shows maturity and composure beyond his young years. It is wonderful when you see a young player who is just starting to realise what he can achieve in the game. Rooney has been outstanding. He is precious. It is a joy for him to play as much as it is for people to watch him play. A young player has the ability to do anything because he is not weighed down by pressure or past experiences. For me, seeing young players come through is one of the most exciting things in football. I just hope that Rooney is allowed to remain focused on his performance and that the only pressure he has to carry is that which he puts upon himself. There is certainly a lot more pressure on a young player like Rooney than there was when I first played for Brazil. It is something Wayne will have to learn to cope with.

Last year Pelé chose a hundred stunning photographs of the world's greatest living footballers for the exhibition to mark the centenary of FIFA, and included Beckham and Owen. Pelé observed: 'When I selected the list, Wayne was a promising talent. In less than a year he has grown up tremendously and would now be a serious candidate for anyone's current list of the world's greatest living footballers. With his tremendous ability both on and off the ball, I am sure England can go on to do extremely well in Euro 2004.'

Eriksson even scared himself by comparing Rooney to Pelé:

I am a little frightened about comparing Rooney to Pelé because of the pressure it will put on him. But when you have someone scoring four goals in three games in a tournament like this, you can't stop that. It's there, in the way he is and the way he plays. So far he has kept his feet on the ground – and that's the only worry for the future. But he seems very happy in the camp, always there with half a smile on his face. I think he has a lot of personality.

Eriksson recalled watching the Brazilian legend at his first tournament, the 1958 World Cup in Sweden, on a pal's TV:

I was only ten but I remember that World Cup because we did not all have televisions in Sweden then. It was the first time I'd seen football on TV. I was staying with a friend and we watched the final and what Pelé did against Sweden and it was something new for me to watch a game. It was the first time I'd seen football on television. It was the summer and I was staying with a friend of mine in the countryside. I remember one of the goals he scored, when he knocked the ball over the shoulder of the defender and then volleyed it in. I am surprised by what Wayne's done. To compare a footballer of today with Pelé is not bad, not bad at all.

Sitting with his best pal in the heart of the Swedish forest, the ten-year-old Eriksson had his breath stolen by the boy he saw taking his country's heroes apart, destroying a nation's dream by scoring twice in a 5–2 win. What Pelé did on that Stockholm afternoon has been forever etched into Eriksson's consciousness, a memory that he has carried with him ever since, something he believed could never be matched.

That goal saw Pelé destroy defender Bengt Gustavsson with one moment of sublime skill, before hammering past keeper Kalle Svensson, yet Rooney's imperious displays in Portugal have been seen by an even wider audience in the multimedia age.

Eriksson added:

I hope he will go on to be one of the greats of football. In football you never know but the way he's started this tournament is incredible. For someone to be eighteen and doing what he's doing, scoring four goals and playing football like that, with good passes, holding the ball strong against defenders, but also defending and coming back to help the team. I've nothing to add to that. He is perfect. I think that if he is eighteen he can be better at everything if he works hard and keeps his feet on the ground. But I mean he has so much. He's strong and quick, not only over five yards but also over long distances when he goes from a long way out like he did for the third goal.

The instinct he showed then said everything. He was ice-cold. It was never in doubt. But he also sees things. He can play people in and knows what to do.

Rooney's second consecutive Man of the Match award – it surely would have been three if it had not been for Zinedine Zidane's injury-time intervention in England's opening game – had turned the boy into a global property.

The FA moved into protection mode, seeking to help Rooney cope with not just the adulation but also the nonstop interest in every aspect of his life.

'I don't know if he needs any help,' said Eriksson. 'But yes, I am surprised by what he's done . . . He had a great game but I will still want to talk to him before we play Portugal. I talked to him before the Croatia game, about not getting any red or yellow cards and things like that. But he's always very, very calm.'

The coach was convinced that if England were to end up as kings of Europe, there would be more to come from Rooney. He added: 'The timing of Wayne coming through couldn't be better, for me and for England. Normally the team winning the big tournaments has the best goalscorer. It's not always like that but it normally happens. Just look at the World Cup and Ronaldo for Brazil. I hope it's the same here, with Wayne.'

Portugal coach Luis Felipe Scolari laughed off claims Rooney could be the new Pelé. Scolari, who led his homeland Brazil to World Cup glory in 2002, was asked to compare the two players. Scolari smiled and said: 'One is white, the other is black. Rooney is an excellent player but Pelé is unique. There will never be another Pelé – not for a thousand years and not even in a computer game.'

Scolari made it clear there would be no special plans for Rooney, 'We will not put one man on him,' he said. 'We will defend our goal in the normal way. England are a very strong team who play to a very strong system and we will have to be attentive to all the different elements the team possesses.' He said English football had made great progress in the last few years and praised the role of Eriksson, whom he famously outmanoeuvred when Brazil eliminated England at the 2002 World Cup. 'Their football has changed a lot in the last eight to ten years. They no longer play the aerial ball and the technical level is much more sophisticated. It is because they have had foreign coaching ideas like Arsène [Wenger] and with Eriksson taking over the national team.'

Soccer pundits throughout Europe heaped praise on the England wonder kid. 'Rooney is the Messiah,' roared Spain's sports daily *AS*, adding: 'One more time the best of England has strength, fight and a shot.'

Under the headline 'Rooney's Cup' another Spanish newspaper, *El Mundo*, described him as 'the boxer's son with the face of a killer who does not take prisoners'.

In Italy, *La Gazzetta dello Sport* ran a photo of the youngster on its front page, and reported: 'Rooney [is] a true talent [and] his two goals take England to the quarterfinals . . . Lisbon's Stadium of Light was illuminated by the brilliance of Wayne Rooney who steered England toward the demolition of Croatia.' The paper awarded his performance 8.5 out of 10 and commented: 'A one-man show, an intelligent assist for 1–1, an explosive delight for 2–1 and a flight of fantasy for the third. A true star.'

Another Italian newspaper, *Corriere dello Sport*, said: 'England belongs to Rooney – another two goals for the baby bomber.'

Germany's newspapers paid their tributes. 'Who is David Beckham?' asked the best-selling *Bild Zeitung*. 'King Rooney – all of England lies at his feet!' they trumpeted, before describing him as 'the undisputed star of this championship'.

'One-man show of the miracle kid,' said the upmarket *Die Welt* newspaper. 'His brilliant play could only have been stopped by yellow and red cards.' In the *Berliner Morgenpost* the headline read: 'Wonderboy Rooney saves England's dreams.' It added: 'The footballing Motherland England owes its thanks to Wayne Rooney who has put England within two games of a major title for the first time since the World Cup 38 years ago.'

France's leading sports paper *L'Equipe* described him as the 'English phenomenon who ruined the Croatians' dreams' and the 'triumphant matador who left the arena with the Croatian bull grounded'.

23

Wazza is Born

'A lot of the fans have got "Roonaldo" on their shirt for him but we haven't nicknamed him that. We call him Wazza.'

– David Beckham

As well as monopolising the sports (and news) pages with his on-field exploits, the size of Wayne Rooney's potential fortune fascinated the media.

There would be a fortune from the Far East to bolster his earnings, more mega-sponsorship deals, and, oh yes, he will still be playing when he returns, so there will be a new bumper contract as a player. Pundits were beginning to estimate that he could even be bigger than England skipper David Beckham in terms of financial return – if not looks!

His agents are being swamped with sponsorship offers from Japan, China and Thailand. The interest is phenomenal. To celebrate his two goals against Croatia, he was in the company of a gathering of corporate sponsors as well as family and agents.

The player has already earned £1.2m in a year from sales in China of club shirts bearing his name. He also has a £5m boot deal with Nike plus sponsorship from Mastercard, Coca-Cola and Ford.

Each of Rooney's Euro 2004 goals were worth £450,000 to his agent's firm, City analysts estimated. Proactive Sports Group's stock-market value has shot up by £1.8m since he started scoring.

Wayne is not the only big earner; fiancée Colleen McLoughlin has grown up with him, and within a matter of a couple of years developed from schoolgirl to covergirl. With short black socks and quilted anorak, Colleen looked like a typical schoolgirl just fifteen months ago. She has been transformed from a shy sixteen-year-old to a professionally groomed beauty. As national hero Wayne has shot to the top of the international stage, Colleen has also grown up at lightning speed. She has swapped her neat little terraced home for the sprawling mansion she shares with Wayne, and her anonymity for life in the public eye. She was pictured by Wayne's side as he promoted soft drinks. Colleen was quickly blossoming into her special role in Wayne's world. Stepping out of a Lisbon restaurant in turned-up jeans alongside a designer-clad Victoria Beckham, Colleen looked as if she was having fun.

A Liverpool radio station changed its name for the day of the quarterfinal with Portugal in goal ace Wayne's honour. Commercial station Radio City became Radio Rooney for twelve hours prior to the game. A spokesperson said: 'We know Wayne listens to us and we're his favourite station. He's a local kid and he's performing brilliantly. We wanted to show our support and we're sure he'll appreciate the gesture.'

Landlord and mad-keen Everton fan Keith Dooley changed the name of his seaside pub from the Half Moon to The Half Roon. He did the job himself after climbing up a ladder outside his boozer in Paignton, Devon, and giving the sign a quick make-over with a paintbrush. Keith said: 'I was told three years ago by a football scout I know to look out for a new kid called Rooney who was going to take the world by storm. He's certainly been proved right. Wayne's the hottest thing around.'

A record company were urged to re-issue a hit record from the 1950s – called, of course, 'Rooney'. The song was a hit in 1958 for Michael Holliday – who was also born in Liverpool – and since Wayne's exploits had started to get radio airplay. Bosses at Sony were said to be considering bringing it out again.

City analysts believed Rooney could have kick-started a potential £400m boost to the British economy if England reached the final, with sports retailers and brewers, in particular, feeling the benefit. Shares in England kit maker Umbro, which only listed the previous month, shot up more than five per cent. Pub group Wolverhampton & Dudley, and drinks companies Scottish and Newcastle and Allied Domecq also made healthy gains. Justin Urquhart Stewart, of Seven

Investment Management, said: 'The further we go, the bigger the impact on stocks.'

Restaurants and some shops are suffering, though, as customers stay away in their droves to watch more Rooney heroics. But while the nation was going Wayne mad, publicity-conscious Becks didn't need to panic just yet. The England captain still led the way on the worldwide web with ten times as many Internet sites devoted to him. Beckham has 111 domain names registered by fans around the globe, up from the 68 listed at the World Cup in 2002, NetNames said. Rooney has ten domains bearing his name, one behind strike partner Michael Owen.

But, of course, the greatest payday for his feats on the field awaited a big-money move.

Chelsea admitted for the first time that they wanted Steven Gerrard if he left Liverpool, but their chief executive Peter Kenyon dismissed any imminent move for Rooney. Anfield chief executive Rick Parry conceded that England's midfielder was 'not happy' and they were struggling to keep him at the club.

His Stamford Bridge counterpart Kenyon, who watched Gerrard play a starring role in the Croatia game with new manager Jose Mourinho and owner Roman Abramovich, returned from Portugal to tell Chelsea TV: 'Steven Gerrard is recognised as one of the best midfielders around and were it possible we would be extremely interested. It's great to see how Frank Lampard and Steven have played together and Steven certainly comes into the Lampard class.'

Gerrard would like to link up with Rooney but Kenyon dismissed reports saying Chelsea are ready to pay a reported £50m to prize Rooney away from Everton. Kenyon admitted he had been impressed, like everyone else, with Rooney's performances in Euro 2004, but played down talk of a bid for the England wonder boy. 'Wayne Rooney's been the talk of the tournament. He's been incredible, particularly coming off a fairly average season. But there's so much speculation, and if we started reacting to all the speculation we would literally do nothing else.'

Chelsea manager Jose Mourinho said he would welcome Gerrard 'with open arms', but no one knew at that point during the tournament that when Gerrard returned to Merseyside he would perform an unexpected U-turn and opt to stay at Anfield – thereby also weakening Chelsea's links with Rooney and increasing his prospects of a move to Manchester United. Mourinho, who won the Champions League with Porto the month before Euro 2004 began, praised Eriksson for his role in helping Rooney adjust to the international stage. 'The only thing I can say is that the kid is playing amazing and Mr Eriksson deserves to take congratulations for that also. Since the first moment Mr Eriksson understood and gave Rooney confidence, and for a young kid his confidence is incredible.'

The tabloid tales of Rooney were becoming even more fanciful as there were pages upon pages featuring every aspect of his life and family.

It was reported that rich fans of Rooney are offering a builder £3m to live next to the wonder kid – they are clamouring to buy a new home being built beside his mansion. Developer Michael McCoomb has been bombarded with offers. The developer had snapped up the plot next to the home shared by Wayne and girlfriend Colleen McLoughlin. He knocked down the existing house and plans to have the new one completed by February next year. The Georgian-style house in Formby, Merseyside, will have seven bedrooms, three living rooms, a cinema and swimming pool. Mr McCoomb said, 'We've been inundated with inquiries since people heard of the Rooney connection, and many have landed serious offers. Roomania has created massive interest in this property.'

Everton ace Wayne and Colleen moved to the six-bedroom pad in February for more peace than their native Liverpool. Mr McCoomb added: 'They are a lovely couple, really down to earth. They often stop and have a chat with the builders.'

The outbreak of Roomania claimed speedway as a victim, with fixtures cancelled at Coventry and Swindon. Swindon owner Terry Russell said, 'There would be little point in going up against thirty million emotionally charged England fans. In fairness to our supporters, many of whom are also passionate about football, we feel it only right to postpone our meeting.'

The FA were in constant touch with Everton, their manager David Moyes and Rooney's agent Paul Stretford to ensure that Rooney-mania didn't entirely engulf the young prodigy. 'We have tried to work within a sensible framework, protecting him from the huge interest while ensuring that the public know what he's thinking and saying,' said an FA spokesman.

Rooney would threaten the legendary Michel Platini's record as the all-time top marksman in European Championship history if he could possibly maintain his rate of scoring. Platini scored nine goals, including two hat tricks, in five games when France won the European title in 1984. The best performance by an England striker is seven goals from a total of eight appearances in the finals of 1996 and 2000 by former England captain Alan Shearer.

The goalscoring successes of these tournaments include some of the greatest marksmen in European football: Shearer, Jurgen Klinsmann, Marco van Basten and Dennis Bergkamp.

'He's got everything that's required to be a great player,' said Sir Geoff Hurst, whose three goals in the 1966 World Cup Final catapulted him to global fame.

'I was six years older than him when that happened to me and probably better equipped to handle all the fuss at the time. If he gets the right support and advice and keeps his feet on the ground, he can have a long and successful career.'

Images of Owen scoring a wonder goal against Argentina in the World Cup began to fade with the exploits of the new kid on the block. Owen had yet to score in the tournament, but England would be taken even more seriously if both their strikers were in form. Owen said: 'There are hopefully three more games to come at Euro 2004 – and I want to be on the scoresheet in every one of them.'

Owen came into the tournament as the deadly finisher feared by all of Europe but, while the astonishing exploits of eighteen-year-old Rooney have captured the imagination of the nation, Owen found himself goalless and desperately short on self-confidence.

It was the first time he had been forced to deal with observers questioning his place in the England team. He confessed:

It always bothers me when I don't score. Even when we've won a game, I still feel there is something missing if I haven't got a goal. Half of me was ecstatic after the Croatia game because England are through to the quarterfinals. But there was still a sense of personal disappointment that

I'd gone another game without scoring. But if you don't feel that way as a striker, then you will never reach the top. I like to have the responsibility of scoring goals and I haven't done that yet.

Owen, 24, still boasted an impressive strike rate of 25 goals in 59 games for England. But he was well aware that his last competitive goal for his country had come way back on 10 September 2003 against Liechtenstein. Yet he remained as driven and single-minded as ever. He insisted: 'I've not got anything to prove here. I've scored in three big tournaments before, so it's not as if I'm doubting myself. But the sooner I score again the better.'

Owen dismissed suggestions that his style is too similar to Rooney's for the pair to work together as an effective strike partnership at the very highest level. He said:

I've played with Wayne for more than a year now and he is such an intelligent striker that anyone can play with him. He likes to link the play and drop deep as well as scoring goals and I think his natural position is to play just off the striker.

Nothing he does surprises me. He has no fear and when he is confident like that anything can happen. He has been on a high right from the start. I think our partnership is working very well and it's great to see him scoring all these goals. In a way it takes a certain amount of pressure off me. But I want to score goals as well and, if we can both click at the same time, it will be very good for England. At the moment it's Wayne who is carrying us forward but I feel I still have a big part to play in this tournament.

Owen admitted his confidence was low after his ineffective performance during the last-gasp 2–1 defeat by France in England's opening Group B game. But he believed he was slowly turning the corner and was encouraged by his role in helping to set up goals for Rooney and Paul Scholes in the victories over Switzerland and Croatia.

I feel I am getting sharper with every game. I don't know why that is. I didn't play badly against France but I did start off quite slowly. Then there was a bit of an improvement against Switzerland and a bit more in the Croatia game. Obviously the next step is to score a goal. That would be nice right now. As a striker, either you've got to create goals or score them. I knocked in a cross for Wayne against the Swiss and helped with a couple of the goals against Croatia. I'd prefer to be scoring myself but hopefully that is still to come. It's not as though I have been missing easy chances. I had one decent opportunity the other night and chipped it over the bar, but apart from that my all-round game is improving. And the bigger the match, the more I relish it.

Owen knew it was time to step up his game against Portugal in Lisbon's Stadium of Light, saying, 'We have played well in every game. Even after being beaten by France, we could hold our heads very high. The Switzerland game was probably our worst performance so far but I feel we are playing very well and deserve to be in the next round. We are creating a lot of chances and scoring a lot of goals. Hopefully, my turn will come against Portugal.'

Eriksson, though, was publicly more forthright about Rooney's blossoming partnership with Owen, commenting: 'Against Croatia, that was the best they've played in the tournament together. Michael's form has been a worry for some people, but not for me. He set up the first goal against Switzerland and was involved in three goals on Monday.'

As for Rooney, the prospect of the kid becoming even more prolific was mouthwatering for Eriksson. Rooney knows he is not the finished article yet. He was putting in hours of hard training to get even *better*.

Three of his goals had come with right-foot shots. But, he said, 'I'm trying to work on my heading and my left foot. I can only improve if I keep working on it. Euro 2004 has been a good experience so far and hopefully one that can get better. I think we can go pretty far in the tournament – hopefully all the way.'

Speaking to the FA website www.fa.com Rooney said:

It's a great experience for me here, a great thing to play with players like David Beckham, Michael Owen and Steven Gerrard. They are all top players and I was watching them on television six years ago in the World

Cup of 1998. Now I'm playing alongside them and that's brilliant for me. We're doing well and I think the standard of the game is better the bigger the game you play in. That can only be good for my game, too, because I want to go out and prove I'm among the top players.

He refused to get carried away with the plaudits and did not even want to think about the attention he was receiving back home. Rooney said, 'I just have to concentrate on what I'm doing. I haven't got time to think about anything else and that's probably a good thing. I just have to keep concentrating on my football and not let anything else get in my way.'

David James revealed the only thing that bothers the kid is the welfare of his dog!

Rooney owns a seven-month-old chow called Fizz, after the *Coronation Street* character. James said:

After every game he gets straight on the phone home to see how his dog is! None of us are worried about Wayne becoming a loose cannon after scoring a few goals in a major competition. He's exactly the same lad he was three weeks ago. It's just annoying I wasn't acting with such maturity when I was his age. There have been a lot of very good teenagers over the years but Wayne is a rare talent, and the guy knows what he is doing. He fits into the side so well and you have to appreciate Mr Eriksson's view that, regardless of his ability, if he didn't fit into the team off the field, he wouldn't be picked.

Rooney relaxes by going for long walks with Fizz near his Merseyside home. He said, 'I take Fizz for walks on Formby beach, which isn't far from the house. It's quiet there so I get a chance to reflect.'

They say that dog owners come to resemble their pets, but some of Rooney's 'victims' know he can be more like a bull terrier than a chow.

Cristiano Ronaldo winced at the memory of his clash with the Everton striker at Old Trafford on Boxing Day 2003. Rooney steamed in with a reckless mid-thigh tackle. Ronaldo said: 'It was an extremely tough challenge and one I remember all too well. In fact, sometimes I can still feel it!' Rooney's full-blooded tackle came after some typical Ronaldo showboating. Everton players were queuing up to have a go when Rooney raced 25 yards to catch the Portuguese winger with the tackle that sent Ronaldo spinning in the air in front of the dugouts.

Rooney picked up a booking and was lucky not to be sent off. Referee Mike Dean later admitted he would have given Rooney a red card if he had seen the foul clearly, but the Everton youngster escaped with a caution. Ronaldo, 19, added: 'I don't want to get involved in anything personal with Rooney and I think he is a wonderful player. But he is very strong and sometimes players mistime tackles. When you have someone quick, like me, the only way to stop them is by fouling them.' To his credit, David Moyes took Rooney off and read him the riot act immediately after the incident.

Rooney had bagged four goals in helping England to the quarter-finals, but Ronaldo insisted Portugal were not afraid. He said:

This Portugal team is not afraid of anybody. Not France, not Spain, not Italy and not England. And not Wayne Rooney. I am not afraid of him. England is not only Rooney anyway. Rooney's a young one who's showing a lot at the moment, but David Beckham and Michael Owen are wonderful players.

Perhaps England will be worrying about us, because there has been a radical change in the Portugal team in the last couple of games. Our team is getting better with every game. Against England, we know we are going to have to work very hard. We respect England and all their team very much. But as Mr Scolari always says, in the nicest possible way, we are going to strike them.

Luis Figo said of the approaching match:

We felt that if we got England in the knock-out, then we would beat them. When the draw was made, we were confident about that outcome. England are a side we like to play. They suit our style. My belief months ago was we would beat them if we met, and I see no reason to change that. We have real confidence. If we play to the best of our ability, I expect Portugal to progress to the semifinals. England are showing good form at the right time and they will come into the match with a great deal of confidence. People expect a goal blitz but when you get to this stage the games are tight and tense, there is too much at stake.

But Figo warned: 'Wayne Rooney is showing incredible potential and ability. I admit he is a worry for us.'

Lisbon newspapers claimed our Wonder Boy had been eating too many hamburgers and branded him 'McRooney'. The porky jibe was the perfect motivation.

Looking ahead to the clash with Portugal, England captain David Beckham praised the youngster's amazing coolness, saying, 'He's so calm, it's as if he was just having a kick-around in the schoolyard or playing in a local Sunday League. Everyone tends to forget that he's only eighteen. He plays like a man but he's still just a boy.'

England last beat Portugal in a competitive game on the way to making history in 1966. Rooney had lifted England players and fans alike and Beckham revealed his team-mates had started calling him 'Wazza' after Gazza. Rooney was only four years old when Gazza burst on to the England scene in 1990. Beckham said:

A lot of the fans have got 'Roonaldo' on their shirt for him but we haven't nicknamed him that. We call him Wazza. We've all seen the comparisons between Wayne and Pelé and that's a great boost for him. I know there's a lot of pressure that will come from that but Wayne doesn't look as if he's worried at all about who he's compared to. When I was younger I was compared to a lot of great players – but never with Pelé. That shows the impact Wayne has had already. He's shown he's a great player and he's an amazing young lad and has been in every game. He has taken absolutely everything in his stride.

Rooney was now the tournament's joint-top scorer but skipper Becks was confident there was much more to come. 'It doesn't feel odd that he's getting all the attention. It's just great that the people in England have got a young talent who is astounding, not just for the other players but for the fans out here and back home as well. It's just fantastic for us that we've got a player that kids and even older men can look up to.'

At England's hilltop hotel to the west of Lisbon, the mood among the players was highly charged; they believed they were within touching distance of this country's first major football triumph for 38 years. The England captain said that for the first time in his memory, there was no fear within the squad, just an expectation of triumph.

> We realise this is a great chance for us. The players are walking around the hotel with confidence oozing out of them. We really believe we can win games and compete with the best and a lot of that confidence is coming from the young players. To have that air of expectancy is a big bonus. I have never known this kind of belief before in an England squad. There is no negativity at all in our hotel. Even from the young players. It is 'We're going to beat them – we're going to win this game.' We watched the Portuguese beat the Spanish and they played well. But we know what their players can do and we are ready. At the hotel, a lot of lads spend a lot of time in the massage room because it's a place we can all go and we can all have a laugh and watch the games and there is a lot of banter in there. Sometimes, in the past, there has been negativity in the squad but in this tournament there has not been one player that has been worried about any game we have gone into. That is the freshness the young players have brought into the squad. I have not heard any player talking about any other team apart from ours. I haven't heard them talking about other team's players. We are not in awe of anybody any more.

Beckham then received a sobering lesson in playing second fiddle to Rooney. 'How's Wayne today?' a television reporter asked him at a packed press conference. But Beckham welcomed the fact that the obsession with the Boy Wonder had taken the attention away from him.

He was asked whether it felt strange that he had been replaced as the country's footballing icon by a teenager from Croxteth. 'I'm not jealous of him at all. I'm not a jealous person. Wayne deserves the attention. I just hope he will be left alone to enjoy his football because he is eighteen and he has a long career ahead of him.'

Someone began to ask him a question about all the players he had been compared to when he first burst on the scene. Beckham smiled wryly and interrupted him: 'Never Pelé!'

Eriksson believed Rooney's impact had injected self-belief to the entire squad. Eriksson described him as 'a bomber'. Asked about how Rooney would set about tackling the Portugal defence the coach said:

It's a test for Wayne, but not only from Costinha. Their two centre-halves, Jorge Andrade and Ricardo Carvalho, are very quick and strong, with a lot of pace. It won't be easy because they defend very well and then hit you on the counterattack very quickly. But I think he's clever and he will find some space wherever because that's in his brain. We're going to try to attack, of course. Portugal will try to keep the ball more than Croatia because that's their speciality. They're technically very good football players. It's an enormous night for Portugal and they're very confident.

Getting momentum in your game depends on where you can win the ball. If you can win it high up, then you can find space. If you win it every time in the back line it's much more difficult. Reaching the quarterfinals is only a partial success, not a complete one. I don't want to go home and neither do the players. The belief inside the players is very big. They're confident and they know it's difficult to beat us. After the French game they were disappointed that they lost but in their heads they knew that they should've won. We made some stupid mistakes and lost it. But as a football player, if you feel that you can cope with France and beat them and then get two positive results, the confidence goes up in all the squad. I hope they believe they can beat Portugal.

In another sign of Rooney's confidence, he volunteered to be one of the penalty takers if the match ended in a shoot-out. Rooney practised spot kicks along with the other players at their final training session. England had lost penalty shoot-outs to West Germany in the 1990 World Cup semifinal, Germany in the semifinal of Euro 96 and Argentina in the quarterfinals of the 1998 World Cup in France. But nothing appears to frighten the eighteen-year-old. Eriksson commented:

I know more or less who will take the penalties if needed. First of all, what you need to know is who wants to be in that situation. Hopefully I will have seven, eight or even nine players who want to be in that situation.

Then, if the match is still not decided after extra time, you have to decide. You can't do it before because you don't know who will be on the pitch. There could be injuries. One player could have played very well and another poorly so confidence comes into it. Another might have cramp. You have to wait and see what happens but the first thing is to have the players from which to choose.

Despite all these caveats, it seemed that England's five first-choice penalty takers would come from Rooney, Owen, Beckham, Lampard, Gerrard and Scholes.

Around 40,000 England fans were set to dominate the 65,000-capacity Stadium of Light. Only 6,000 originally had tickets but touts had cashed in on the demand, charging up to £350 for a seat. Beckham said: 'Fans will do anything to get in and watch this game.'

Wayne's granddad, Billy Morrey, flew out to Portugal at the last minute to be a VIP guest at the big game. 'He has the heart of a lion – and you will see him roar!' he declared to a posse of local sports reporters after landing in Lisbon. Wearing a T-shirt saying 'I could murder a pint', Billy was taken for a preview visit to the magnificent Stadium of Light. The tubby Scouser, who has 37 grandchildren, jogged towards the pitch and joked: 'I'm only coming on as sub and won't be starting the match.'

He added: 'When I see our Wayne run out on that turf my heart will go bump, bump. And when he puts a couple in the back of that onion bag it will be bumping more.'

Asked why he thought Wayne had done so well, he replied: 'He has been well brought up, that's the secret. He has a good family. His dad's a wonderful person and so is his mum, my daughter.' Billy told ITN: 'Watching Wayne has been brilliant. It makes me cry when I think about him and I go to bed with tears on my pillow. I wouldn't care if I snuffed it after this. He is dead shy and quiet but he's got the heart of a lion. Football is in his blood. That's what it's all about. When he comes out here tomorrow I will have a nice clean hanky because I know the tears will come.'

Billy's wife, Pat, 73, who had a pacemaker fitted earlier in the year, could have gone but the family reckoned the excitement might get a bit too much for her. She said, 'Wayne is determined to do his best for his country . . . and I'm sure he'll win the game for the fans.'

She was determined, too, to follow every kick on TV – contrary to rumours that she couldn't face the pressure and would be going to bingo instead. 'I'll be going to the bingo in the morning if I feel up to it, but I'll be watching Wayne and England on telly – in bed that is! I'll be rooting for them all the way.'

24

Game Over for England

'Maybe it would have been different if Wayne had been out there. He had been on fire for us.'

— Frank Lampard

After all the build-up and hype, and all the expectation and hope, Wayne Rooney left the field after 27 minutes with a broken foot, and English hearts were later broken with yet another sorrowful penalty shoot-out exit in a major competition. The 1990 World Cup, Euro 1996 and the 1998 World Cup all brought cruel knockouts from the spot. Now it was the turn of David Beckham and Darius Vassell to miss from the spot.

England lost their quarterfinal to Portugal in a dramatic penalty shoot-out long after Rooney had limped off midway through the first half after being trodden on by defender Jorge Andrade. He was desperate to continue, prepared to play in pain, as he limped back to the halfway line before collapsing to the ground. After two minutes of treatment from physio Gary Lewin, he tried to go on. But it was hopeless, as it was far too painful for him to run, and he hobbled tearfully down the tunnel. Certainly his departure gave Portugal a huge lift and seemed to negate Michael Owen's early opener. The initiative swung back to Portugal as soon as Rooney limped off. Margins are fine in the knockout stages and England never fully recovered from the loss of Rooney. Deprived of their talisman they visibly sagged.

Rooney was replaced by Darius Vassell, who saw Portugal substitute Helder Postiga, who plays for Spurs, equalise with just eight minutes to spare. England thought they had won it minutes later when Campbell headed in. But referee Meier disallowed the goal, citing a foul on the keeper.

The match went into extra time and just ten minutes from the end Rui Costa put Portugal ahead, only for Frank Lampard to level for England. In the penalty shoot-out, Beckham missed the opener, but Owen, Lampard, Terry and Hargreaves all scored and, as Portugal's Rui Costa had also blazed over, it went to sudden death. Ashley Cole scored for England, but Postiga equalised. Vassell's shot was saved by Ricardo, who then scored Portugal's winner.

Up to 40,000 fans had backed England inside the Stadium of Light and an estimated 25 million watched on TV at home, leaving streets across the country deserted. In Liverpool, more than 400 'Roonatics' packed into the tiny pub run by Wayne's uncle, John Morrey. The Old Stanley Arms was festooned with red and white England bunting and banners. Chants of 'miss it' bounced off the walls every time a Portugal player stepped up for a penalty. At Glastonbury, more than 70,000 pop festival-goers watched on giant screens. Nearby Bristol was a ghost city from 7.30 p.m.

Rooney was taken straight from the stadium for an X-ray, which showed he had broken a bone in his right foot, and even had England got through Rooney would have played no further part in the tournament. A distraught Wayne received news of the penalties defeat while in hospital having the X-ray. He was deeply upset at missing out on the chance to spearhead England's campaign in the later rounds. Colleen left the match early to check how he was. She had been watching from the stand together with his mum and dad, his two brothers, his granddad, Bill Morrey, and his uncle Robbie from Australia.

No one will forget the way Rooney burst on to the world stage in this tournament. The images of Rooney will be England's fondest memory of Euro 2004, and brightest hope for the future. Despite England's exit, Rooney had become the country's new-found star of Euro 2004, and needless to say, his transfer value rocketed during the tournament.

It would take at least four weeks for the Beckhamesque metatarsal in his right foot to heal, the same injury that hampered David

Beckham before the 2002 World Cup. Rooney was chasing after the ball on goal when he lost a boot and then was trodden on. Sven Goran Eriksson said: 'It is a pity because he got injured rather badly, very similar to the problem Beckham had, and he will be out for some weeks, maybe a month.' Eriksson refused to blame the departure of England's leading scorer for the defeat, saying, 'I wouldn't say that if Rooney was on the pitch then we would have won. That's just an excuse I don't want to use.'

There were wild celebrations across the host nation as Portugal won 6–5 on penalties. But there was anger among England fans at the Swiss referee Urs Meier who disallowed what would have been a Sol Campbell winner, ruling that John Terry had fouled the Portuguese keeper. BBC TV pundit Alan Hansen branded Meier's decision a 'disgrace'. Former England striker Ian Wright added: 'It's just a joke, he's meant to be the best referee in the world and he gives a decision like that. The referee cost us the game.'

England coach Sven Goran Eriksson said: 'Unfortunately we lost on penalties. That's very hard.' Asked about Campbell's disallowed goal, Eriksson commented: 'We were not lucky with some things out there today. That's football. From the bench it looked all right. The referee said it was a push. He decides. The spirit has been fantastic. I have no complaints at all. The players have been fantastic and the supporters. Losing in this way is very hard.'

There was also controversy about the pitch. Eriksson said England had twice complained to Uefa about conditions underfoot on the penalty spot. Players had been unhappy with the state of the pitch there during training before the two games England played in the stadium. Eriksson said officials 'suggested we should take away the grass and then put the ball down on it'.

Michael Owen, who scored the first goal, said: 'It's a big disappointment. Going out on penalties again is a bitter blow. I couldn't see the problem with it [Campbell's 'goal']. It was the same against Argentina in 1998. He scored a very good goal then.'

Lampard admitted: 'Maybe it would have been different if Wayne had been out there. He had been on fire for us. It's a horrible way to go out, though. I had a feeling they were going to miss one. Credit to them though, they didn't.'

Gary Neville believed the match hinged on two incidents. He said: 'The first was Wayne Rooney's injury and the second was the disallowed goal. Other than that I don't think we can have any complaints. Portugal played very well. They didn't deserve to lose but we didn't either.'

The England team headed home with the bookies wondering who Rooney would kick off the new season with, on the day the fixture list was published. Eriksson concluded: 'I'm sad for the fans and the team and now we will have to look to the next World Cup, and unfortunately we will have to wait two years. It is very disappointing to lose like that and I feel for the players.'

The 2006 World Cup in Germany looks set to be an even bigger stage for Rooney, who in two years time will be at the ripe old age of twenty!